THE STORY OF THE

THE STORY OF THE

HITLER'S INFAMOUS
LEGIONS
OF DEATH

AL CIMINO

This edition published in 2022 by Arcturus Publishing Limited
26/27 Bickels Yard, 151–153 Bermondsey Street,
London SE1 3HA

AD006183UK

Printed in the UK

MIX
Paper from
responsible sources
FSC® C171272

Contents

Introduction

The SS was the armed wing of the Nazi Party and the Waffen-SS *was the party equivalent of the regular army. You had to be 18 to join up*

To this day it still beggars belief that right here in the 20th century a civilized European country such as Germany could descend into the unimaginable abyss that was Nazism. Leading this march through the gates of hell was the SS – the *Schutzstaffel*, or 'Protection Squadron'. Its members were the black-uniformed elite of the Nazi Party, who looked down on the *Sturmabteilung* (SA) – the brown-shirted thugs who ruled the streets. One member of the SS, a young man named Horst Mauersberger, carried an annotated copy of

Goethe's *Faust* in his pocket. Germany, it seems, had sold its soul to the devil in exchange for power and worldly pleasures.

Mauersberger came from Weimar, once the poet Goethe's home. As an SS sergeant major, he worked at Buchenwald concentration camp. This repulsive symbol of man's inhumanity to man was built on Ettersberg hill outside Weimar, the very place that Goethe used to visit when he sought inspiration. Yet Mauersberger was a normal young man from a decent home.

This is the most chilling thing about the SS. While the force contained more than its share of psychopaths, most of its members seemed to be ordinary men who in other times would have gone on to become book-keepers, accountants, lawyers, bank managers, general practitioners, academics and even priests and theologians. But when they became part of an organization in which the normal rules and constraints of society had been abandoned, they turned into some of the most vicious killing machines the world has ever seen. It is true that a handful of SS members were brave soldiers who faced their military opponents on equal terms, but many of them killed babies and children and liquidated millions of innocent citizens without a qualm.

Some committed their heinous crimes for personal gain or power. Others were sucked into a spiral of evil because they did not dare to disagree with Adolf Hitler, the man to whom the SS had sworn a personal oath, or Heinrich Himmler, the second-most powerful man in Germany. Even worse than that, many SS members derived pleasure from inflicting all kinds of degradation and humiliation on their victims. They raped and tortured anyone who fell into their hands and they practised cruel and fatal medical experiments on selected subjects.

But the real horror of the situation is that the entire SS organization was directed towards murder and oppression. The SS was a law unto itself. It was answerable to no one except Hitler, or his henchman Himmler. Every member of the SS was complicit. If they did not commit crimes against humanity themselves, they stood by and watched them take place. Simply being a member of the SS was to be part of a huge criminal conspiracy. This was the banality of evil writ large.

'All my life I have wrestled with one question,' said Mauersberger. 'How could it be that a man from such a respectable home, with those humanist ideals, with those visions and aspirations, could end up in the SS?'

Many of the SS leadership, including Himmler and Heydrich, imagined they belonged to a line of Nordic knights from Germany's mythical past

It cannot be said that the answer can only be found deep within the German psyche. When we look into the glass we are met with our own reflection. As well as German nationals, the ranks of the SS were swollen by French, Dutch, Belgian, Danish, Latvian, Ukrainian, Hungarian, Italian, Croatian and even Bosnian Muslim recruits. A number of Britons and Americans also joined, though they tended to be half-hearted in their approach. Most SS men did not appear to be at all discouraged by the losses they sustained and, when it became clear that Germany was going to lose the war, they went about their murderous activities all the more fanatically.

When the war was over, only a handful of SS murderers showed any remorse. Those who were executed often went to the gallows protesting the justness of their cause. Many did not pay such a high price, however. A large number of war criminals had their death sentences commuted. After a relatively short period of imprisonment they were allowed to resume their daily lives in the normal world, a million miles away from their hideous crimes. Others fled to South America or the Middle East, where they continued to extol the virtues of National Socialism. Some even found safe havens in Britain, the United States and Canada, where they lived out their lives in comfort, without ever having to answer for their foul crimes.

The story of the SS has been told before, but it is well worth telling it again before the events fade from living memory. Hopefully we can all take heed of this warning from history. Germany is a country that has produced some of the greatest scientists, philosophers, musicians and artists the world has ever seen and yet it was able to experience a moment of terrifying madness. It could all happen again somewhere else if we do not remain vigilant. We must make sure that the seeds that blossomed as the stinking flower of the SS are not sown again. The people who joined the SS were not monsters or aliens but human beings who were not so very different from ourselves.

Al Cimino

Chapter One

THE SCHUTZSTAFFEL

Hitler was a complete nonentity until 1919, yet he ended up dominating the political landscape of the 20th century. A number of factors contributed to his meteoric rise to power, but a significant part of his success can be attributed to the physical intimidation of his opponents, and the German people, by the *Sturmabteilung* (SA) and the *Schutzstaffel* (SS).

————ᛋᛋ——————————————————————————

Although he was an Austrian by birth, Hitler served in a Bavarian infantry regiment during the First World War. He never rose above the rank of corporal, but he was awarded the Iron Cross and several regimental decorations. Hitler's war experiences turned him into a zealous German patriot and he was incensed by what he saw as Germany's premature surrender in 1918.

The peace treaty that ended the war, the Treaty of Versailles (see p.22), had imposed a number of onerous conditions on Germany – such as the restriction of the newly-named *Reichswehr* (German Defence Force) to a complement of 100,000 men. As a result the German army was anxious to compensate for its military shortcomings by forming a 'Black *Reichswehr*', or secret army. But first of all it would have to find out where its support lay. As a member of the *Reichswehr* intelligence arm, Hitler was given the job of penetrating small right-wing groups to check on their political reliability.

Political beginnings

The recently formed National Socialist German Workers' Party (DAP) was still very small, but its activities had come to the attention of the authorities, so Hitler was sent along to check it out. Although he was not very impressed with the organization of the party, he was greatly taken with its ultra-nationalist, anti-Semitic views, which mirrored his own. At that time, a document known as the *Protocols of the Elders of Zion* was being taken seriously in racist circles. A fraud fabricated in Russia in 1895 and published in Germany in 1920, it suggested that the whole of recent history, including the First World War, was caused by a conspiracy of Jews who sought to rule the world.

Having impressed the party members with his oratorical skills, Hitler was persuaded to join the organization. In September 1919 he became its propaganda chief. He immediately changed its name to the National Socialist Workers' Party (NSDAP) – the words 'national' and 'socialist' were a cynical ploy to attract new members from both the right and the left. More commonly known as the Nazi Party, the membership of the NSDAP had grown to around 3,000 by 1921 and it operated from a dozen branches outside its Munich powerbase.

Hitler was rapidly becoming the natural leader of the NSDAP, thereby undermining the status of Anton Drexler, the party's founder. Stung into action, Drexler tried to rid himself of Hitler by proposing a move to Berlin, where he would merge the NSDAP with the German Socialist Party, but he had unwittingly played into Hitler's hands. After calling for a ballot of the membership, Hitler resigned. As a charismatic propagandist, Hitler had a considerable following within the party, but he declared that he would only rejoin if he could take over as chairman. With the party in turmoil, Drexler had no option but to agree. Hitler then placed his own henchmen in all of the key positions. In 1923, Drexler left the party he had founded.

ADOLF HITLER (1889–1945)

Hitler was born in Austria on 20 April 1889. He dreamt of becoming an artist but after being refused entry to the Academy of Fine Art in Vienna he became a down-and-out.

After five years of living from hand to mouth in Vienna, a small inheritance enabled him to move to Munich in 1913, where his life was as aimless as before. However, everything changed when the First World War broke out in 1914. Although Hitler had been declared unfit to join the Austrian army he managed to get into the

16th Bavarian Reserve Infantry Regiment. He then served in the trenches of the Western Front, where he enjoyed the discipline and camaraderie of combat and won several awards for bravery. On 15 October 1918 he was temporarily blinded by mustard gas, but he was left with a belief in the heroic virtues of war.

After the war, Hitler joined the German Workers' Party. He quickly changed its name to the NSDAP or Nazi Party and then became its head. His confrontational political style meant that his life was often in danger, so he always carried a gun. Following a failed attempt to take over the government of Bavaria, known as the Beer Hall Putsch, he was imprisoned in Landsberg Castle. It was there that he dictated *Mein Kampf* (My Struggle), a book in which he combined his autobiography with a statement of his political ideology. He condemned the politicians who had ended the war before Germany had been decisively beaten on the battlefield; repudiated the Versailles Treaty; called for revenge on France; attacked Marxism; demanded *Lebensraum*, or living space, in the east at the expense of the Slavs; and spelt out a racist creed which maintained that so-called 'Aryans' were a race of geniuses while Jews were parasites.

In 1930, the Nazi Party won 18 per cent of the vote and 107 seats in the Reichstag, Germany's federal parliament. Hitler took German citizenship in 1932 and in the following year he became chancellor, after winning 44 per cent of the vote. He then assumed dictatorial powers over what he called the Third Reich. The Holy Roman Empire, which lasted from 800 to 1806, was known as the First Reich (realm or empire) and the German Empire, which lasted from 1871 to 1918, was the Second Reich.

In contravention of the Treaty of Versailles, Hitler then began to rearm Germany. After sending troops into the demilitarized Rhineland, he signed treaties with Fascist Italy and Imperial Japan. He then annexed Austria in 1938 and demanded the return of the Sudetenland, an area of Czechoslovakia that was populated by Germans. The territory was conceded by Britain and France in the Munich Agreement, but it was still not enough for Hitler. In the following year he seized the rest of Czechoslovakia.

After signing a non-aggression pact with the Soviet Union, Hitler invaded Poland. France and Britain responded by declaring war on Nazi Germany. The German army then invaded much of western Europe, but Britain remained unconquered. In 1941, Hitler invaded Russia and when Japan attacked Pearl Harbor he declared war on the United States.

Germany's progress was eventually halted by the Russians in the east and the British in North Africa. After an Anglo-American force had established a toehold in Italy, the Western Allies landed in Normandy in June 1944. Germany was besieged from all sides. Hitler committed suicide on 30 April 1945, as the Soviet army fought its way into Berlin.

After the failed Munich Putsch in 1923, Hitler is driven away by his supporters

FIRST WORLD WAR (1914-18)

On 28 June 1914, Serbian nationalists sought to liberate the southern Slavs of the Austro-Hungarian Empire by assassinating Archduke Franz Ferdinand in Sarajevo. In retaliation, Austria declared war on Serbia. As a Slavonic nation, Tsarist Russia came to Serbia's defence. The German Kaiser, Wilhelm II (1895–1941), urged Austria–Hungary to attack, while warning Russia not to mobilize. He also insisted that the French stay neutral in any war between Germany and Russia. Both Russia and France ignored these demands, so Germany declared war on France. Germany then attacked France through Belgium, whose neutrality was guaranteed by Britain. Italy and Japan sided with Russia and the Western Allies, while Turkey and its Ottoman Empire joined the Central Powers.

After the development of the machine gun had halted Germany's western advance, the German and Allied armies built barbed wire barricades, and dug lines of trenches, that ran across northern France from the Channel to the Swiss border. Then a prolonged stalemate followed, during which the opposing armies stood facing each other. Periodic battles resulted in massive slaughter, but few gains. At sea, the British sought to blockade Germany, while the Germans used submarines in an attempt to cut Britain's supply lines. There was more fighting in the Dardanelles, the Middle East, Germany's African colonies and along the Italian front.

In the east, the battle was more fluid. The Germans' superior tactics and high industrial output brought them battlefield victories, but the Russians could call on massive manpower reserves. Tsar Nicholas II took command of the Russian forces in September 1915, but he proved to be an inept commander. In the following year, he launched an offensive that cost a million Russian lives. This senseless slaughter sounded the death knell for the Russian monarchy.

The tsar was deposed by the February Revolution of 1917. When the Communist Party leader, Vladimir Lenin, seized power in the following October, the new Soviet government withdrew from the war by signing a peace treaty. With the Soviet Union out of the way the German army seemed set for victory, but by then the United States had entered the war on the side of the Allies. By that time, Britain had developed the tank, which broke the battlefield stalemate and proved a war-winning weapon, and its naval blockade had brought Germany to its knees.

The German sailors mutinied when they were ordered to break the blockade. Councils of soldiers and workers took over in some places, following the Soviet example, and then on 8 November 1918 the Bavarian Soviet Republic was proclaimed. The German Kaiser, Wilhelm II, went into exile in the Netherlands where he lived until his death. An armistice was called on 11 November 1918 and the German troops marched home to a country where the old order had been destroyed. Many of them, including Hitler, felt that they could have fought on if they had not been betrayed by politicians and agitators back in Germany.

Sturmabteilung (SA)

But the NSDAP had a rival in the form of the German Communist Party (KPD). Despite their failure to take over in Berlin and Bavaria, the communists had been buoyed by the success of the Russian Revolution of 1917. Fearful of a Bolshevik uprising, the German authorities organized a huge army of unemployed First World War veterans into more than 65 *Freikorps* groups which were secretly armed by the *Reichswehr*. Their task was to secure political stability by opposing the communist threat. The *Freikorps* units were unswervingly loyal to their commanders, whose names they bore. Brigade Ehrhardt was led by Hermann Ehrhardt, for instance. However, they were often hostile to the government because they felt that the politicians had foisted a treasonous peace on them. In 1920, a monarchist element in the *Freikorps* tried to overthrow the new Weimar Republic, but the putsch was thwarted by a strike of socialist and communist workers.

Unsurprisingly, there was a continuing struggle between the left and the right, which often erupted into violence at political meetings. Determined to maintain order, the Nazi Party created a troop of stewards, the *Ordnertruppe* – also known as *Saalschutz* or 'assembly-hall protection'. In practice, however, the Nazi thugs took things a stage further by physically ejecting anyone who disagreed with the National Socialist speaker. When quasi-military formations were banned in an attempt to suppress the *Freikorps*, who were becoming troublesome, the *Ordnertruppe* became the *Turn- und Sportabteilung* (athletics and sports detachment).

Its members were recruited from the *Sturmabteilung* (stormtroopers; SA), which had been organized by Chief of Staff Ernst Röhm. Stormtroopers – small squads of men using infiltration tactics – had originally been used on the Western Front instead of employing costly mass frontal assaults. Röhm's SA was made up of former members of the *Freikorps*, which had been officially disbanded after its failed 1920 putsch. SA troops wore distinctive brown shirts, in emulation of the black shirts worn by the followers of Benito Mussolini, who came to power in Italy after the March on Rome (see box, p.30) in 1922.

Street fighting man: Ernst Röhm (centre) was the leader of the SA, which specialized in beerhall brawls, a key tactic in the early days of the Nazis

As well as 'keeping order' at Nazi Party meetings, the SA also used coshes and knuckledusters to disrupt the meetings of rival parties. On one occasion in 1922, Hitler himself stormed on to a rival's platform and physically assaulted the speaker. He was sentenced to three months' imprisonment.

THE TREATY OF VERSAILLES (28 JUNE 1919)

The peace treaty that ended the First World War attributed all of the guilt to Germany alone. Germany was in no position to resume hostilities, so the nation's politicians were forced to accede to the harsh terms within the contract. For a start, it was ordered that reparations totalling 132 billion gold marks should be paid to the Allies. In addition, a number of European territories had to be surrendered. These were handed over to the newly re-established state of Poland and newly created Czechoslovakia. The Rhineland, lying between Germany and France, was demilitarized and the German army was reduced to 100,000 men. Germany would not be allowed to possess tanks, military planes or poison gas and the naval fleet could only retain a dozen battleships. All submarines were banned. On a more personal note, the Kaiser was declared a war criminal, together with a number of other Germans.

Germany was already heavily in debt after the war, so it could not pay the reparations. As a result, France and Belgium occupied the Ruhr, Germany's industrial heartland, in 1923. The German workers went on strike in the same year, but the government continued to pay them, thereby pushing the already devalued currency into a state of hyperinflation. For example, a loaf of bread that cost 20,000 marks in the morning cost 5 million marks by nightfall. The German state experienced complete economic collapse on 15 November 1923, when the exchange rate stood at over four trillion marks to $1. A lifetime's savings would not even buy a ticket for the U-bahn (the rapid transit railway in Berlin).

Catastrophe was averted when the Allies ended the occupation of the Ruhr and granted Germany 800 million gold marks in loans. The situation was eased still further when reparations were cut by two-thirds and the payments were rescheduled. This was not good enough for press and movie baron Alfred Hugenberg, leader of the German National People's Party. He employed Hitler to lead a campaign against the settlement, in which he demanded the end of all reparations and the removal of the so-called guilt clause.

Stosstrupp Adolf Hitler

From the very start Hitler realized that he was constantly in personal danger. He had upset too many people for things to be otherwise. At first he had looked to Röhm's SA for protection, but by 1923 he began to see the SA as a threat. Röhm could call on the support of his brown-shirted thugs whenever they were needed, even against Hitler if he so desired. Unnerved by this thought, Hitler ordered the formation of a personal bodyguard, which would be commanded by two of his trusted comrades, Julius Schreck and Joseph Berchtold. At first it was called the *Stabswache* (Security Guard), but it was quickly renamed *Stosstrupp Adolf Hitler* (Adolf Hitler Shock Troop).

As Hitler said:

> *Being convinced that there are always circumstances in which elite troops are called for, I created in 1922–3 the*

'Adolf Hitler Shock Troop'. It was made up of men who were ready for revolution and knew that some day things would come to hard knocks.

Hitler described his *Stosstrupp* as 'the first group of toughs'. Its original members were:

Julius Schreck (1898–1936)

Veteran of the First World War and the *Freikorps*, he had helped form the *Stabswache*. As Hitler's bodyguard and chauffeur, he took part in the Beer Hall Putsch and was incarcerated with Hitler in Landsberg Prison. A founder member of the SS, he was given a state funeral.

The Stosstrupp-Hitler *in September 1923 shortly before the Munich Putsch; five men were killed in the uprising and the squad was disbanded*

Joseph Berchtold (1897–1962)

Former second lieutenant and stationery salesman, he succeeded Schreck as *Reichsführer* of the SS, the only holder of the post to survive the Second World War.

Ulrich Graf (1878–1950)

Former butcher and amateur wrestler, he joined Hitler in confronting the communists in Coburg in 1922. He saved Hitler's life during the Beer Hall Putsch of 1923 and was elected to the Reichstag in 1936. After the war, he served five years in a labour camp.

Emil Maurice (1897–1972)

Watchmaker and convicted embezzler, he was imprisoned in Landsberg Prison after the Beer Hall Putsch. There he acted as Hitler's secretary when he dictated *Mein Kampf*, until Rudolf Hess took over. He fell out with Hitler over his relationship with Hitler's niece Geli Raubal, but was reconciled. Himmler tried to have him expelled from the SS over his Jewish ancestry, but Hitler stood by him. He participated in the Night of the Long Knives and after the war he served four years in a labour camp.

Christian Weber (1883–1945)

Former army sergeant, horse dealer and publican, he participated in the Beer Hall Putsch and the Night of the Long Knives. He gradually fell from favour and was killed in Bavaria at the end of the war.

Rudolf Hess (1894–1987)

He served in the same regiment as Hitler in the First World War and then he joined the *Freikorps* and the NSDAP. After marching beside Hitler in the Beer Hall Putsch, he was imprisoned in Landsberg Prison, where he took over the transcription of *Mein Kampf* from Emil Maurice. Tried at Nuremberg, he died in Spandau Prison in 1987.

Josef 'Sepp' Dietrich (1892–1966)
After serving in the fledgling German tank unit during the First World War, he became a runner and a hatmaker. Following his participation in the Beer Hall Putsch and the Night of the Long Knives, he went on to become a Panzer commander and Nazi Germany's most decorated soldier. At the end of the war, he was first jailed for ordering the massacre of United States prisoners of war at Malmédy, during the Battle of the Bulge, and then for murder during the Night of the Long Knives.

Stosstrupp members wore the same uniform as the SA – a khaki brown shirt with a swastika armband on the left arm and khaki brown trousers with a brown belt and brown combat boots. However, instead of brown forage caps they wore black ski caps, adorned with a skull-and-crossbones badge.

The *Totenkopf* or death's head was an important symbol in the German military, for it had been the traditional badge of the elite hussar units of the Imperial Guard.

In 1916, Crown Prince Wilhelm of Prussia conferred the right to wear the death's head on the elite unit, whose troops operated flame-throwers ahead of the front line. They were known as men who had a particular relish for battle.

The Beer Hall Putsch

Although some members of the SA harboured left-wing sympathies, the *Stosstruppen* were fanatically right-wing in their beliefs. Confident of their backing, Hitler began planning a coup – a March on Berlin that would be similar to Mussolini's successful March on Rome. He found a willing ally in General Erich Ludendorff, who had been the German military leader during the First World War. When faced with the punitive terms of the armistice, Ludendorff's knee-jerk reaction had been to urge the continuation of the war.

On the evening of 8 November 1923 the SA surrounded the *Bürgerbräukeller*, a large beer hall in Munich, where a right-wing meeting was being addressed by the leader of the Bavarian government, Gustav Ritter von Kahr. Brandishing a pistol, Hitler burst in with his men. He announced that the revolution had begun and that the governments in Bavaria and Berlin had been deposed. Röhm took over a number of key government buildings in Munich while Ludendorff released von Kahr and his officials, after securing a gentleman's agreement from them.

On the following morning, Hitler and Ludendorff led their men out of the beer hall with the *Stosstrupp* in the vanguard. They marched on the War Ministry, which had been occupied by Röhm but was now beginning to be besieged by the *Reichswehr*. Outside the *Feldherrnhalle* (field marshals' hall), a military memorial in the Odeonsplatz (a square in Munich), the 2,000 marchers were met by a force of 100 armed policemen. Wearing the death's head badge, *Stosstrupper* Ulrich Graf stepped forward.

'Don't shoot,' he said. 'His Excellency Ludendorff and Hitler are coming.'

A shot rang out and a police sergeant fell dead. The policemen replied with a salvo. Max Erwin von Scheubner-Richter, who had linked arms with Hitler, was shot through the lung. Mortally wounded, he dislocated Hitler's arm as he fell. Graf threw himself in front of Hitler and was peppered with bullets, but he survived. Hermann Göring was shot in the groin and Joseph Berchtold was also wounded. A total of three policemen and 16 Nazis were killed – five of the Nazi dead were members of the *Stosstrupp*.

Hitler left the Odeonsplatz without a word while Ludendorff continued the march, believing Hitler to be a coward. This drove a wedge between the two men.

The failure of the Beer Hall Putsch led Hitler to seek power by legitimate means, but it also provided the Nazi Party with a revered relic. The swastika flag that had been carried at the head of the column became the *Blutfahne*, or 'Banner of Blood'.

After being left behind in the square it was kept for a short time in the vaults of the Munich police headquarters. It was then used to consecrate the new flags of the SA and the SS. Anyone who had participated in the abortive putsch was awarded the badge of the *Blutorden* or 'Blood Order', and from 1933 the SS mounted a 'guard of honour' at the *Feldherrnhalle*. It remained there until the last SS guards were captured by the incoming American troops in 1945.

On the day after the putsch Hitler was arrested and charged with treason. A sympathetic judge gave him the minimum sentence of five years' imprisonment, but he served just eight months in considerable comfort in Landsberg Castle, accompanied by some of his closest cohorts. The Nazi Party and the SA were then briefly outlawed. With Hitler in prison, Röhm countered the ban by creating an organization called the *Frontbann*, which was the SA under a different name, to all intents and purposes. And in its temporary form the membership of the SA mushroomed from 2,000 in November 1923 to 30,000 at the time of Hitler's release in December 1924.

Although Hitler did not escape imprisonment, a badly wounded Göring managed to flee. Born in Bavaria, Göring trained as a soldier before joining the embryonic German Imperial Air Force. In 1918 he took command of Manfred von Richthofen's celebrated fighter squadron after the Red Baron was killed.

After the war, Göring moved to Scandinavia where he married a Swedish baroness. Returning to Munich in 1921, he met Hitler and joined the Nazi Party. As a former officer, he was given command of the SA. He took part in the Beer Hall Putsch in 1923, was wounded and fled into exile in Austria. When he returned he was addicted to morphine.

In 1928 he was elected to the Reichstag, where he helped manoeuvre Hitler into a position of authority, and in 1933 he was instrumental in passing the Enabling Act, which gave Hitler absolute power. Göring then founded the Gestapo – the secret police – and set up concentration camps for the 'corrective treatment' of political opponents. Later on he became head of the *Luftwaffe*, which was disguised as a civilian operation until 1935. After the *Luftwaffe*'s failure to win the Battle of Britain, Göring was given the special title of *Reichsmarschall des Grossdeutschen Reiches*.

Seen as Hitler's successor, he tried to take over when Hitler was encircled in Berlin. He later surrendered to the Americans. At Nuremberg he denied complicity in the Holocaust, but he could not deny the evidence of the orders he had signed, in which he had authorized the murder of Jews and prisoners of war. He was sentenced to death for his crimes, but he cheated the hangman by committing suicide with the aid of a cyanide capsule.

MARCH ON ROME

Athough Italy was on the winning side in the First World War, the hostilities had left the country in a state of social and economic turmoil. This situation was exploited by the radical journalist and politician Benito Mussolini (1883–1945) and his Fascist Blackshirts. On 30 October 1922 the Blackshirts marched on Rome in a show of strength, forcing the Italian king, Victor Emmanuel III, to invite Mussolini to form a government. This event greatly inspired the Nazi Party.

When Hitler came to power he proclaimed the Rome–Berlin axis with Mussolini, which in 1939 became the 'Pact of Steel'. Once France was on the verge of collapse Mussolini declared war, which led to the Italian forces in North Africa being routed by the British.

After an Anglo-American invasion force landed in Sicily in July 1943, Mussolini was deposed and imprisoned. That September he was rescued by the SS, but by then the Allies had established a presence in southern Italy. The Nazis then installed Mussolini as the ruler of the Italian Social Republic in northern Italy, a German puppet state. When it collapsed, Mussolini was captured by partisans and shot.

Birth of the SS

Shortly after Hitler had been released from Landsberg Castle he realized that the SA had become too unwieldy and too unruly to control while Röhm had become dangerously powerful. In fact the SA was now an embarrassment to him. He no longer needed a paramilitary force because he now sought power by peaceful means.

Hitler and Göring at Tempelhof airport, Berlin in 1932: Hitler was on the campaign trail against President Hindenburg

—*ϟϟ*————————————————————

His only requirement was a small squad of men to protect him at public meetings. In 1925 a disgruntled Röhm resigned from the SA and emigrated to Bolivia.

Hitler explained his reasoning later:

> *I said to myself at the time that I needed a bodyguard which, though small, would be made up of men unquestioningly dedicated to me, ready even to go into action against their own brothers. Better to have just twenty men from a single city – provided they could be relied on absolutely – rather than an unreliable mass.*

Hitler had been impressed by the behaviour of the *Stosstrupp* during the putsch, but it had been officially disbanded while he was in prison. Unsure of the SA and now without a personal bodyguard, he quickly ordered Schreck to recruit a new elite unit. At the suggestion of Göring it would be called the *Schutzstaffel* ('protection squad'; SS) – a reference to the aeroplanes that had flown on escort duties during his time with the elite Richthofen squadron. Initially it consisted of only eight men, all former members of the *Stosstrupp*, but on 21 September 1925 Schreck sent out a circular asking all Party cells to form SS squads.

But the SS would remain a select band. While the SA continued to accept just about anyone, SS recruits had to undergo a rigorous selection process. They could be no younger than 23 years old and no older than 35 and they had to be healthy and powerfully built. And their personal characters needed to be unblemished. They were required to have been resident in the same area for five years and they had to provide two personal guarantors, be of good standing and have no criminal record.

According to the guidelines issued by the SS, 'Habitual drunkards, gossip-mongers and other delinquents will not be considered.'

While the SA continued to grow, the SS was restricted to units of ten men under one officer in each district, with twenty men under two officers in Berlin. Each man would have to swear his unswerving loyalty, not just to the Nazi Party but to Hitler personally.

The SS troops wore a distinctive black-bordered swastika armband and a black ski cap which bore the death's head badge of the *Stosstrupp*. Early recruit Alois Rosenwink said: 'We carry the death's head on our black cap as a warning to our enemies and an indication to our *Führer* that we will sacrifice our lives for his concept.'

Using one of his favourite tactics – divide and rule – Hitler sought to stir up the rivalry between the SS and the SA. At a national meeting of the Nazi Party in Weimar in 1926, the *Blutfahne* was delivered into the 'loyal hands' of the SS – much to the resentment of the SA, whose members were there at the time. Its new bearer would be Jakob Grimminger of the Munich SS, a tall, imposing man with a Hitler moustache.

A veteran of the First World War, Grimminger joined the Nazi Party in 1922. As a member of the SA he took part in the Beer Hall Putsch. He was seen carrying the *Blutfahne* in the 1935 Nazi propaganda film, *Triumph of the Will*. After surviving the war he was tried for being a member of the SS. Although he managed to escape imprisonment, his property was confiscated. He later became a city councillor in Munich, but his past stood in the way of his political progress and he died in poverty.

Nevertheless, Hitler left the SS under the control of the new SA *Reichsführer*, Franz Pfeffer von Salomon. Predictably, the SS did not fare too well under an SA man's command. It was forbidden to form squads in situations where the SA was not fully up to strength, while local SA men used the SS troops as errand boys. The hand-picked elite force was reduced to selling newspapers and subscriptions, pasting posters on walls and soliciting for new Party members from door to door.

Throughout all of this period the SS troops were not allowed to waver from the strict rules of conduct that had been imposed upon them, though they occasionally involved themselves in brawls.

In Dresden, the local SS chief boasted that his men had not only beaten off an attack by 50 communists 'but they threw some of them out of the window'. Normally, though, the SS avoided the limelight. The Munich police noted the discipline that was demanded of SS men:

> *Even the slightest infringement of order, according to SS regulations, is threatened with cash fines, the withdrawal of the armband for a specified period, or dismissal from the service. Particular emphasis is placed on the conduct and dress of the individual SS man.*

When his papers were checked, each SS man was found to be carrying a Nazi Party membership card, an SS card and a song book. The words of one of the songs were:

> *When all are becoming disloyal*
> *We ourselves stay true*
> *So that forever on this soil*
> *A flag will fly for you.*

The SS emerges victorious

Marching songs formed a central part of the SS culture.

> *March on, SS, the road is clear!*
> *The storm-troop ranks stand firm!*
> *Freed from the grip of tyranny*
> *They'll tread the path to liberty.*
> *So up and ready for the final thrust,*
> *Just as our fathers were,*
> *Let death be our comrade-in-arms,*
> *We are the black-clad hordes!*

But while the SS might sing, they did not talk. When Berchtold recovered from his injuries he took over from Schreck as *Reichsführer-SS*. In 1926, he set up the *SS-Fördernde Mitglieder* (SS Supporting Members; SS-FM), a group of people who supported the SS financially and wore a tiny silver pin in their lapels. But Berchtold could not bear the thought of subordinating himself to the SA, so he stood down in favour of his deputy, former *Stosstrupp* member Erhard Heiden. The following order demonstrates his perception of the role of the SS:

> *The SS never participates in discussions at members'*
> *meetings. For the duration of the lecture no SS man shall*
> *smoke and none is allowed to leave the building. The*
> *purpose of these evenings is political education. The SS man*
> *must remain silent and never become involved in a matter*
> *that does not concern him.*

There were no such strictures on the SA.

But Heiden was no more able to withstand the pressure from the SA than Berchtold. Under Heiden, SS membership dwindled from 1,000 to 280 and there was talk of the unit being disbanded. However, Heiden then took on a deputy who would not only prove to be his nemesis – he would also become the saviour of the SS. That man was Heinrich Himmler. A former member of Röhm's *Reichskriegsflagge* (Imperial War Flag) unit, who had carried the imperial flag at the War Ministry during the Beer Hall Putsch, Himmler was now a chicken farmer. But he was gifted with exceptional organizational abilities.

Heiden fell into disgrace after allegations surfaced that parts of his uniform had been customized by a Jewish tailor. On 5 January 1929 he was dismissed by Adolf Hitler and his position was taken by Himmler. Four years later, in April 1933, the now all-powerful Himmler ordered Heiden's arrest. Members of Reinhard Heydrich's *SS-Sicherheitsdienst* (Security Service; SD) went off to capture him. He was killed shortly afterwards, presumably at the SD headquarters in Munich, though his discarded corpse was not found until five months later.

In 1930 Hitler asked former SA leader Röhm to return from his voluntary exile, so that he could reorganize the SA. Röhm had always been close to Hitler, not least because both men had been deeply involved in the creation of the Nazi Party. Röhm began his autobiography *History of a Traitor* with the sentence: 'On 23 July 1906, I became a soldier.' Wounded three times during the First World War, he rose to become a major. After the war, he joined the *Freikorps* and the German Workers' Party and then organized the *Sturmabteilung*. As a homosexual he used the organization to acquire lovers. Arrested after the Beer Hall Putsch, he was discharged from the *Reichswehr* and sentenced to 15 months' imprisonment, but he was released after sentencing.

However, by 1934, and with SA membership running at around a million, Röhm had become Hitler's main rival. His army of brown-shirted thugs was much larger than the *Reichswehr* and his troops were behind him to a man. Furthermore, he wanted to push the *Reichswehr* aside and turn the SA into the new German army, with himself at the helm. As an old friend, Röhm thought Hitler would support him in his endeavours – but Hitler had other ideas. On the Night of the Long Knives, 30 June 1934, Hitler personally oversaw the arrest of Röhm from a hotel at Bad Wiessee and on the following day Röhm was shot without trial.

In the absence of any significant rivals, Himmler and his SS could now race forward to a position of unassailable power.

Chapter Two

HEINRICH HIMMLER

Although *Reichsführer-SS* Erhard Heiden saw Heinrich Himmler as little more than a gifted clerk with no leadership potential, it was Himmler who saved the SS from extinction. He was not content for the SS to be merely a unit of the *Sturmabteilung*. He established it as a separate force with its own distinct identity, greatly expanding it until it eclipsed, then snuffed out, Ernst Röhm's SA.

—⚡⚡————————————————————————

Born in Munich to a middle-class Catholic family in 1900, Himmler was too young to fight in the First World War, though he was eager to do so. By 1918 he had become an officer cadet, but the war ended before he could be commissioned. His lack of front line experience remained an embarrassment, particularly in view of the fact that his godfather and namesake, Prince Heinrich of Bavaria, had died on the battlefield in 1916.

After the war, Himmler studied agriculture at the Munich Technical Institute, where he took a special interest in breeding and genetics. Although he did not know it at the time, he would eventually have the power to put his theories into practice. A small, sallow man with a pince-nez, he tried unsuccessfully to prove himself on the sportsfield, but he only succeeded in obtaining a small, though highly prized, duelling scar. He still fantasized about becoming a soldier but without an outlet for his passion he became a fertilizer salesman. It was at about this time that Himmler began to develop his obsession with Teutonic mythology and racial purity.

Himmler's gurus

Robbed of physical prowess by nature, Himmler became fascinated with the myth of the Nordic warrior, particularly the version that appeared in the operas of Richard Wagner. Himmler shared his passion for Wagner's works with Hitler. Bursting with Germanic mythology, the operas were the embodiment of both men's vision for the German nation.

Himmler was also beguiled by tales about Henry I of Germany (the Fowler), who defended Germany against a Slavic invasion in the 10th century. Another of his obsessions was the Order of the Teutonic

Knights, a religious order that Christianized Prussia – albeit by the sword – in the 13th century. The knights were defeated by a Polish–Lithuanian army at the Battle of Tannenberg in 1410, but legends of their chivalry lived on. The Austrian emperor, Ferdinand I, revived the order in 1834, but it faded away with the ending of the Habsburg Empire in 1918. Later on, Himmler made a reference to the Order of the Teutonic Knights by naming *SS-Panzer Battalion 11* after Hermann von Salza, the order's 13th-century grand master.

Himmler's enthusiasm for German mythology was surpassed only by his obsession with racial theory, a study that was influenced by Alfred Rosenberg (1893–1946). The two men would have met in 1918, when they were both involved with the semi-mystical Thule Society in Munich. Rosenberg was born to German parents in Estonia, but following the Russian revolution he fled to Munich, where he joined the nascent Nazi Party and became editor of the *Völkischer Beobachter*, the Party newspaper. Within its pages he denounced Jews, communists, Freemasons and Christians, and he announced Nazism as a 'new faith'. Even Hitler called his writings 'ideological rubbish'.

In 1930 Rosenberg published a book called *The Myth of the Twentieth Century*, which purported to show that black people and Jews were at the bottom of the racial ladder while Germans were the 'master race'. According to Rosenberg, Germans were even set above other 'Aryans', such as Nordic peoples and Indo-Iranians. The book sold two million copies, but few managed to read it beyond the first chapter. At a later date he railed against 'degenerate' modern art and homosexuality, on the grounds that they inhibited the growth of the Nordic races.

'Ideological rubbish' or not, Rosenberg's racial theories came into their own during the Second World War, when they served to justify the genocidal policies of the Nazi Party. As well as being chief Nazi

—ᛋᛋ———————————————————————

philosopher, Rosenberg went on to hold various positions of power. One of his functions was to steal art and other belongings from Jews and eastern Europeans. Captured by the Allies, he was tried at Nuremberg, where he was found guilty of crimes against humanity. He was sentenced to be hanged.

Himmler also came into contact with Richard Walther Darré (1895–1953), a leading 'blood and soil' ideologist. Born in Argentina, Darré was educated in England and Germany. After serving in the First World War, he went on to study agrarian economics and animal breeding before becoming an active member of the Nazi Party. Spurred on by his interest in the relationship of people with the land, he published *The Peasantry as the Life Source of the Nordic Race* in 1929 and *New Nobility from Blood and Soil* in 1930, which carried the argument that the Nordic races faced extinction because they suffered from a lower birth rate than other peoples.

One of his roles in the Nazi Party was to define racial standards for the SS. Himmler eagerly put Darré's findings into practice by drawing up a genealogical register of SS members, which he pored over as if it were a stud book. His men would marry pure Nordic women and then breed a new Germany.

Darré's SS Race and Resettlement Office (or RuSHA) employed 'race examiners' – white-coated technicians armed with tape measures and callipers, with which they checked suspect citizens for non-Aryan characteristics. After Darré became Minister of Agriculture in the Nazi administration, SS men were also encouraged to set up model farms in accordance with his 'blood-and-soil' philosophy. Arrested in 1945, Darré was sentenced to seven years' imprisonment. He was released in 1950, but suffering from alcoholism he died three years later.

The family man

Official pictures of Himmler portray a small, unsmiling man, a cold ideologue who believed single-mindedly in the Nazis' murderous creed. But like many other mass murderers he was able to lead a double life. It is chilling to think that the man who was perfectly at ease with the extermination of the Jewish population could also be a devoted husband and father.

Himmler met his future wife in a hotel lobby in 1926, while escaping a storm. The story goes that when he gallantly removed his hat he soaked her with water from its brim. But Margarete Siegroth was both divorced and a Protestant, so the future tyrant was afraid to take her home to meet his Catholic parents.

'I would rather clear a hall of a thousand communists single-handed,' he declared.

Parents or not, Himmler found Margarete irresistible – she was blond-haired and blue-eyed, the epitome of the Nazi ideal. The daughter of a Prussian landowner, she had worked as a nurse during the First World War. She owned a clinic in Berlin when she met Himmler, but she sold it to pay for a chicken farm when the couple married on 3 July 1928. The couple's hopes were high when they purchased some land at Waldrudering near Munich, on which they built a small wooden house and some chicken coops. This was only the start, they thought. They would soon own several farms. But in May 1929, only ten months after their wedding, Margarete was moved to write a pitiful note: 'The hens are laying frightfully badly: only two eggs a day. I worry so much about what we're going to live on…'

They had a daughter, Gudrun, who was born in August 1929. Himmler adored her and he called her *Püppi* (Dolly). Margarete later

—*SS*—

adopted a son, but Himmler showed no interest in him. By then he was spending most of his time away from home on Party business, which did not please his wife. In her surviving letters she repeatedly refers to him as a 'naughty husband'.

The couple separated in 1940, but they avoided the scandal of seeking a divorce. Himmler then became involved with his secretary, Hedwig Potthast, who left her job in 1941. He borrowed 80,000 marks from the Party chancellery and built a house for her at Schonau, near Hitler's Bavarian retreat at Berchtesgaden, which they called 'Haus Schneewinkellehen'. There she became friends with Greda, the wife of Hitler's secretary, Martin Bormann. Himmler had two children with Hedwig – a son, Helge, born in 1942 and a daughter, Nanette Dorothea, born in 1944.

Himmler takes over the SS

Always trying to prove himself physically, Himmler was a member of a student duelling group. It was there that he met Ernst Röhm, who was seeking suitable recruits for his *Reichskriegflagge*, a super-nationalist group whose chauvinistic and anti-Semitic views Himmler shared. Röhm later encouraged him to join the NSDAP. Thus it was that Himmler ended up carrying the banner of the *Reichskriegflagge* during the 1923 Beer Hall Putsch. He did not cut a very dashing figure. Surviving photographs depict a small, puny man wearing a helmet that was several sizes too big for him. He was fortunate enough to escape injury and arrest, but he lost his job after taking unauthorized leave to attend the march. It was then that he began to work full time for the Party. During his short time in the army he had been an orderly-room clerk, so he had learnt how to keep meticulous records. In order to

Preacher of Hate: Himmler listens demurely as right-wing evangelist Bruno Doehring holds forth to a Nazi congregation at Bad Harzburg, 1931

prove his abilities he claimed to have compiled a list of the people who befriended Jews in Lower Bavaria, but at that stage he was dismissed as a fanatic. However, his organizational abilities proved useful and in 1925 he became district leader of the newly formed SS in Bavaria. Just two years later, in 1927, he was appointed deputy leader of the entire force, serving under Erhard Heiden – though at that time the SS was nothing more than a small unit within the SA.

With the beginning of the Great Depression in 1929 came a huge fall in industrial output and many workers suddenly found themselves unemployed. Large numbers of them found their way into the SA, along with a sizeable proportion of criminals. A dramatic rise in violent incidents was inevitable. The number of SA men 'wounded in the course of duty' rose from 110 in 1927 to 2,506 in 1930. In 1929 the Prussian authorities registered 580 major disturbances involving the SA – this figure had risen to 2,500 in 1930 and 5,300 in 1933. In the first half of 1932 the SA's bloody street campaign had resulted in 86 deaths, 72 of them in the six weeks before the election. Even the far smaller SS lost ten men that year.

On 6 January 1929 Himmler took over Heiden's position as leader of the SS. While the members of the SA were an undisciplined rabble, the SS troops were seen as an elite corps, which appealed to the middle and professional classes. At the same time the stern discipline of the SS attracted former *Freikorps* men to its ranks, who quit the SA to join.

But not just anyone could enrol in Himmler's SS. For a start, candidates had to display the outward signs of Nordic ancestry and be over 5ft 8in (1.73m) tall. Himmler would pore over photographs of potential recruits with a magnifying glass, looking for traits of the Mongol or the Slav. Recruits had to supply evidence of their lineage going back at least three generations, to prove they had no Jewish blood in them. Ordinary SS men were asked to provide records that went back to 1 January 1800 while officers were required to trace their ancestry back to 1 January 1750. The men under Himmler's command also had to be tall, blond-haired and blue-eyed. Unfortunately, a large proportion of the existing membership – including Himmler himself – could not fulfil these criteria, so Himmler made an exception for those who had served in the First World War and, of course, himself. Despite these exacting standards, SS numbers had climbed back to 1,000 by the end of 1929 and by the end of the following year that figure had tripled.

As the membership of the SS swelled, Hitler decreed that it should be an independent organization. The old system of ten-man units was abandoned and a military-style hierarchy was introduced with a proper officer structure. Himmler also redesigned the uniform. Members wore a new black kepi with a death's head badge, together with a black tie, breeches, boots and a crossbelt. Shirt collars were edged in black-and-white twist cord except for those of senior leaders, which were trimmed in silver. SS shirts also carried black patches bearing symbols denoting units and rank.

THE GREAT DEPRESSION (1929-39)

The Great Depression could be described as the most severe and sustained economic downturn ever to hit the Western industrialized world. In 1929, the United States government began to tighten monetary policy as a way of curbing excessive speculation, but no one realized that the economy was already slipping into recession. The resulting stock market crash was sudden and violent. Between 1929 and 1933 industrial production fell by 47 per cent, the wholesale price index dropped by 33 per cent and gross domestic product (GDP) tumbled by 30 per cent. By comparison, GDP slid by just 2 per cent in the recession of 2008–9.

Almost every country in the world was hit, but the economic decline in Great Britain was only about a third of that experienced in the United States and the downturn suffered by France was relatively short-lived. In Germany, the decline in industrial production was roughly equal to that in the United States. However, it started from a low base because the German economy was only just recovering from the bout of hyperinflation that had taken hold earlier in the decade. As a result, mass unemployment and personal privation paved the way for the 'economic miracle' that would allow the Nazi Party to take power.

The SA threat

Although the SS was beginning to grow under Himmler's leadership, its existence, and that of the Nazi Party, was still being threatened by the SA.

The Nazi Party itself was in disarray in the mid-1920s. Leftist members such as the Strasser brothers had proposed an alliance with the Soviet Union, while Joseph Goebbels had demanded Hitler's expulsion from the Party. However, Goebbels changed his tune when he realized that Hitler would win any internecine struggle within the Nazi Party. Any future threat to the Party would not come from the Party itself but from the SA.

Gregor Strasser joined the Nazi Party in 1920 and he took part in the Beer Hall Putsch of 1923, after which he was jailed briefly. Being present at the putsch was a good career move for many of those who took part. Strasser went on to become the Party's propaganda chief, employing Heinrich Himmler as his secretary. His brother Otto followed his example by joining the Party in 1925. The brothers were committed socialists who appealed to the lower-middle and working classes and they helped build the Nazi Party into a mass movement.

However, Otto became disillusioned with Hitler when he discarded any vestige of socialism and began courting wealthy industrialists, so he left the Party in 1930. Like his brother, Gregor was opposed to Hitler's alliance with big business, and he also disliked Hitler's anti-Semitism, but he carried on heading the left wing of the Party. He resigned two years later, but by then the damage had been done. During the Night of the Long Knives he was arrested by the Gestapo and shot in the back of the head.

Otto managed to escape to Canada but Goebbels denounced him as 'Public Enemy Number One' and put a price of $500,000 on his head. Canada proved to be a safe refuge, though, because he was able to return to Germany in 1955, when he continued to promote National Socialism.

Like many of Hitler's henchmen, including Himmler, Goebbels was something of a failure before he joined the Nazi Party. He was exempted from service during the First World War because of a club foot and after graduating from the University of Heidelberg he tried unsuccessfully to become a journalist and a playwright. Then in 1924 he made friends with a group of National Socialists who encouraged him to join the Party. Because he was a gifted speaker he was made *Gauleiter* (district leader) in Berlin, where he railed against socialists and communists.

When Hitler came to power, Goebbels became the Nazi Party's propaganda chief. His task was to organize mass rallies, newspapers and films. He became a protagonist of 'total war' and he proved himself a master of wartime propaganda, especially in the face of repeated defeats. In April 1945, he was the only high-ranking Nazi leader to remain with Hitler. Goebbels and his wife took their own lives in Hitler's bunker, along with those of their six children.

Although Hitler saw the SA as nothing more than a tool that would facilitate the expansion of the Nazi Party, some members of the SA viewed the force as a glorious military organization that could completely absorb the *Reichswehr*. This clash of views led to a rebellion in the summer of 1930 and the spring of 1931.

In Berlin, the SA and the communists joined together to oppose

———*ϟϟ*———————————————————————————————

an increase in public transport fares. Some Brownshirts even took the 'socialism' in National Socialism seriously by consulting the communists about a planned economy. As a result, some SA formations became known as 'beefsteaks' – that is, brown on the outside and red on the inside. They even went as far as attacking Hitler personally. The slogan 'Adolf is betraying the proletariat' appeared and leaflets attacked the 'treachery of the party clique headed by Hitler'. Then there was a poem:

> *Entschlossen, seinen Geldgebern dankbar zu sein,*
> *Stellt er seinen 'Kampf' gegen das Finanzkapital ein.*
> *Was kümmern ihn des Volkes Sorgen?*
> *Was kümmert ihn, was wohl sein mag morgen?*
>
> *(Determined to be grateful to his benefactors,*
> *He ceases his 'struggle' against financial capital.*
> *What does he care for the people's woes?*
> *What does he care what tomorrow may bring?)*

The SA's resentment of Hitler was brought into sharp focus when he bought an expensive new Mercedes from the Berlin Motor Show. He was seen to be betraying 'socialism' to further his own ends. This was not what the Brownshirts were getting broken bones and cracked skulls for.

As the 1930 election approached, the leader of the SA in Berlin, Walter Stennes, supplied Hitler with a list of demands. If he wanted the SA to support him at the polls he would have to add SA men to the list of candidates to the Reichstag; provide the SA with the sole responsibility for security at Nazi Party meetings; and stop Nazi *Gauleiters* interfering in SA matters. This was a direct challenge to the SS and the SA wanted paying well for the privilege. Hitler refused even to discuss the matter and then he issued a list of prospective candidates that did not even include Stennes' name.

In retaliation, Stennes sent a troop of Brownshirts along to break up a meeting at the Palace of Sports, where Goebbels was giving a speech. Goebbels called on the SS for protection, but two days later a mob of SA troops smashed up the Nazi Party headquarters in Berlin and attacked the SS men on guard.

The affair ended with the arrest of 25 SA men. Hitler rushed to Berlin, apparently to make peace with Stennes, and he seemingly caved in to all of his demands. He then recalled Röhm from Bolivia and asked him to take over as head of the SA. While Röhm was not Hitler's greatest fan – 'Dolf is an ass' he wrote to a friend in 1928 – he still had a considerable following in the SA.

But even Röhm could not restrain Stennes, who accused Hitler and Goebbels of betraying the National Socialist ideal. At a secret meeting of SA commanders in Berlin, it was decided to take no further orders from Hitler.

Then the SA took over the Party headquarters in Berlin, along with the offices of the Nazi newspaper *Der Angriff* (The Attack). The SS fought back but its troops were heavily outnumbered. Finally a leaflet was circulated, which carried the message that Goebbels had been deposed as *Gauleiter* of Berlin.

'The SA is on the march. Stennes is in command,' it said.

In response, the Nazi Party expelled any SA units that rebelled. This deprived the rebels of the funds that Hitler had brought in from the business corporations that backed him. Stennes' support melted away and in 1933 he left Germany to command Chiang Kai-shek's bodyguard in China.

—44—————————————————————————

Heydrich and the SD

Throughout the rebellion, the SS had remained loyal and Hitler now depended on the force to root out any further dissent. Himmler's obsession with record-keeping now came into its own and his records of suspect Party members were used to purge all those who opposed Hitler. Himmler was helped in this enterprise by a new recruit named Reinhard Heydrich.

Although Heydrich became Himmler's most trusted henchman, Himmler was not at first interested in the would-be recruit, to the extent that he cancelled an appointment with him. Undeterred, Heydrich turned up anyway. When Himmler saw him he was impressed with his Nordic looks and his rabid anti-Semitism.

'I want to set up a security and information service within the SS and I need a specialist,' Himmler said. 'If you think you can do this management job, will you please write down on paper how you think you would tackle it? I will give you twenty minutes.'

Off the top of his head, Heydrich sketched out a plan for the *Sicherheitsdienst* (SD; Security Service). He was instantly hired. Heydrich then moved into the Brown House, the Nazi Party's new headquarters in Munich. After being shown into a shared room with only one typewriter, he was put to work at a kitchen table. In spite of the conditions, he set up a system of index cards that held details of aristocrats, communists, Catholics, conservatives, politically active Jews and Freemasons. He also kept a record of any Nazis who had been made unreliable by heavy debts or scandal of any kind. Jewish communists, socialists or Freemasons went into a special 'poison' file.

According to one of Himmler's confidants, Heydrich's mind was a 'living card index, a brain with all the threads woven together'. After less than four months in the job Heydrich told a meeting of SS officers that the Party was riddled with spies and saboteurs. He recommended that every SS unit should create a security detachment in order to root out any disloyal members.

Heydrich was rapidly promoted and all was going well, but then a Nazi Party member in Halle recalled an old rumour that he was a Jew. Himmler ordered a full genealogical investigation, which eventually concluded that: 'Heydrich is of German origin and free from any coloured or Jewish blood.' Nevertheless, Himmler realized that Heydrich's fear of being considered Jewish was a weakness that could be used to control him.

Members of the SS elite at Wannsee, 1934: (front row) Daluege, Himmler, Milch, Krügel, von Schütz; (back row) Wolff, Bonin, Heydrich

—ᛋᛋ——————————————————————

Heydrich then moved out of the Brown House so that he could set up the SD in a secret location. The organization soon created a network of SS spies that penetrated every aspect of German life. Heydrich also manoeuvred the SD out of the SS chain of command so that its men would be loyal only to him. Meanwhile, he reported directly to Himmler, though he disliked him intensely. He told his wife that he disguised his hatred for his boss by imagining him 'in his underpants, then everything is all right'.

But who was the man that had so impressed Himmler? Born a Catholic in the stoutly Protestant city of Halle, Heydrich had first-hand experience of being a member of a minority group. His father's real name was Süss, which had distinctly Jewish overtones, and as a youth he was taunted about it. Even though he had no Jewish ancestry, Heydrich was so sensitive about the subject that he had the name Sarah erased from his mother's gravestone. He was also teased about his high-pitched voice and feminine figure, which resulted in frequent beatings by his fellow pupils. As if that were not enough, he was frequently thrashed by his mother, who was a strict disciplinarian.

By contrast, Heydrich's father was a musician who introduced his son to the cult of Richard Wagner and encouraged him to become an accomplished violinist. Tall and Nordic, Heydrich was also a talented sportsman. In fact, he was everything that Himmler longed to be.

With the family fortune in ruins after the First World War, Heydrich joined the *Freikorps* in 1919. Then in 1922 he joined the German navy as a cadet under the command of Admiral Wilhelm Canaris (1887–1945), who was later head of the *Abwehr* (German military intelligence), a rival to the SD. However, after being charged with dishonourable conduct towards a shipyard director's daughter, Heydrich was discharged just a year before he would have been eligible for a pension. It was a blow to his finances, his career prospects and his honour.

The Nazi Party was more forgiving, so in 1931 he joined the Party and the SS. By 1936, Heydrich was in charge of the SD, the criminal police and the Gestapo. Universally feared, the Gestapo was a secret police force that ruthlessly eliminated the enemies of the Nazi state and rounded up Jews to be sent to extermination camps. As head of the Gestapo, Heydrich could imprison his political enemies at will.

In 1938, the SD became the state's official intelligence service, which brought it into conflict with the *Abwehr*. Using his greatly increased powers, Heydrich rooted out any suspect elements in the German High Command and then fed false information to Stalin. This caused him to purge the Red Army, thereby leaving it chronically weakened in the run-up to the Second World War. Not content with that, Heydrich turned his attention to Germany's Jewish population. On *Kristallnacht* (the 'Night of Broken Glass'), which took place on 9 November 1938, he had thousands of Jewish citizens arrested and sent to concentration camps while the synagogues and their property were attacked.

Having displayed his Nazi credentials, Heydrich was made head of the Reich Security Head Office or RSHA, which put him in charge of all of the security and secret police forces in the Third Reich. However, he still found the time to organize a fake 'Polish' attack on the radio transmitter in Gleiwitz, Silesia, which provided Hitler with a pretext for his invasion of Poland. Soon afterwards, he joined SS Captain Adolf Eichmann in deporting Jews from Germany and Austria to ghettos in Poland. He also organized the *Einsatzgruppen* – the mobile killing squads that murdered almost a million Polish and Soviet Jews and communists in the German-occupied territories.

In 1941, Göring asked Heydrich to come up with a plan for the extermination of the Jews. Efficient as ever, Heydrich presented his 'final solution' plan to the Wannsee Conference in the following January. Heydrich's ruthless personality had not escaped Hitler's notice, so in September 1941 he appointed him *Reichsprotektor* (governor) of Bohemia and Moravia, because the previous *Reichsprotektor*, Konstantin von Neurath, had not been harsh enough. Heydrich did not disappoint his master. Anyone who did not collaborate was either shot or sent to a concentration camp, while ration cards were issued to factories on the basis of the productivity of their workers. Needless to say, industrial production quickly rose.

But fate was working against Heydrich. When Emile Hácha, the puppet president of the rump of Czechoslovakia, showed him the Czech crown jewels in Prague Castle, he warned him not to put the crown on. According to the legend, anyone who was not the rightful heir would die. But by now Heydrich felt invincible, so with a laugh he placed the crown on his head. Eerily enough, the British government had just sent two Czech soldiers to assassinate Heydrich as he drove through Prague in his open-topped car. Fatally wounded in the incident, he died a week later.

Heydrich had kept files on all of the leading Nazis, including Hitler himself, so Himmler's first task was to locate the key to the vault that held the evidence. Once everyone was in the clear Heydrich was given a state funeral and was posthumously awarded the German Order, the highest Party and state award.

The two assassins escaped, so the Gestapo retaliated by executing hundreds of Czechs and wiping out the entire village of Lidice. After a reward of a million Reichsmarks had been offered to anyone who knew the whereabouts of the killers, the family who had harboured them was betrayed. The woman of the house committed suicide, while her son was tortured and plied with drink. He was then shown his mother's severed head in a fish tank. Understandably, he told the Gestapo all he knew. The assassins were cornered in a church, where they held off 700 SS men. With no means of escape, they committed suicide. Anything was better than being taken alive.

SS RANKS

The approximate British army equivalent rank in 1939–45 is shown against the SS rank. US army ranks are shown in brackets if they differed from British army ranks.

Reichsführer-SS
SS-Oberstgruppenführer – General
SS-Obergruppenführer – Lieutenant-General
SS-Gruppenführer – Major-General
SS-Brigadeführer – Brigadier (US: Brigadier General)
SS-Oberführer – Senior Leader (no UK or US equivalent)
SS-Standartenführer – Colonel
SS-Obersturmbannführer – Lieutenant-Colonel
SS-Sturmbannführer – Major
SS-Hauptsturmführer – Captain
SS-Obersturmführer – First Lieutenant
SS-Untersturmführer – Second Lieutenant
SS-Sturmscharführer – Regimental Sergeant Major (US: Sergeant Major)
SS-Hauptscharführer – Battalion Sergeant Major (US: Master Sergeant)
SS-Oberscharführer – Company Sergeant Major (US: Sergeant First Class)

—⚡—

SS-Scharführer – Platoon Sergeant Major (US: Staff Sergeant)

SS-Unterscharführer – Sergeant

SS-Rottenführer – Corporal

SS-Sturmman – Lance Corporal (no US equivalent)

SS-Oberschütze – Private First Class (no UK equivalent)

SS-Schütze – Private.

The Nazis come to power

Under Himmler's leadership the SS grew rapidly, its ranks swollen by recruits who were too young to have fought in the First World War. The organization increased its membership from 2,000 in 1931 to 30,000 in 1932, despite a further tightening of the racial criteria. Himmler was so obsessed with race that he even vetoed the marriage of any SS man whose prospective wife could not produce sufficient evidence of Aryan ancestry. His purpose, he explained, was to create 'an order of good blood to serve Germany'. To achieve his aim he would instigate a programme of selective breeding.

'Tomorrow belongs to us,' he declared.

Now that the SS was becoming a powerful force in its own right it needed a uniform to match, one that would distinguish it from the other branches of the German military. In 1932 two SS members, Professor Karl Diebitsch and Walter Heck, designed the famous black SS uniform, with its black jodhpurs and riding boots, black jacket and military-style peaked cap. The red swastika armband and the brown shirt of the SA were retained, but the SS insignia was transferred to the collar of the jacket, with the unit denoted on a band around the cuff. Like other Nazi uniforms, it was manufactured by Hugo Boss. The lightning bolt SS insignia in old Germanic pagan runic script,

The Leibstandarte SS Adolf Hitler *barracks at Berlin Lichterfelde: in 1939, these troops took part in the invasion of the Sudetenland*

modified by Walter Heck, was added the following year, first for the *Leibstandarte SS Adolf Hitler* – Hitler's personal bodyguard – and then for the entire SS.

Professor Karl Diebitsch was an interesting mixture of serviceman and artist. He served in the Imperial Navy during the First World War and then resumed his art education by enrolling in the Design School of the Academy of Plastic and Graphic Arts in Munich. In 1920, he joined the Nazi Party while he was making a living as a painter and graphic artist. When Hitler came to power he moved to Berlin, where he joined the National Association of German Visual Artists and the SS. As an artist with an interest in military matters he was very useful to the SS. He served as the director of the SS porcelain company until 1936 and he designed the SS ceremonial dagger and sword, as well as many other SS items. All of his designs were manufactured in the Dachau concentration camp. He also designed postage stamps and served as a staff officer in the *Waffen-SS*.

Despite the new uniform and its growing numbers, the SS remained in the background. Himmler was almost unknown to the general public. In newsreels, he was glimpsed in the third tier, behind Hitler and Röhm. But Himmler was not looking for publicity. It was enough for him to see his creation flourish.

'The SA are the line infantry; the SS are the guards,' he said.

In 1932, the SS became responsible for security in Munich's Brown House. The organization was effectively the Party's police force and Himmler marked the occasion by giving the organization a new motto: 'SS-man, loyalty is thy honour.'

Fearing that the SA was planning a coup, the German government banned the wearing of political uniforms. However, when Franz von Papen, a moderate from the Catholic Centre Party, was appointed chancellor, he lifted the ban three months later. In the election that followed in July, the Nazi Party gained 230 of the 608 available seats and became the largest party in the Reichstag, but Hitler refused to join the government.

Von Papen had only been in office for three months when his defence minister, General Kurt von Schleicher, persuaded President Paul von Hindenburg, the hero of the First World War, that the army had no faith in him. A further election was called in November 1932, when the Nazis lost 34 seats. In spite of the Nazis' loss, Papen was still unable to gain a majority, so he was persuaded to resign.

Schleicher then tried to form a coalition with Gregor Strasser, who was still a member of the Nazi Party, but it soon became obvious that he would not be able to maintain a parliamentary majority. Finally, on 23 January 1933, Schleicher was forced to admit his failure to Hindenburg. This was Hitler's chance. He knew he could form a government and Hindenburg knew it too, though the president had vowed to keep Hitler out of office. It was Papen who managed to persuade the old warrior to make Hitler chancellor. He did it by assuring Hindenburg that he would be able to control Hitler when they were both in the government.

On 30 January 1933 Hindenburg invited Hitler to become chancellor, with von Papen as vice-chancellor. Göring was made Minister of the Interior, which gave him control of the police force, a power he relished.

'Every bullet that leaves the barrel of a police pistol now is my bullet,' he said gleefully, as the Prussian police began rounding up leftists. 'If one calls this murder, then I have murdered.'

However, the majority of the posts in the government were given to non-Nazis. This was not good enough for Hitler. He called for fresh elections, but before they could take place the Reichstag burnt down.

Hitler blamed the communists and rushed through an emergency decree that suspended civil liberties and invested the SS and the SA with sweeping powers 'for the protection of the people and the state'.

Twenty-five thousand bloodthirsty troops took to the streets alongside Göring's police force. They rounded up so many of the Nazi Party's political opponents that the prisons could not cope with them, so they were herded into hastily constructed concentration camps.

It is thought that the SS had started the Reichstag fire as part of a plot devised by Goebbels, gaining access through a tunnel that led from Göring's official residence. However, the incident was blamed on Dutch communist Marinus van der Lubbe, who was executed.

In the March elections, the Nazis won only 288 seats, but they could claim a majority when the 52 seats of Alfred Hugenberg's German National People's Party were added in. This was the green light that Hitler had been waiting for. He could now assume dictatorial powers – and this time he could do it legally. On 23 March 1933 Hitler's government passed the Enabling Act, which gave his cabinet the authority to pass laws without parliamentary control. It also removed presidential oversight. Over the next three months, all political parties except the Nazi Party were banned.

Hitler feared that he might lose control of his power base in Munich now he was based in the chancellery in Berlin, so he sent orders that a Nazi governor was to be appointed in Bavaria. Heydrich delivered the telegram to the Bavarian chancellery at pistol point.

The *Gauleiter*, Adolf Wagner, became Minister of the Interior and Himmler and Heydrich took over the police force.

'How tragic my new duties will bring me into contact only with the lowest species of humanity,' said Himmler, 'with criminals, Jews and the enemies of the state, when all my thoughts and endeavours are for the elite of our race. But the *Führer* has assigned this duty to me. I shall not shirk it.'

Heydrich's index cards then came into play. First the communists were taken into 'preventive detention', followed by the socialists, the trade unionists and the Catholic politicians. With the prisons full to bursting point, they were herded into a barbed-wire stockade that had been set up around a disused munitions factory in Dachau. This was Bavaria's first concentration camp. Himmler boasted that it had room for 5,000 inmates. He was eager to fill it up, so he wrote to Berlin for money.

'The central Bavarian card index of foreign citizens, which is newly to be made,' he said, 'requires the writing of some 200,000 index cards.'

Heydrich boasted that he had made 16,409 arrests by the end of 1933, though many did not remain in his clutches for long. He reported that 12,544 people were released during that nine-month period. However, those that had been detained had gone through a frightening and humiliating experience, so it is hardly surprising that opposition to the Nazis in Bavaria wilted. More arrests followed – clergymen, journalists and anyone else who was regarded as a reactionary. Heydrich's men even hauled in a factory owner who had paid his workers less than the standard rate. He had made the mistake of standing up to the Nazis when they took him to task. But mere control of the police force was not enough for Heydrich.

'Now the SS should penetrate the police and form a new organization within it,' he said.

For Himmler too, domination of the police force was crucial.

'A nationwide police is the strongest lynchpin that the state can have,' he said.

Meanwhile in Berlin, the traditional army guard outside the chancellery was replaced with an SS guard. Made up of veterans of the *Stosstrupp* and the *Stabswache*, it was led by Josef 'Sepp' Dietrich. That September two SS *Sonderkommando* units – *Zossen* and *Jüterbog* – were combined to form *Leibstandarte SS Adolf Hitler*, Hitler's new bodyguard, whose members had to be over 5ft 11in (1.80m) tall. Ironically, the prisoners who disposed of the corpses in the concentration camps were also called *Sonderkommandos*. On 9 November 1933, the tenth anniversary of the Beer Hall Putsch, the *Leibstandarte* swore an oath of allegiance to the *Führer* in front of the *Feldherrnhalle* in Munich. Hitler's thoughts must have drifted back to his time in Landsberg Prison only ten short years earlier. But no one could challenge him now.

THE SS OATH

All SS men swore a personal oath of allegiance to Hitler, rather than to the state or the constitution. *Waffen-SS* men did this after they had completed their basic training and had been presented with their ceremonial daggers – which they had to pay for themselves. The oath was renewed on 20 April, Hitler's birthday. SS men pledged:

'I swear to thee, Adolf Hitler
As Führer *and Chancellor of the German Reich*
Loyalty and bravery
I vow to thee and to the superiors that you appoint
Obedience unto death
So help me God.'

Himmler's quest

The Nazi bandwagon now seemed unstoppable – and so did the SS, whose membership had now reached 50,000. But the SA was mushrooming too. Its numbers had risen from half a million at the beginning of the year to three million by the end. New members were called 'March violets', after the month in which Hitler had assumed dictatorial powers. They were generally looked down on by veterans of the Beer Hall Putsch, who were entitled to wear the *Blutorden* (Blood Order – decoration of the Munich Putsch).

One of Himmler's main ambitions was to turn Germany into a police state, but he had not lost his early obsession with racial purity and mysticism. Hitler called Himmler 'my Ignatius Loyola' after the founder of the Jesuits, from whose structure and rituals Himmler borrowed freely. However, unlike Loyola he did not act from any religious motives, because he tried to root out churchgoing among the SS. He believed in pagan mysticism and he set up a series of *Ahnenerbe* institutions in order to study the pagan runes that were incorporated into the SS insignia. The institutions also studied old Germanic languages, ancient history and the genealogy of the German people in an attempt to prove his racial theories. Sites related to Henry the Fowler and the Teutonic Knights were excavated and expeditions were sent to Tibet in order to search for Aryan roots. Like Hitler, Himmler was a vegetarian. He recommended that SS officers should only have leeks and mineral water for breakfast. Himmler also believed in astrology and the occult.

To Himmler, the SS was not just a political formation that was loyal to Hitler but a mystical order of Nordic men, a brotherhood inspired by medieval legends and tales of the Teutonic Knights. It held torchlit parades on the anniversary of the Beer Hall Putsch, where members reaffirmed their loyalty to Hitler, repeating their oath as if it were a prayer.

Men were given rings, ceremonial swords and daggers decorated with pagan runes. In 1936, Himmler sought to abolish Christian holidays and replace them with Nazi and pagan celebrations. His list of approved festivals included 20 April, which was Hitler's birthday, May Day, the summer solstice, a harvest feast, and 9 November, the anniversary of the Beer Hall Putsch. Christmas was replaced with Yuletide at the winter solstice, when the SS and their wives had candlelit banquets and celebrated around giant bonfires. SS men were married, and their children were named, at other 'pagan' ceremonies, though some remained stubbornly Christian in their affiliations, if not their actions.

Himmler restored the medieval castle of Wewelsburg outside Paderborn, using slave labour from concentration camps. Within its walls he installed a round table, in emulation of King Arthur, and a hall dedicated to the 12 'knights', Himmler's trusted lieutenants. It was said that each knight of Himmler's round table received a coat of arms. On his death, this was to be incinerated in the Hall of the Supreme Leader. The clifftop castle also contained a library of Aryan folklore.

It has been suggested that Himmler's apparently cranky notions had a serious purpose, that his focus on ritual and mysticism fostered a spirit of idealism in his men, which transcended guilt and rationalized mass murder. Or was he just trying to justify his own enormous crimes to himself by pretending to be on a heroic mission?

On a more mundane note, Himmler was also interested in money-making schemes. In 1934, he set up a publishing company to propagate his racial ideology and two years later the SS purchased a porcelain factory that made Aryan knick-knacks. Eventually Himmler set up the SS Economic and Administrative Main Office (WVHA) which employed slave labour from concentration camps in its commercial ventures. This organization even took over the lucrative business of bottling and distributing mineral water. Perhaps Himmler was trying to wipe out the memory of his failed chicken farm? Backed by the infinite resources of the Party, and with a slave labour force to call upon, he could hardly fail in business this time around.

Mythology and theories of race aside, Himmler's mind was still set on creating a police state. He and Heydrich were already forging ahead in Bavaria, where they had separated the political police from the regular force. After sacking those they found unreliable, they did not fill the vacant posts with Nazi Party members. Instead, they retained their former opponents if they were competent and they recruited any men that Heydrich considered to be intellectuals. Degrees in law, economics, engineering or accountancy were more important than Party credentials. Such men could be coerced into working for the National Socialism cause. Indeed, the needs of the Party were sidelined altogether. What Himmler and Heydrich wanted was a police force that was loyal only to them, while they would be loyal only to Hitler.

It was well known that the SA was a brutal organization but Himmler was more fastidious about the reputation of the SS. However, in 1933 rumours of torture, beatings and murder leaked from Dachau. Munich's public prosecutor investigated and charged three top SS men with incitement to murder. Himmler was forced to fire the camp commandant for the sake of appearances, but he instructed Minister of the Interior Wagner to ban any future investigations of concentration camps on the grounds of state security. He then offered the senior state attorney a post in the SS. The official became deputy chief of the Bavarian political police and no further complaints were heard about Dachau, though the torture, beatings and murders continued.

The new commandant of Dachau was Theodor Eicke, an SS man with a violent reputation. After winning the Iron Cross in the First World War, Eicke joined the *Freikorps*. He then worked as a policeman

Theodor Eicke, a man with a fearsome reputation for brutality,
became commandant of Dachau concentration camp in 1933

but he was dismissed for his outspoken political views. After that he went to work for IG Farben, the chemical industry conglomerate, as an industrial counter-intelligence agent.

His next move was to join the Nazi Party and the SA, but in 1930 he moved into the SS. In 1932 he received a two-year prison sentence for bombing his political rivals, but he was protected by the Minister of Justice, Franz Gürtner, who had secured Hitler's release from Landsberg Prison. Eicke fled to Italy, returning only when Hitler came to power. He was put in charge of the new concentration camp at Dachau, where he tightened discipline and punishment and formed a new SS formation to guard the concentration camps. It was called the *SS-Totenkopfverbände* (SS Death's Head Unit). Members were granted the right to wear the skull and crossbones on their collar patches.

After killing Röhm on the Night of the Long Knives, he was promoted to the role of inspector of concentration camps. His first task was to ensure that all camps conformed to the Dachau model. During the Second World War, he joined the *Waffen-SS* as commander of the *Totenkopf* Division. Although he fought with distinction, he was responsible for several war crimes, including the murder of 97 prisoners of war from the 2nd Royal Norfolk Regiment at Le Paradis on the Pas-de-Calais on 27 May 1940. Under Eicke's command the *Totenkopf* Division murdered a number of Soviet prisoners of war and plundered defenceless villages. While making a reconnaissance flight in the preliminary stages of the Third Battle of Kharkov, he was shot down and killed.

In the early 1930s, Himmler and Heydrich went about creating a national police force, along the lines of the one they had set up in Bavaria. But Göring stood in their way.

'Himmler and Heydrich will never get to Berlin,' he vowed.

The Prussian police force was full of SA and SS men. Even its police chief, Kurt Daluege, was an SS major-general. Wounded several times during the First World War, Daluege was an engineer by profession. While retaining a number of professional posts he joined the *Freikorps*, the Nazi Party, the SA and finally, at Hitler's behest, the SS. His job was to spy on the SA and any dissidents within the Nazi Party. He was one of the group that fought Walter Stennes' SA troops when they invaded the Party headquarters in Berlin.

In November 1932, Daluege was elected to the Reichstag. He then joined the police force, first as a *Kommissar* and then as chief of informants. His efficiency was rewarded when he became chief of police in Prussia in May 1933. During the reorganizations that followed he was regularly promoted, eventually becoming an SS general, the only police officer to attain that rank.

Heydrich disliked him, nicknaming him 'Dummi-Dummi', which makes it ironic that Daluege took over as deputy *Reichsprotektor* of Bohemia and Moravia when Heydrich was assassinated in 1942. In May 1943 he suffered a heart attack and retired to a property given to him by Hitler, but two years later he was arrested by United States troops in Lübeck. In the following year he was extradited to Czechoslovakia, where he was convicted of war crimes and condemned to death. When he was hanged, he was so ill that he was barely conscious.

THE SS TIBET EXPEDITION (1938-39)

Himmler's *Ahnenerbe* institutions promoted some bizarre ideas. One was glacial cosmology. In 1913 the Austrian engineer Hans Hörbiger came up with the notion that outer space was made of ice. This explained why Nordic man was superior – he had grown strong in snow and ice. Hörbiger's hypothesis was also a refutation of Albert Einstein's Theory of Relativity and other 'Jewish science'. Glacial cosmology also explained how Atlantis came to be destroyed. Himmler was a great believer in all of this.

Another popular theory was that the Aryans had come from Atlantis, but traces of them could be found in Tibet. It was then but a short step to the idea that Hinduism and Buddhism had Aryan origins. It is said that Himmler carried a copy of the Hindu scripture, the *Bhagavad Gita*, during the Holocaust, believing that somehow it absolved him of his guilt.

In 1938, Himmler sent an expedition to Tibet under SS officer Ernst Schäfer, a hunter and zoologist. Schäfer was asked to find proof that the Aryan people had migrated from Tibet to Europe 15 centuries earlier. In an exercise that was curiously reminiscent of the Nazi 'race examiners', the expedition scientists measured the craniums of the local people and took plaster casts of their features. The mission also returned with a number of ancient Tibetan texts, which were said to have been of Aryan origin.

The quest proved nothing. After the Second World War Schäfer distanced himself from the embarrassing episode by claiming that he had joined the SS under duress.

Göring's Gestapo

Göring was intent on checking the headlong progress of Himmler and Heydrich, so on 26 April 1933 he used his position as interior minister of Prussia to hive off the political and intelligence departments of the Prussian police force. He then manned it with Nazis. But he was careful to put a civil servant with no Party affiliation, Rudolf Diels, in charge.

—𝓈𝓈———————————————————————

The new organization was to be called the *Geheime Staatspolizei* (secret state police). It was moved out of the police headquarters to an address that would become infamous, 8 Prinz Albrechtstrasse. A postal clerk who was making a franking stamp contracted the organization's name to 'Gestapo'. He had created a name that would strike fear into the hearts of millions of people.

Diels was told to disregard the restrictions of state law.

'I have no obligation to abide by the law,' said Göring. 'My job is simply to annihilate and exterminate – nothing more.'

He then hired gangs of SA thugs, who dragged people from their homes or off the streets. Hundreds were crammed into makeshift detention centres. There were 50 of these temporary prisons in Berlin alone. Diels was appalled, so he sent his Gestapo men to track down the torturers. On one occasion, his men surrounded an SA detention centre and forced the Brownshirts to surrender. Inside, Diels discovered that a number of prisoners had been savagely beaten.

'When we entered, these living skeletons were lying in rows on filthy straw with festering wounds,' he said.

A dozen or so thugs had been employed to beat their victims with rubber truncheons, whips and iron bars. The SS was also capable of such things but it was more discreet – its torture chambers were hidden. No one was safe at that time. Even the chief of criminal police, SS Major-General Artur Nebe, was reduced to going in and out of his office by a back stairway, with a cocked pistol in his pocket.

Then the Gestapo began to arrest one another. An SS squad raided Diels' home, locking his wife in the bedroom while they searched the place. Himmler protested when Diels ordered the arrest of the man who had led the raid, so Göring forced Diels to hand the man over to the SS for trial. Meanwhile, Reich interior minister Wilhelm Frick, a former associate of Gregor Strasser, made another attempt to take over the Prussian police force so that he could incorporate it into a national force. In order to outmanoeuvre him, Göring forged an alliance with Himmler. It would put Himmler in charge of all of the political police forces in Germany.

Chapter Three

THE NIGHT OF THE LONG KNIVES

Although Hitler had seized dictatorial power in 1933, he realized that his position was not secure. Most of all his position was threatened by the SA, led by his old friend Ernst Röhm. However, with a force of over three million men, the SA could well have absorbed the much smaller German army, which would have made Röhm its overall leader. That was why Hitler had to act, and act quickly he did.

itler was aware that power was linked to money. He was already funded by a group of wealthy businessmen and industrialists, who had supported him for fear of a communist takeover. But they were uneasy about Röhm's revolutionary views and would be glad to see him ousted. Added to that, a number of Party members disapproved of the fact that Röhm and some of the other SA leaders were homosexuals. The SA was a penniless, disruptive force that threatened Germany's economic stability and Hitler's own position. A ruthless move against the organization would not only remove a thorn in his side but it would also cow all of the remaining opposition. And the SA could then be blamed for all of the Nazi Party's previous excesses. Hitler already had the perfect weapon to hand in the shape of the SS, who had already proved their unswerving loyalty. However, the dictator

The Banner Company of the SS in Bavaria, 1932: that year the SS and the SA were banned in Germany for plotting a coup, but the ban was lifted

still hesitated. Röhm was the only one of his political associates that he could call '*du*', the familiar form of address in German.

Although Himmler and Göring constantly played on Hitler's sense of insecurity by supplying him with false information about Röhm's planned coup, any remaining doubts were removed by Röhm himself. On 28 February 1934, the SA leader made a speech in which he declared that the SA was the true army of National Socialism and that the *Reichswehr* should be demoted to the status of a training corps. It seemed clear that Röhm was angling to become the new Minister of Defence. This would obviously not sit very well with the German generals and it was a threat to Hitler himself, who had ambitions far outside the borders of Germany. Besides, President Hindenburg was now mortally ill. When he died, Hitler intended to seize the presidency as well, a move that only the army had the power to prevent.

One of Hitler's ploys was to encourage his senior commanders to compete with one another so that they would be too busy to organize a coup against him. As a result Göring, Himmler and Röhm were at daggers drawn – but both Göring and Himmler were fearful of Röhm's motives. Göring had intended to make an independent move against the SA, but he realized that his Gestapo was not strong enough, so he curbed his dislike of Himmler in order to make a deal with him.

On 20 April 1934, control over the Gestapo was handed to Himmler, which made him the head of all of the political police forces in Germany. Himmler seized the opportunity to move from Munich to Berlin, so that he would remain in the inner circle of Nazis who now had national power. Rudolf Diels, the first commander of the Gestapo, was dismissed and Reinhard Heydrich became its new leader, while remaining at the head of the SD.

Hitler met with Röhm on 2 June 1934. They agreed to send the SA

—ᛋᛋ—

on leave for the whole of July, but while they continued their talks Hitler had Göring, Himmler and Heydrich draw up a death list with Viktor Lutze, an SA insider. The meetings continued, with Röhm agreeing to make peace with the seemingly conciliatory Hitler, but when Hitler left the room Röhm was heard to say: 'What that ridiculous corporal says means nothing to us. I have not the slightest intention of keeping this agreement. Hitler is a traitor and, at the very least, must go on leave.'

While Hitler dithered, the others pressed ahead. Heydrich ordered Théodor Eicke to prepare his men to take on the SA in nearby Munich. Eicke's troops, the *SS-Totenkopfverbände* (SS-TV), were the ferocious band of thugs that ran the concentration camps. Although Himmler had long admired Röhm, not least because of his war service, he knew that the SA chief of staff stood between him and even more power. Göring also fancied being Minister of Defence and commander of the army. There was no way that he was going to let Röhm take that role.

With Hindenburg on his death bed, Hitler feared that von Papen might attempt to gain power by making a deal with the army. But while visiting Hindenburg, Hitler was upbraided by the normally quiescent defence minister, General Werner von Blomberg, for not curbing the SA. Two days later, the army was ordered to put its arms at the disposal of the SS.

Röhm's execution

For Himmler, this was an opportunity that was too good to miss. With the SA out of the way his SS would reign supreme. Together with Göring, Goebbels, Heydrich and Rudolf Hess, he manufactured 'evidence' that pointed to Röhm having been paid 12 million marks by France to overthrow Hitler. It was also claimed that Gregor Strasser, one of Hitler's mortal enemies, was part of the coup against him. All of this was backed up by a report that the SA had not been sent on leave but had instead been put on alert in Berlin, ready to take over the government buildings. SA men had also been seen loading rifles on to trucks. The first account was a complete fabrication but the second one was true – SA troops had been loading up old arms from the *Freikorps* days, to hand over to the Bavarian police.

SS teams in cities across Germany were put on the alert. Sepp Dietrich and two hand-picked companies of the *Leibstandarte SS Adolf Hitler*, equipped by the army, were sent to Bavaria where Röhm and his principal lieutenants were relaxing at a spa at Bad Wiessee. Despite warnings to be more discreet about his homosexuality, Röhm was indulging himself in one last orgy.

On 30 June news came from Munich that the SA had taken to the streets, so Hitler flew there with Viktor Lutze. He was met by the Nazi *Gauleiter* (district governor), two *Reichswehr* officers and old *Stosstruppe* (stormtrooper) comrades. The SA chief in Munich was summoned.

'You're a traitor,' said Hitler as he tore off the man's insignia. 'You will be shot.'

He was.

Hitler then travelled to Bad Wiessee. Sepp Dietrich had ordered his men to surround the hotel in which Röhm was staying. Hitler burst into Röhm's room brandishing a pistol and again screamed: 'You are a traitor. You will be shot.' In an adjoining room, the SS found SA leader Edmund Heines in bed with an unidentified 18-year-old SA troop leader. They were shot on the personal order of Hitler.

Röhm was taken to Stadelheim Prison in Munich, along with six others. He was thrown in a cell, while the other six were lined up in the courtyard and shot. Some made the Nazi salute and shouted, 'Heil

Hitler!', thus paying homage to the man who had ordered their deaths, while others cursed. SA Lieutenant-General August Schneidhuber cried out: 'Sepp, old comrade! What's going on? We're innocent!'

Dietrich clicked his heels.

'You have been condemned to death by the *Führer*, Heil Hitler!' he exclaimed. And the shooting began.

At a meeting in which he literally foamed at the mouth, Hitler affirmed Röhm's death sentence. Then he changed his mind, promising that Röhm's life would be spared. Göring and Himmler were terrified that Hitler might believe Röhm when he asserted that he had never been involved in a plot against his leader, so they convinced Hitler to overcome his squeamishness. He finally gave the order.

Rudolf Hess pleaded excitedly: '*Mein Führer*, it is my job to shoot Röhm.'

Instead two dependable SS murderers were sent – the commandant of Dachau, Theodor Eicke, and his adjutant, SS Major Michael Lippert. Prison governor Lechler directed them to Röhm's cell.

Hitler had told them to take along the latest edition of the *Völkischer Beobachter*, which carried the news of the failure of the so-called 'Röhm-Putsch'. The newspaper was wrapped around a pistol that was loaded with just one bullet.

'You have forfeited your life,' said Eicke. 'The *Führer* gives you one more chance to draw the right conclusions.'

Then they left Röhm alone for 15 minutes. Hearing no shot, they returned. Eicke and Lippert then took aim at Röhm.

'Take it slowly,' Eicke said to Lippert, who was trembling.

The SS men shot twice. Röhm fell, groaning.

'*Mein Führer, mein Führer*,' he said.

'You should have thought of that before,' said Eicke. 'Now it's too late.'

While the killing was going on, Hitler was throwing a garden party for members of the cabinet and their wives and children. He was said to be in an expansive mood, drinking tea and ruffling the hair of the youngsters.

The new SA leader

Röhm's successor was Viktor Lutze. He rose to the rank of company commander in the First World War, when he was wounded four times, losing one of his eyes. After the war, he became a policeman before joining the Nazi Party in 1922. Together with the SA, he organized the resistance to the French occupation of the Ruhr in 1923.

When Hitler came to power, Lutze became police chief in Hanover and later provincial governor. It was Lutze who told Hitler of Röhm's speech of 28 February 1934, in which the former leader of the SA had outlined his ambitions. He also decided which members of the SA should be murdered on the Night of the Long Knives. Unlike Röhm he posed no threat to Himmler and Hitler when he became leader of the SA, because he was seen as a weak man who was happy to serve his leaders. His job was to root out disloyal elements and reduce the size of the organization. At the Nazi Party Congress in Nuremberg in September 1934 he reaffirmed the SA's loyalty to the Party. In Leni Riefenstahl's film *Triumph of the Will,* Lutze was seen making a speech and being mobbed by the SA, though elsewhere it was recorded that he was far from popular.

In 1937, Lutze ordered the SA to support the anti-Christian efforts of the Nazi Party, which included banning religious ceremonies, seizing Church property and jailing the clergy. Then following the *Anschluss* he organized the SA in Austria, where they terrorized the Jews alongside the SS during *Kristallnacht*. He also reviewed a parade of 20,000 Blackshirts in Rome in February 1939 and he later visited North Africa.

Lutze remained head of the SA until he died in 1943 following a car accident. He was posthumously awarded the highest grade of the German Order and was given a state funeral, which Hitler attended.

The killings begin

Meanwhile, the secret code word *kolibri* (hummingbird) had been sent out – the Night of the Long Knives was called 'Operation Hummingbird' – and in every part of the Reich SS and Gestapo officers were opening sealed envelopes. The death list was circulated and old scores were settled, though nearly half of the victims were not even members of the SA. One of them was Wilhelm Schmid, the music critic of the *Münchner Neueste Nachrichten*. It is thought that this was a case of mistaken identity and that he had been mistaken for SA Major-General Wilhelm Schmidt.

Schmid had been playing the cello with his wife and children in the next room when the SS came to take him away. He was returned to his widow in a casket.

She was given strict instructions not to open it. When Rudolf Hess dropped round later to express his regrets, he offered Schmid's widow a pension, adding gratuitously that Schmid had died 'for a great cause'.

Former chancellor Kurt von Schleicher was executed on the spot. When two SS men arrived at his Potsdam home late at night, the door was opened by a cook. She was roughly pushed aside as the SS men headed for the ex-chancellor's study.

'Are you General von Schleicher?' they asked.

'Yes, I am von Schleicher,' he replied.

They shot him dead.

Hearing the gunfire, his wife came running. They killed her too.

Seventy-one-year-old Gustav von Kahr, leader of the Bavarian government during the Beer Hall Putsch, was taken to Dachau where he was tortured on Eicke's orders. His body was later found in a swampy part of Dachau heath. It had been hacked to pieces with a pickaxe. Then Gregor Strasser, whom Himmler feared might be reconciled with Hitler, died in a Gestapo cellar in Berlin. Shot from behind, his death was declared a suicide.

Rudolf Diels was the one that got away. After acting as the main interrogator of Marius van der Lubbe, the man accused of setting fire to the Reichstag in Berlin, he became head of the newly formed Gestapo, only to be dismissed by Himmler in April 1934. During the Night of the Long Knives he fled to Czechoslovakia, returning after five weeks.

He then married Göring's cousin. Göring honoured the family connection by saving him from prison twice – once when he declined an order to arrest some Jews and again after the plot to assassinate Hitler in July 1944.

Diels gave an affidavit for the prosecution at the Nuremberg trials but was also summoned to testify by Göring's defence lawyer. He served in the postwar government of Lower Saxony from 1950 onwards and then in the Ministry of the Interior until his retirement in 1953. He died following a hunting accident.

A statute was signed by Hitler on 3 July, retrospectively legalizing the murders. It contained just one sentence: 'The measures taken on 30 June and 1 and 2 July to crush treasonable attacks on our nation are a legal act of self-defence.'

Who the killers were

On 30 June 1934 a squad of SS men burst into Erich Klausener's office at the Ministry of Transport. The surprised official was just about to cry out in protest when SS Captain Kurt Gildisch pulled out a revolver and shot him. Klausener was the leader of the police department in the Prussian Ministry of Internal Affairs and a member of the Catholic Action Group, but Gildisch did not even know him. He only knew that Klausener had criticized the National Socialists in a speech he had made a couple of weeks earlier.

On Heydrich's orders Gildisch also arrested several SA men, who were taken to the *Leibstandarte* barracks in the suburb of Lichterfelde. One was a doctor and another thought his comrades were playing a joke on him, because his death had already been announced in the local newspaper.

Gildisch joined the SS after being dismissed from the police force. In April 1933 he took command of Hitler's personal bodyguard commando, but he was dismissed for heavy drinking. When he had played his part in the Night of the Long Knives he was dismissed from the SS and the Nazi Party, but after taking a leadership course in the *SS-Junkerschule* in 1941 he was made a second lieutenant in the *Waffen-SS*. He fought on the Eastern Front, but after several more drunken incidents Theodor Eicke sentenced him to house arrest, which was followed by time spent recuperating in the barracks of Buchenwald concentration camp. Later, he was wounded and captured during the Battle of Berlin, but the Soviets returned him in 1946 when he needed his right leg amputated. In 1949, he was recognized by a friend at a Berlin train station, after which he was arrested. He was sentenced to 15 years in jail for the murder of Erich Klausener, but he died in hospital of an incurable liver disease.

Born in Pomerania the son of a Junker, Erich von dem Bach-Zelewski was responsible for the mass murder of civilians in eastern Europe (see pp.86-8)

SS police commander Udo von Woyrsch also took delight in carrying out Hitler's killing orders to the letter, particularly when it meant settling old scores. He ordered his men to chase his rival Emil Sembach through a forest before blasting him to death with shotguns.

A first lieutenant and winner of the Iron Cross First Class during the First World War, Woyrsch first joined the *Freikorps* and then the Nazi Party and the SS. In 1933, he was elected to the Reichstag. On 30 June 1934 he took command in Silesia and on the orders of Göring he arrested a number of SA leaders, disarmed all of the SA headquarters' guards and then occupied the Breslau police headquarters.

Woyrsch's men murdered a number of SA officers as the result of a private feud. In 1935 Woyrsch was promoted to SS lieutenant-general, when he served on Himmler's private staff. Then in September 1939 he commanded an *Einsatzgruppe* (special operations unit), which terrorized and murdered the Jews in Poland. His campaign around Katowice was so brutal that *Wehrmacht* officers asked the Gestapo to have the *Einsatzgruppe* withdrawn. Between 20 April 1940 and February 1944, he was the Higher SS and police leader in military district IV and district leader in Dresden. Captured by the British, he became a prisoner of war from 1945 to 1948. He was then sentenced to 20 years' imprisonment, but he was released in 1952. Although he was tried again in 1957 for his part in the Night of the Long Knives, he was released in 1960.

SS Lieutenant-General Erich von dem Bach-Zelewski also took the opportunity to eliminate an old enemy. He sent two SS men to kill his rival, *Reiterführer* Baron Anton von Hohberg und Buchwald. They shot the baron from behind in his own drawing room. When his 17-year-old son rushed in to find out what was happening, they said: 'We have just shot your father.'

Born Erich von Zelewski, he added the 'dem Bach' in the late 1930s and then had the Zelewski officially removed in 1941 because it sounded Polish. One of the youngest recruits to the Prussian army, he was wounded twice and won the Iron Cross during the First World War. As a member of the *Reichswehr*, he fought against the Polish uprisings in Silesia in 1919–21. To his annoyance, three of his sisters married Jewish men. After serving in the Border Guards, he joined the Nazi Party in 1930 and the SS in 1931. He won rapid promotion, serving as a Reichstag deputy from 1932 to 1934, but he then fell out with his staff officer, Anton von Hohberg und Buchwald, which is why he had him killed during the Night of the Long Knives.

In November 1939 he went to Silesia where he became Commissioner for the Strengthening of Germandom and then Higher SS and police leader. His duties included mass resettlements and the confiscation of private property. By August 1940 his units had forced more than 20,000 families to leave their homes. Later on he started the building of a concentration camp at the Polish artillery barracks in the Zasole suburb of Oswiecim, which would become known as Auschwitz.

In July 1943, he became commander of the *Bandenkämpfverbände* (Bandit-fighting Units) that were responsible for the mass murder of 35,000 civilians in Riga and more than 200,000 people in Belarus and eastern Poland. He was chosen as the future Higher SS and police leader in Moscow, but the Germans failed to take the city, so his new post did not materialize.

He was then assigned to anti-partisan duties, but he suffered a nervous breakdown. However, in August 1944 he took command of the German troops fighting the Warsaw Uprising. While the Red Army looked on, units under his command killed approximately 200,000 civilians – more than 65,000 in mass executions – and an unknown number of prisoners of war.

After more than two months of heavy fighting and the total destruction of Warsaw he finally managed to take control of the city and was awarded the Knight's Cross. After the war he went into hiding, but was arrested by the Americans in August 1945. To avoid being extradited to Poland to face a war crimes trial, he became a witness for the prosecution at Nuremberg. In 1951, he was sentenced to ten years' special labour, which amounted to house arrest.

It was only in 1958 that he actually served time, after being sentenced to four-and-a-half years' imprisonment for the murder of Anton von Hohberg und Buchwald. He was sentenced to another ten years for the murders of ten German communists in the early 1930s. But he escaped punishment for murdering countless Jews and perpetrating other crimes again humanity. He died in Munich-Harlaching Prison in 1972.

The aftermath

At least 85 people died immediately in the purge – Hitler himself admitted to 77 deaths at a meeting of the Reichstag on 13 July 1934, which was temporarily accommodated in the Kroll Opera House. But the death toll climbed into the hundreds as thousands more were arrested and incarcerated. Flanked by steel-helmeted SS men, Hitler justified the murders in his speech.

In that hour I was responsible for the fate of the German people, and thereby I became the supreme judge of the German people. I gave the order to shoot the ringleaders in this treason, and I further gave the order to cauterize down to the raw flesh the ulcers of this poisoning of the wells in our domestic life. Let the nation know that its existence – which depends on its internal order and security – cannot be threatened with impunity by anyone. And let it be known for all time to come that if anyone raises his hand to strike the state, then certain death is his lot.

The SS also had its reward. On 26 July the *Völkischer Beobachter* carried a decree from Hitler, which read:

In consideration of the great services rendered by the SS, particularly in connection with the events of 30 June 1934, I hereby promote the SS to the status of an independent organization within the NSDAP.

Himmler was a step closer to gaining control of all of Germany's security organizations. From then on the Night of the Long Knives ('Operation Hummingbird' – the Röhm-Putsch), would become the 'Blood Purge' and those who had taken part in it would be lauded alongside those who were at the Beer Hall Putsch of 1923.

The arbitrary arrests and imprisonments in concentration camps appalled even some senior Nazis. Franz Gürtner, Hitler's Minister of Justice, and the Party's top legal expert, Hans Frank, recommended that the camps should be closed and those in custody should be tried in regular courts. Himmler, who was at the meeting, glared at them. Hitler merely declared that such a move would be 'premature'.

Further protests were silenced by Werner Best, whom Heydrich had appointed as chief legal adviser to the Gestapo. According to Best: 'Insofar as the police are acting in accordance with the rules laid down by their superiors – right up to the highest level – they can never be acting "lawlessly" or "contrary to law".'

In other words, the police and the Gestapo could do what they liked.

But what qualified Best to award such powers to the German security services? As an early member of the German National Youth Movement and the German National People's Party, Best was imbued with German myths and the *Völkisch* 'return to nature' world view. He then studied law and was arrested twice by the French authorities for his activities in the Ruhr.

In 1931, he was sacked by the Hessian Department of Justice when he was found in possession of the Boxheim documents, named after the estate near Worms where the National Socialists met to discuss what they should do in the event of a communist revolution. Their plans were drastic:

1. Fascist 'Storm Divisions' were to seize government in a counter coup d'état.

2. Any citizen caught bearing arms or disobeying the orders of a 'Storm Commander' was to be shot without trial.

3. Private property was to be 'abolished provisionally', all bank deposits were to be 'immobilized in the banks' and interest payments stopped.

Reinhard Heydrich was responsible for the slaughter of millions while imagining he was saving the world from 'intellectual and moral decay'

4. The Fascist Dictatorship was to abolish wages, enrol the able-bodied citizenry (except Jews) in state labour divisions and distribute food by a system of rationing to everyone (except Jews, who would starve).

The documents, which bore Best's signature, embarrassed Hitler who was seeking power by legal means at the time. Best then joined the Nazi Party and the SS, quickly rising through the ranks. He became head of legal affairs for the Gestapo and Heydrich's deputy. At the Reich Main Security Office (RSHA), Himmler and Heydrich depended on Best to give some legal gloss to the deportation and murder of Jews and Polish intellectuals. In 1942, Best was sent as Reich Plenipotentiary to Denmark, where he remained until the end of the war. He was arrested and sentenced to death by a Danish court, but the sentence was commuted. After being released in 1951 and returned to Germany, he was fined 70,000 marks as a senior SS man under the de-Nazification programme. He was imprisoned again in 1969 and he was charged with further war crimes in 1972, but he was released when he was found unfit to stand trial.

Growth of the Gestapo

'Soon no one dared to utter anything that might be construed as hostile to the regime or even critical of it,' said the journalist Bernt Engelmann, who was studying in Berlin at the time. 'No one knew whether there might be an SD spy among their close friends, or even their own family.'

Engelmann told the tale of a widow named Meinzerhagen who

bought a new radio. That night she wanted to try it out, so she closed the windows and drew the curtains. With only her daughter present, she went around the dial to find out what stations it could pick up. Shortly afterwards she was arrested by the Gestapo, who accused her of listening to 'horror stories about Germany' put out by foreign broadcasters – or worse, 'nigger jazz'. She could well have been denounced by her next-door neighbour, who once complained that she beat carpets during his afternoon nap. Fortunately, Mrs Meinzerhagen was let off with a warning on that occasion. But even a few careless words could cost a life. Engelmann recalled being at a boozy New Year's Eve party when a Brownshirt stood up and gave a speech, which ended with the words: 'God save our *Führer…*'

'… And us from him,' whispered an elderly attorney at Engelmann's table. A few days later, the attorney was arrested as a 'dangerous enemy of the state' and was sent to a concentration camp. Later his ashes were returned in an urn.

Under Heydrich, the Gestapo grew from a staff of 35 in 1934 to 607 in 1935. Coupled with the SD, it became a formidable tool of oppression. Heydrich's index cards proliferated. They had different-coloured tags on the right-hand side denoting whether the subject was a communist, a Marxist, an assassin or a 'grumbler' – that is, someone who complained about the regime. And Heydrich had already anticipated war. On the left-hand side other colour-coded tags indicated whether the subject should be picked up before or after mobilization, or should merely be kept under close surveillance.

In a rare speech in 1935, Heydrich would claim that 'enemy organizations have been smashed'. These were 'world Jewry, world Freemasonry and the clergy, who are to a large extent political'.

Between 1935 and 1936, the Gestapo arrested over 7,000 people

——*ϟϟ*——————————————————————————————

whose crime, Best maintained, was to make 'any attempt to gain recognition for, or even to uphold, different political ideas'. Meanwhile, in Bavaria the political police followed Wagner's directive to 'arrest without pity persons strolling about in a suspicious manner'.

'It is enough to drive one to despair,' said Reich justice minister Gürtner.

Himmler becomes chief of police

The only apparent solution to these excesses was once again to consolidate all of the state police into a national force. This time interior minister Wilhelm Frick negotiated with Himmler. On 17 June 1936 he agreed that Himmler would be made head of the national force as long as it was under the control of the interior ministry. Fortunately for Himmler, Heydrich was in charge of the negotiations between the SS and the ministry. He insisted that Himmler be made a government minister as well as chief of police and *SS-Reichsführer*. Frick found himself outmanoeuvred so Himmler was named chief of police. Not only was he in charge of the SS and the SD, he was now head of all the national and state police forces, including the Gestapo. And although he was not given ministerial status, he was answerable only to Hitler.

Heydrich followed his boss up the greasy pole. The criminal police were added to his portfolio, along with the Gestapo and the SD. And his card index expanded as he went along. By 1937, the categories included communists, Marxists, Freemasons, Jews, political malcontents, the nationalist opposition, reactionaries, economic saboteurs, habitual criminals, traitors to the country and the state, abortionists and homosexuals. These last two were thought to endanger the defence of the state by not contributing to the increase of the population.

Homosexuals were also thought to be particularly prone to espionage.

The problem with including habitual criminals in Heydrich's card index was that they were under the jurisdiction of the criminal courts, so Best was ordered to come up with a legal argument for their summary detention. In 1937, the criminal police were sent out to arrest 2,000 habitual 'offenders against morality' and 'antisocial malefactors'. They were sent to concentration camps. Citizens could no longer count on the protection of the law, for guilt or innocence was no longer something to be decided by the courts. The police could arrest anyone for what they thought they might do in the future. Those who had been arrested had just three minutes in which to pack their belongings. After that they were required to 'agree' to being sent to a concentration camp by signing Form D-11. A signature would be obtained one way or another, so there was little point in resisting. The severity of their punishment would be decided by the commandants of the concentration camps. Theodor Eicke had reorganized these camps into just four large units – Dachau near Munich, Buchenwald near Weimar, Sachsenhausen near Berlin and Lichtenburg near Wittenberg.

Like Himmler, Heydrich was greedy for power. He wanted to take over the concentration camps from Eicke. After citing the human rights abuses that had been reported, he said that he could run them much more 'efficiently'. But Himmler had problems of his own. The police forces he had taken over had not been racially screened. Nor had they been infused with the Nordic mythology that permeated the SS.

Hitler takes over the army

Hitler had even bigger problems. Although the army – redesignated the *Wehrmacht* in 1935 – had supplied weapons and transportation during the Night of the Long Knives, it opposed his plan for foreign expansion. However, in November 1937 Hitler declared that he would give the German people the *Lebensraum* or living space that he had promised them in *Mein Kampf* within six years – even if it meant risking war. The commander-in-chief of the army, General Werner Freiherr von Fritsch and the newly-promoted Field Marshal Werner von Blomberg, formerly Minister of Defence, now Minister of War, said this was impossible.

Hitler did not want to ruin the army's effectiveness by filling it with loyal Party men, nor did he dare oppose it. The army had the weapons to overthrow him, but Heydrich had the means to assist his plans. In the previous year, a thief and blackmailer named Otto Schmidt claimed to have witnessed a homosexual incident involving an army officer named Fritsch.

He was prevailed upon to identify the man as General von Fritsch, although the Gestapo could find no evidence when they investigated the case. Undaunted, Heydrich's men turned their attention to von Blomberg, who had recently remarried at a private ceremony attended by Hitler and Göring. A few days later, the criminal police reported that the new Frau Blomberg had been a prostitute – and they had some obscene pictures to prove it.

As the nominal head of the Prussian Gestapo, Göring gave the information to Hitler. Fritsch and Blomberg were dismissed and Hitler then seized the opportunity to reorganize the army. Sixteen other generals were sacked and 44 were reassigned. But Göring did not become Minister of War and commander-in-chief as he had hoped. Instead Hitler dissolved the War Ministry altogether. He replaced it with the *Oberkommando der Wehrmacht* (OKW) and he became commander-in-chief of the armed forces himself.

The plot thickens

However, Fritsch would not take his dismissal lying down. When he was told of the allegations of homosexuality, he exclaimed, 'It's a stinking lie!', and he demanded a court martial to clear his name. While the case was being prepared, it became clear that the officer involved was not General Fritsch but a Captain Frisch. Nevertheless, Himmler and Heydrich did not tell Göring, who had recently been promoted to the rank of field marshal. Göring was going to be chairman of the court.

Fritsch was so confident that he was going to be cleared that he submitted to an interrogation by the Gestapo. Meanwhile, Himmler assembled 12 SS officers in an adjacent room and told them to use their mental powers to make Fritsch 'tell the truth' and admit his homosexual dalliance. Heydrich's assistant Walter Schellenberg walked in on what he took to be a séance. The officers were 'sitting in a circle, all sunk in deep and silent contemplation … a remarkable sight,' he said.

Schellenberg was an interesting character in his own right. After studying law, he joined the SS in 1933 and went to work in the counter-intelligence department of the SD. In 1939, posing as a member of the resistance, he organized the kidnapping of two British agents from Venlo in neutral Holland, providing Hitler with the excuse to invade. It is also thought that he was involved in a plot to abduct the Duke of Windsor and that he was given the job of compiling a list of 2,820 prominent people to be arrested in the event of a successful invasion of Britain.

From 1939 to 1942 he was Heinrich Himmler's personal aide and a deputy leader of the Reich Main Security Office under Heydrich. On Heydrich's order Schellenberg took over a high-class brothel called Salon Kitty at Giesebrechstrasse 11 in Berlin. The madam, Kitty

Schmidt, had been smuggling money out of Germany and was caught trying to flee to Britain in June 1939. She was told that she could either co-operate with the SD or go to a concentration camp. Microphones were installed in the bedrooms, while girls supplied by the vice squad were taught how to wheedle information out of their clients – who included top Nazis, businessmen and diplomats.

After the downfall of Heydrich's nemesis, Admiral Wilhelm Canaris, in February 1944, Schellenberg took over the *Abwehr* (military intelligence organization), which was then dismantled. He then became head of all of the secret services. It was said that he had an 'office fortress' desk with two guns built into it, that fired at the touch of a button.

In 1945, he acted as a negotiator between Swedish diplomat Count Folke Bernadotte and Himmler, who wanted to surrender to the Western Allies. He flew to London in the same year, carrying a list of his agents, and he testified against other Nazis at Nuremberg. Sentenced to six years' imprisonment in 1949, he was released in 1951, when he moved to Italy, where he died of cancer.

Word spread to the army that the allegations against Fritsch were a case of mistaken identity and the Gestapo expected reprisals. On the evening before the trial, Heydrich invited Schellenberg to dinner and told him to bring a gun. As the time ticked by, Heydrich grew increasingly nervous. Finally, Heydrich said: 'If they don't start marching from Potsdam in the hour and a half, the danger will have passed.'

He then revealed that certain army officers had talked of marching on the Gestapo headquarters – but they missed their opportunity. However, the truth did come out. In court, Göring forced Schmidt to admit that he was committing perjury. Himmler had him shot and Fritsch was cleared, but the general's former position had been taken. However, he was recalled in time for the invasion of Poland. While he was inspecting the front lines, he was shot dead. It is thought that he wanted to die.

Heydrich then achieved his ambition. While Eicke went into action with the *Waffen-SS*, Heydrich took over the concentration camps. In September 1939 Himmler merged the SS, the SD, the Gestapo, the criminal police (Kripo) and all of the other police forces under his control into the Reich Security Head Office (RSHA), making Heydrich its head. But the entire operation was subordinate to chief of police and *SS-Reichsführer* Himmler, who was answerable only to Hitler.

Chapter Four

MAKING WAR

Although several countries had signed peace treaties with Hitler, SS commanders were aware that nothing would prevent him from going to war. If Hitler's fellow world leaders had taken the trouble to read *Mein Kampf*, they would have known that his first foreign policy objective would be the annexation of Austria. As always, Himmler was eager to help in any way he could.

—ᛋᛋ——————————————————————————

J ust as the earth is attracted to the sun, so was Austria attracted to Germany, its much larger neighbour. It was inevitable, therefore, that Austria formed its own DAP in 1903 – the German Workers' Party in Austria. In May 1918, the DAP changed its name to the National Socialist German Workers' Party (DNSAP) and it produced a National Socialist programme which possibly influenced the later Nazi German manifesto. In 1923, the party split into two factions, but by 1930 most former members of the DNSAP had become members of the German NSDAP, which was led by Adolf Hitler. Between 1930 and 1933 the Austrian membership of the Nazi Party swelled from around 300 to 40,000.

It was clear that tiny Austria would not be able to survive alone during the Great Depression. Many ordinary Austrians favoured a customs union with Germany, but the Austrian chancellor, Engelbert Dollfuss, wanted to keep the Nazi Party at arm's length. His solution was to turn to Italy for support. In 1933 he signed a deal with Mussolini, which guaranteed Austria its independence provided it abolished all political parties and reorganized its constitution along Fascist lines. Consequently, the Nazi Party was outlawed in Austria. That was the signal for thousands of Austrian Nazis to flee into the arms of Himmler, who was waiting for them in Bavaria. The fugitives were then formed into an Austrian legion, after being armed by the SS. Other Party members were recruited inside Austria. When the force's numbers reached 5,000, a campaign of sabotage and political assassination began.

One of Himmler's recruits was former sergeant major Fridolin Glass, who had been thrown out of the Austrian army after bringing six companies of Brownshirts together to create his own force. Following a visit to Himmler in Berlin, Glass was made an officer in the SS and his private army became *Standarte 89*. The plan was to seize Dollfuss and the radio station in Vienna and then proclaim a Nazi government.

At 1 pm on 25 July 1934, a convoy of Austrian army trucks pulled up outside the chancellery on the Ballhausplatz, Vienna's central square. One hundred and fifty *Standarte 89* troops swarmed out, disguised as soldiers and policemen. Armed and ready for action, they stormed upstairs to the room in which Dollfuss should have been in a meeting with his ministers. However, a traitor had warned the rest of the cabinet and Dollfuss sat there alone. After being shot in the neck he was laid out on a couch. His assassins denied him medical attention and he bled to death while they were haranguing him.

The radio station was occupied by *Standarte 89*, who announced that Dollfuss had resigned. However, the promised SA reinforcements did not materialize because the SA troops still felt bitter about the role of the SS in the Night of the Long Knives. When the army and the police force surrounded the chancellery, Glass's force was too small to put up a fight, so the putsch failed. Hitler was attending a performance of Wagner's *Das Rheingold* at the Bayreuth festival while the putsch was going on. He was delighted by the news that Dollfuss was dead, but when he discovered that Dollfuss's wife and children had been staying with Mussolini in Italy at the time of the assassination, he disowned the attack.

Dollfuss's successor, Kurt von Schuschnigg, tried to organize a referendum which he hoped would demonstrate that the Austrian people wanted independence. But Hitler had other ideas. The German Ministry of Propaganda issued reports that riots had broken out in Austria and that the Austrian people had called for German troops to restore order. In the face of mounting pressure from Hitler, who was threatening invasion, the referendum was cancelled and Schuschnigg resigned.

Then on 11 March the Austrian Nazi Party took over Austria's state institutions and many members of the government were arrested. The Austrian president, Wilhelm Miklas, was finally forced into appointing Arthur Seyss-Inquart as chancellor. After all of this turmoil, the *Wehrmacht* was greeted by cheering crowds when it entered Austria on 12 March 1938. Austria had been annexed without a struggle.

Born in Austria, Seyss-Inquart fought with the Austro-Hungarian army during the First World War, when he was seriously wounded. In 1921 he became a lawyer in Vienna, after which he devoted himself to achieving *Anschluss* through political means.

Following the assassination of Engelbert Dollfuss, Seyss-Inquart joined the government led by his successor, Kurt von Schuschnigg. In 1938, Schuschnigg made Seyss-Inquart Minister of the Interior with control over the police force – but that was because Hitler had threatened invasion. On 11 March, with Hitler's troops at Austria's borders, Seyss-Inquart became chancellor, and two days later he became a member of the Nazi Party. Instead of keeping Austria as a satellite state, as he had first intended, Hitler decided to call it Ostmark and make it a province of the Reich. Seyss-Inquart signed the necessary act on the same day.

As *Reichsstatthalter*, Seyss-Inquart remained head of Ostmark, with Ernst Kaltenbrunner as his chief minister and Josef Bürckel as *Reichskommissar* for the union of Austria with the German Reich. Bürckel's duties included dealing with the 'Jewish Question'. Seyss-Inquart then became an honorary SS major-general and in May 1939 he was promoted to Minister without Portfolio in Hitler's government.

After the invasion of Poland, Seyss-Inquart was the administrative chief for southern Poland, becoming deputy to the governor-general, Hans Frank. During this period Polish Jews were being moved into ghettos, strategic supplies were being seized and 'extraordinary pacification' was being employed against the resistance movement.

In May 1940 Seyss-Inquart moved again, becoming *Reichskommissar* of the Netherlands, where he made sure that the country's resources contributed to Germany's war effort. Five million Dutch people were forced to work for the Nazis. Answering only to Hitler, he employed draconian measures to deal with cases involving resistance or dissension. He also deported 117,000 Jews.

However, Seyss-Inquart was not always so compliant. When the Allied troops were advancing into the Netherlands in late 1944, Hitler ordered a 'scorched earth' policy which would have destroyed the infrastructure of Germany, but Seyss-Inquart joined Albert Speer in resisting the *Führer's* plans. In the spring of 1945 he was even persuaded to allow Allied planes to drop supplies to starving people in occupied areas of Holland. But he refused to surrender. At a preliminary meeting to discuss food supplies on 4 May, United States General Walter Bedell Smith snapped at him: 'Well, in any case, you are going to be shot.'

'That leaves me cold,' Seyss-Inquart replied.

'It will,' Bedell Smith retorted.

Seyss-Inquart remained *Reichskommissar* until 8 May, when he was captured on board a German U-boat by Canadian sailors, after a meeting with Hitler's successor, Karl Dönitz. At Nuremberg, he was convicting of planning, initiating and waging wars of aggression, war crimes and crimes against humanity. He was sentenced to be hanged. As the last defendant to mount the scaffold, his last words were: 'I hope that this execution is the last act of the tragedy of the Second World War and that the lesson taken from this world war will be that peace and understanding should exist between peoples. I believe in Germany.'

THE *LEBENSBORN*

The key to fighting a war was manpower, but by 1935 the German birth rate had fallen to half of the level that had been seen 50 years earlier. A complete generation of young men had been killed off in the First World War and Germany's economic situation did not encourage marriage. Alarmed by the prospect of a depleted army, Himmler campaigned against contraception, abortion, homosexuality and even pet ownership, because pets might serve as a psychological substitute for children.

SS men were told that it was their patriotic duty to father at least four children, though Himmler fell short of his own target as usual. In 1936, the RuSHA set up the *Lebensborn* (Fount of Life), a network of maternity homes 'to accommodate and look after racially and genetically valuable expectant mothers'. After springing up all over Germany they began to appear in the occupied territories. In 1939 it was decided that a little more haste was needed, so SS men were ordered to impregnate their wives and, whenever possible, serve as 'conception assistants' to unmarried women aged 30 or older. As a result, the *Lebensborn* came to be seen as legalized brothels or Aryan stud farms. The project was personally supervised by Himmler, who took an interest in every detail, right down to how much breast milk nursing mothers were producing. Particularly fertile women were rewarded with honours.

Himmler was the nominal godfather of thousands of *Lebensborn* children and those that were born on his birthday, 7 October, were given toys and presents. If a *Lebensborn* child died, Himmler's eyes filled with tears. However, he refused to receive reports about children born with physical or mental defects. Such a thing was not possible in the Aryan super-race.

SS men conduct a Lebensborn *christening as putative family members*

————*ϟϟ*————————————————————————————

Bridging the population gap

The *Anschluss* had boosted Germany's declining population by about 6.5 million 'racially pure' German speakers. This gave Himmler an idea. Why wait around for an increase in the birth rate? In 1936 the Nazi Party set up the Ethnic German Welfare Office (VoMi). One of its functions was to contact the ethnic Germans who lived outside the Reich and invite them to join Greater Germany.

Since the Middle Ages, millions of Germans had spread out across central and eastern Europe. They had settled in the Baltic states and the Caucasus. When Prussian-born Catherine the Great took the Russian throne in 1762, she invited her fellow Germans to go to Russia. As a result, a large number of Germans settled along the Volga, where they maintained their German culture. But Stalin feared their disloyalty when he came to power, so he had them deported to the remote reaches of Kazakhstan. However, the Nazis saw the ethnic Germans in the east as the key to bolstering Germany's flagging population – and their land would provide Germany with the *Lebensraum* that Hitler had promised. Himmler was particularly keen on this idea, so he sought to take over the VoMi.

'I intend to take German blood from wherever it can be found,' Himmler vowed, 'to rob and steal it wherever I can.'

Always on the lookout for a chance to take a hand in foreign affairs, Himmler installed SS Lieutenant-General Werner Lorenz as the VoMi's director. After serving as a pilot in the First World War, Lorenz joined the Nazi Party in 1929 and the SS in 1931. He was later elected to the Reichstag. In 1937, he set up the VoMi and in 1939 he became directly subordinate to Himmler in his role as Reich Commissioner for the Strengthening of Germandom. No source of ethnic Germans was overlooked. In 1942 he was injured in a car accident while overseeing the evacuation of ethnic Germans from Bosnia. Apart from the repatriation of ethnic Germans, Lorenz was also responsible for the 'Germanization' of kidnapped children, largely Poles and Slovenes, who met Himmler's ethnic criteria. At the end of the war, Lorenz was captured in Flensburg in Germany and interned in England. He was sentenced to 20 years' imprisonment at Nuremberg, but he was released in 1955.

Hitler was so impressed with the organization of the VoMi that it was supplied with funds to build hospitals and clubhouses, in order that it could spread German propaganda.

Meanwhile a veteran of Heydrich's SD, *SS-Oberführer* Hermann Behrends, was appointed as Lorenz's deputy, so that the VoMi could be used to investigate ethnic Germans who were not politically reliable in the eyes of the SS. The SS also took over such seemingly innocuous organizations as the German Bulgarian Society.

After attaining a doctorate in law at the University of Marburg, Behrends joined the Nazi Party and the SS in 1932. He became the first head of the SD in Berlin and he is thought to have been responsible for some of the death lists that were used on the Night of the Long Knives. In 1937 he joined the VoMi, where he built up lists of ethnic Germans who were not considered politically reliable abroad. He also joined the *Waffen-SS*.

Later on he became the Higher SS and police leader in Yugoslavia, where he was responsible for a number of atrocities. In 1945 he was arrested by the British in Flensburg. Handed back to the Yugoslavs, he was executed in Belgrade in 1946.

Nazi foreign policy

Himmler soon had another opportunity to get involved in Nazi foreign policy. Following the reorganization of the army that had followed the

---*ϟϟ*-----------------------------------

allegations against Blomberg and Fritsch in 1938, Hitler also sacked his foreign minister, Konstantin von Neurath, a veteran who had been inherited from von Papen. Von Neurath was replaced with Himmler's man, Joachim von Ribbentrop. Himmler had been cultivating Ribbentrop since he first joined the Party in 1932 and he had made him an honorary SS colonel. Ribbentrop was a vain man who liked to wear the black uniform of the SS, so he welcomed the opportunity to be a member of the foreign ministry staff, working with SS men.

After being educated in Germany, Switzerland, France and England, Ribbentrop was in Canada when the First World War broke out in 1914. Eager to serve his country, he returned to Germany and served as a hussar on the Eastern Front, before becoming an intelligence officer in Turkey. After the war, he married the daughter of a producer of *Sekt* – the German version of champagne – and he persuaded a distant, noble relative to adopt him so he could add the prefix 'von' to his name. Then in 1932 he met Hitler and joined the Nazi Party, becoming Hitler's chief foreign policy adviser by the simple expedient, it is said, of memorizing Hitler's words and repeating them back to him. Between 1936 and 1938 he was the German ambassador to the Court of St James's, where his mission was to forge an alliance between Germany and the British Empire. Instead he completely alienated the British. First of all Ribbentrop had an affair with Wallace Simpson, who became the wife of Edward VIII after his abdication. Then he greeted George VI at a court reception with a shout of 'Heil Hitler' and a Nazi salute that almost knocked the king over when he stepped forward to shake the German's hand.

Göring warned Hitler to recall Ribbentrop because he was a 'stupid ass', but Hitler dismissed Göring's fears. Ribbentrop knew 'quite a lot of important people in England', he said. '*Mein Führer*, that may be right,' Göring replied, 'but the bad thing is, they know him.'

Ribbentrop might have failed to woo England, but he had a little more success with the Japanese, having negotiated the Anti-Comintern Pact with them in 1936. The Comintern (Communist International) was a communist organization that was founded in Moscow in 1919. Its aim was to promote a worldwide communist revolution. When Ribbentrop returned from England in 1938, he was promoted against all expectations, becoming the German foreign minister in von Neurath's place. Some say that it was because he flattered Hitler; others say that it was because he was an ardent warmonger.

One of his first moves was to sign the 'Pact of Steel' with Mussolini. Then in August 1939 he signed the German–Soviet Non-Aggression Pact – which is sometimes known as the Molotov–Ribbentrop Pact, because it was also signed by Soviet foreign minister Vyacheslav Molotov. Germany immediately gained the ability to invade Poland without retaliation by the Soviet Union. When the Second World War broke out, Ribbentrop signed the Tripartite Pact with Italy and Japan, which established the Axis Powers. However, he gradually lost favour with Hitler and faded from prominence. After being captured in Hamburg, he was sentenced to be hanged at the Nuremberg trials.

Invasion of Czechoslovakia

After the *Anschluss*, Hitler's next foreign policy objective was Czechoslovakia. Formed after the collapse of the Austro-Hungarian Empire at the end of the Second World War, Czechoslovakia was home to three million people of German descent. Most of them lived in the Sudetenland, an area in the western half of the nation. Working behind the scenes, the SS funded the Sudeten German Party (SdP) which looked to Hitler and National Socialism. In addition, Heydrich deployed SD

─── ⚡⚡ ─────────────────────────────

spies in the Sudetenland. They collected so much information that two more telegraph lines had to be built between the German–Czech frontier and Berlin.

Hitler's aim, and that of the SdP, was to integrate the Sudetenland into Germany, but the leader of the Sudeten German Party, Konrad Henlein, was seen as too moderate. Indeed, he was seeking independence for Czechoslovakian Germans, not union with the Reich. So Heydrich took steps to undermine him. First of all, the VoMi formed a fifth column to undermine the Czech government and then the SS cultivated the Nazis within the radical wing of the party. This forced Henlein's hand and he quickly adopted the Nazi slogan: '*Ein Volk, ein Reich, ein Führer!*' ('One People, One Country, One Leader!').

Fearing that a German invasion of Czechoslovakia would spark a war, the leaders of Britain, France, Italy and Germany met in Munich. On 30 September 1938, they attempted to appease Hitler by instructing the Czechoslovak president, Edvard Beneš, to hand over the Sudetenland to Germany. Henlein was made an SS lieutenant-general and he became a member of the Reichstag and governor of the Sudetenland. He committed suicide in Allied custody after the war.

Throughout the whole crisis the SS had bypassed Ribbentrop and the German ambassador to Prague, who opposed the annexation of Czechoslovakia. However, buoyed by their success in the west, Heydrich and the SD then set about inflaming the Slovak campaign for independence in the east of the country.

At first they tried a diplomatic approach, with Wilhelm Keppler being sent to talk to the ultra-nationalist Slovak People's Party. However, the Slovak Minister of State, Karel Sidor, got cold feet and the independence negotiations stalled.

Keppler joined the Nazi Party in the 1920s and was one of a circle of businessmen who provided it with financial backing. He was elected to the Reichstag early in 1933 and he became Commissioner for Economic Affairs later in the same year. At that point he fell into Himmler's circle. In 1938 Keppler became attached to the German embassy in Vienna, where he prepared the ground for the *Anschluss*. During the war, he was chairman of many of the SS's businesses and in January 1942 he became an SS lieutenant-general. In 1945, he was sentenced to ten years' imprisonment, but he was released in 1951.

The time for talking was over, as far as the Nazis were concerned, so Heydrich sent a sabotage squad under SS Major Alfred Naujocks. After the saboteurs had set off a bomb in a chocolate factory in the Slovak capital, Bratislava, a state of emergency was declared.

Described as an 'intellectual gangster', Naujocks studied engineering at Kiel University, though he seems to have spent most of his time brawling. In 1931 he joined the SS, where he became one of Heydrich's most trusted agents. He was then involved in a number of chaos-provoking stunts. For instance, he led an attack on a radio station in Gleiwitz, Czechoslovakia, that effectively started the Second World War; he provoked a purge of the Red Army; and he set off bombs in Czechoslovakia in order to incriminate the Slovak nationalists.

Naujocks also participated in the Venlo incident with Walter Schellenberg and he took part in Operation Bernard, which employed prisoners in Sachsenhausen concentration camp to forge British bank notes. But then he made the mistake of disputing one of Heydrich's orders, which resulted in him being demoted and sent to the Eastern Front with the *Waffen-SS*. While he was with his new unit he murdered members of the Danish resistance and terrorized Denmark.

In November 1944 he defected to the Americans, but thinking better of it, he escaped from the internment camp he was being held

*'Intellectual gangster' Alfred Naujocks spread chaos wherever he went and has
even been credited with starting the Second World War*

in. He is thought to have been one of the men behind ODESSA, the
organization that smuggled former SS men out of Europe.

The pressure on Czechoslovakia mounted. While the VoMi was
organizing demonstrations in Prague, the SD took the head of the
Slovak People's Party, Jozef Tiso, along to visit Hitler. Swayed by
the prospect of power, Tiso announced that he was willing to head

an independent Slovakia under German protection. Hitler then issued an ultimatum that demanded independence for Slovakia, the formation of a new puppet government in Prague and the payment of gold and foreign exchange for Germany's 'protection'. On 15 March 1939, the German army marched in. Hitler then made a triumphant entrance in an open-topped car. As he drove through the streets of Prague he was flanked by Ribbentrop and Himmler – the man who was really responsible for the annexation. Tiso remained president of Slovakia until the Red Army arrived in 1945. He was hanged for treason in 1947.

Invasion of Poland

The next task of the SS was to provide Hitler with the pretext to invade Poland. On 31 August 1939 – a week after Germany and the Soviet Union had signed a non-aggression pact – Alfred Naujocks and a team of five SD operatives took over the radio station in the border town of Gleiwitz. They were dressed in Polish uniforms and one of them broadcast an inflammatory anti-German speech in Polish. As a way of making the attack look more convincing, they had with them the body of Franciszek Honiok, a German Silesian known for sympathizing with the Poles, who had been arrested by the Gestapo on the previous day. Honiok was dressed to look like a saboteur and then his dead body was riddled with bullets and left at the scene, along with the corpses of other Dachau inmates.

Like Honiok, they had been prepared by the Germans, who called them 'Konserve' (canned goods).

A number of American journalists were summoned, but no one was particularly convinced. However, the Völkischer Beobachter carried the headline: 'Unprecedented attack by bandits on Gleiwitz radio station'.

The attack was one of a series of incidents that were designed to discredit Poland. Before the newspaper headline was even published, the *Wehrmacht* had crossed the border.

The Polish killings

The SS then carved itself out a new role. Its job was to go in behind the army and liquidate Poland's political and cultural elite. With no one to lead the country, it was thought that Poland would become a vast reservoir of *Untermenschen* (subhumans) who could be put to work as slaves. Hitler realized that the *Wehrmacht* commanders would not approve of wholesale murder, so members of the SS were formed into *Einsatzgruppen* – innocuous-sounding 'deployment groups'. There were six units, each consisting of between 400 and 600 men. Each of the five armies was followed by an *Einsatzgruppe* and the sixth group was sent into the border province of Poznan, which Hitler intended to incorporate into the Reich.

The agency in charge of the *Einsatzgruppen* was the RSHA. Heydrich, its chief, had already had death lists drawn up. His intended victims included all aristocrats, businessmen, selected priests, doctors, teachers, civil servants and political leaders. At that point, there was no specific order for the murder of Jews, but SS General Udo von Woyrsch took it upon himself to kill them anyway.

Within a week of the invasion, SS commanders were boasting of killing 200 Polish citizens a day and by 27 September Heydrich was able to report that only 3 per cent of the Polish upper classes had survived. Taking advantage of a secret protocol to the German– Soviet Non-Aggression Pact, the Soviet Union invaded eastern Poland on 17 September. Following the German example, the

Soviets also deprived Poland of its elite by murdering over 4,000 army officers in the Katyn Forest.

The *Einsatzgruppen* allied themselves with the *Selbstschutz* – 'self-defence squads' of ethnic Germans who had been attacked by their Polish neighbours when Germany invaded. Some 5,000 ethnic Germans had been killed and a further 50,000 had been forced from their homes, so they were in the mood for revenge. Backed by the *Einsatzgruppen,* they massacred large numbers of Poles. The situation was particularly inflamed in West Prussia because a large part of the province had been given to Poland after the First World War. The *Gauleiter* in Danzig, Albert Forster, did his utmost to stir up hatred between the different factions.

Ex-SA member Forster was no fan of the SS. In the years between 1933 and 1939 he had been embroiled in a feud with the Nazi president of the Danzig senate, SS Lieutenant-General Arthur Greiser, over who should oversee the pro-German activities of the ethnic Germans who lived in the parts of West Prussia then under Polish control. The VoMi stepped in. Himmler certainly did not want to see Forster gaining influence, so he sent in his recruiting officer, SS Lieutenant-General Gottlob Berger, to bring the *Selbstschutz* under SS control. Berger divided them into four units and then put an SS officer in charge of each. They served as an auxiliary police force but they remained undisciplined – their vicious acts of revenge made even the sadistic Heydrich complain.

Greiser and Forster had never seen eye to eye. A pilot during the First World War, Greiser had co-founded the veterans' group in Danzig. Initially a member of the SA, he joined the SS in 1931 after he had fallen out with Party boss Albert Forster. In 1939 the two of them were responsible for creating tensions between Danzig (now Gdansk) – a

———ᛋᛋ————————————————————————

'free city' under the Treaty of Versailles – and the Polish government, by demanding reunion with Germany.

After the German invasion, Greiser became *Gauleiter* of Warthegau (roughly equivalent to pre-war Poznan) which became part of Germany, while Forster remained as governor of Danzig–West Prussia, a newly-created Nazi province. They both instituted 'Germanization' policies, but while Forster was ready to accept any Pole with a claim to German ancestry, Greiser implemented a strict ethnic cleansing policy by expelling ethnic Poles. And Greiser was prepared to resettle ethnic Germans from the Soviet-occupied zone, while Forster resisted.

However, both men were united in their brutal treatment of Jews. Forster was responsible for the murder of 12,000 Jews, sending thousands more to concentration camps, while Greiser was responsible for the experiments with gas vans at Chelmno – large panelled trucks that could hold up to 70 people. At least 150,000 Jews died at Chelmno between late 1941 and April 1943.

In 1945, Greiser surrendered to the Americans in Austria and Forster handed himself over to the British in Germany. Both men were returned to Poland, where they were tried and hanged for their war crimes.

Hitler did his best to hide the actions of the *Einsatzgruppen*, and Berger's *Selbstschutz*, from the *Wehrmacht*, who feared that they might be blamed for the atrocities being committed. The SS, he maintained, were merely undertaking 'counter-espionage work'. However, many soldiers wondered why young, able-bodied SS men were removed from the front line so that they could take on defenceless civilians.

By the end of September, the fighting in Poland was over and the country was partitioned between Germany and the Soviet Union. The western regions were absorbed into Greater Germany while the bulk of the country became a German colony called the General Government, which was a separate region of the Greater German Reich. The *Wehrmacht* was then relieved of its occupation duties and Himmler stepped in. The colony would be run by his *Einsatzgruppen* and the killing would continue. Eventually the whole of Poland would become an SS colony. SS Major-General Otto Hofmann of the RuSHA simply said: 'The East belongs to the SS.'

THE SECOND WORLD WAR

War in Europe began on 3 September 1939 when Britain and France declared war on Germany after Hitler refused to remove his troops from Poland. There was little the Western Allies could do about the situation in Poland and by April 1940 Germany occupied Denmark, Norway, Belgium, the Netherlands and Luxembourg. On 10 May 1940 a coalition government was formed in Britain, under Prime Minister Winston Churchill.

From Luxembourg the German army drove on into France. The British Expeditionary Force (BEF) was outflanked, but it had control of a corridor which ran to the sea, which allowed Britain to evacuate its army via Dunkirk. As the Germans entered Paris the French signed an armistice and then set up a collaborationist government under Marshal Pétain in the southern town of Vichy. Victory in the Battle of Britain (July to October 1940) prevented Germany from invading Britain. Meanwhile, Italy joined the war on the side of Germany, which took the conflict to the neighbouring British and Italian colonies in North Africa. An easy victory over the Italians was prevented when Hitler sent along Erwin Rommel and his Afrika Korps.

However, in April 1941 Mussolini was experiencing problems in

———𝟰𝟰———————————————————————

Albania and Hitler had to help his ally by sending troops to invade Yugoslavia and Greece. At that point Hitler was about to break the German–Soviet Non-Aggression Pact by attacking the Soviet Union, but that part of his plan would now have to wait until 30 June 1941. The late start of the offensive is seen as the main reason for the Germans' failure to reach Moscow before winter set in.

On 7 December 1941, the Japanese Imperial Navy bombed the US Pacific Fleet's base at Pearl Harbor in Hawaii, as well as a series of British, French and Dutch colonies in the Far East. Hitler then declared war on the United States. His act was as unnecessary as it was futile because United States president Franklin Roosevelt and Churchill had already agreed that they would take on Germany first, before dealing with Japan. The United States Army Air Force joined the RAF's bombing campaign against a number of German cities and the United States army entered the fight in North Africa after the British army had won a convincing victory over the Germans at El Alamein in Egypt.

German ambitions in the east were crushed when the 6th Army was defeated at Stalingrad in January 1943. The Red Army then forced the Germans back relentlessly. Following the Anglo-American victory in North Africa, the Allies made landings in Sicily and Italy in the summer of 1943. Mussolini was deposed and jailed, but he was rescued by the SS in September 1943. The unwilling ex-dictator was then forced to set up a short-lived puppet Fascist state in northern Italy, under German protection.

But the Allies' relentless move north threatened to cut the Red Army off from its prize – it had a large account to settle with Germany. Accordingly, Stalin urged the Western Allies to land in France, which they did in June 1944. Stalin and Eisenhower then raced for Berlin, uncovering SS death camps as they went. The non-Soviet Allies suffered two reversals as they went. An advance party of British and Polish paratroopers was crushed by a German counter-attack as it tried to secure the bridge at Arnhem in the Netherlands and a further German counter-attack was mounted through the Ardennes, in what is known as the Battle of the Bulge. The battle was long and wide-ranging and the Allies suffered huge losses, but the German fighting machine was almost totally destroyed.

In early 1945 the Supreme Allied Commander, General Dwight Eisenhower, diverted American forces to the south in order to prevent the German army from establishing a redoubt in Bavaria, thereby allowing the Red Army to take Berlin. Hitler killed himself in his bunker and the war in Europe ended on 7 May 1945. The place where the Red Army met the Western Allies became the frontier between East Germany and West Germany for the next 45 years.

In the Far East, the British forced the Japanese out of Burma, while United States forces fought their way from island to island across the Pacific. Meanwhile the Chinese held their own on mainland Asia. They had been fighting the Japanese since 1937. The war in the Far East ended when newly developed atomic bombs were dropped on the Japanese cities of Hiroshima and Nagasaki. Peace was declared on 14 August 1945.

It is estimated that 55 million people lost their lives during the Second World War. Few attempts have been made to estimate how many were wounded or permanently disabled. The best estimates of the losses sustained by each country are: Russia, 18 million dead, including civilians; Germany, 4,280,000 dead and 5 million military personnel wounded; China, 1,310,000 servicemen dead and 1,752,951 wounded; Japan, 1,300,000 servicemen dead and 4 million wounded, as well as 672,000 civilian deaths; Poland 5,675,000 dead plus the 5.7 million Jews who were murdered in the death camps; United States, 298,131 dead, including 6,000 civilians, and 671,801 wounded; Britain, 357,116 dead, including 92,673 civilians, and 277,077 military wounded; British Commonwealth, 466,045 dead and 475,047 wounded.

Poland lost approximately 20 per cent of its total population, Russia and Yugoslavia lost around 10 per cent and Germany only slightly less. The millions of civilians who died as a result of battle and bombardment, or who were murdered or died of famine and pestilence, were not counted.

Gathering up the Aryans

The VoMi took charge of the resettlement of 136,000 ethnic Germans in the Soviet zone of occupation, along with 120,000 ethnic Germans from the Baltic states, which had been invaded by the Soviet Union under the secret protocol of the German–Soviet Non-Aggression Pact. For Himmler this was a gift. He had long believed in the superiority of the noble German peasant and now he could put his theories into practice. The Jews and Slavs in Poland would be dispossessed and their places would be taken by ethnic Germans, who would compensate for Germany's low birth rate by peopling the east with their Nordic descendants. Himmler persuaded Hitler to allow him to take over this project and a decree was issued on 7 October 1939 – Himmler's birthday. Heydrich then oversaw the resettlement of what Hitler called 'Jews, Poles and similar trash'.

It was plain that more bureaucracy would be needed. Himmler set up the Reich Commission for the Strengthening of German Ethnic Stock (RKFDV) to co-ordinate the operation. Its chief would be Ulrich Greifelt, who had liaised with Göring on behalf of Himmler during Göring's stewardship of Hitler's Four-Year Plan to rearm Germany and boost its economy. After serving in the army in the First World War, Greifelt managed a manufacturing plant before losing his job in the Great Depression. As many others had done before him, he turned to the Nazi Party in his hour of need, joining both the Party and the SS in 1933. He began as a second lieutenant but he was promoted rapidly, reaching the rank of SS major-general by 1941.

Before becoming head of the RKFDV, Greifelt had successfully organized the repatriation of the ethnic Germans from the South Tyrol, just inside the Italian border. Although Greifelt was more at home with organization and technology than racial theory, he was prosecuted at

—ϟϟ—————————————————————

Nuremberg along with 14 other members of the RKFDV and RuSHA. He was found guilty of crimes against humanity, war crimes and being a member of a criminal organization – which is how the Allies saw the SS. Sentenced to life imprisonment, he died in Landsberg Prison.

Himmler's dream of a German peasant idyll in Poland was shattered when Greifelt pointed out that recruitment into the army had created a labour shortage within Germany, so half a million extra workers were needed. Greifelt's realism triumphed over Himmler's fantasies. The Slavs and the Jews were deported eastwards while 500,000 ethnic Germans were uprooted and forcibly returned to the Reich, where they were put to work in the armament factories.

Many of them did not want to be resettled thousands of miles from their homes, but Himmler saw this as a good sign. It was, he exclaimed, 'in the very nature of German blood to resist'. But long stays in the resettlement camps had left the returning Germans 'disappointed, embittered and hopeless', according to an SS official.

The ethnic Germans were processed in 1,500 camps run by the VoMi, where they were tested by officials for their racial purity. They were given a rating from I-a-M/1 – racially very valuable – to IC-3-C – racial reject. This determined whether they would go on to work in a German munitions factory or be settled on a farm taken from a Jew or a Pole. Those who were considered racially inferior or politically unreliable stayed on in the camps for more tests. Meanwhile a million Poles and 300,000 Jews were deported from western Poland. In the winter of 1939–40, when temperatures fell to 40 degrees below zero, they were packed into unheated trains. When they arrived in eastern Poland, many had frozen to death. This was tough work, Himmler assured his men.

'Gentlemen, it is much easier in many cases to go into combat with a company than to suppress an obstructive population of low cultural level, or to carry out executions or to haul away people or to evict crying and hysterical women,' he told the troops of the *Leibstandarte SS Adolf Hitler*.

In the midst of all of this confusion stood the governor-general of the Polish territories, Hans Frank, who oversaw the segregation of Polish Jews into ghettos and the use of Polish civilians as forced labour. He also carried out the Special Pacification Operation (AB-Action), whose function was 'to destroy the cultural fabric of the Polish nation'. In the summer of 1940, more than 30,000 Polish citizens were arrested and some 7,000 political leaders, professors, teachers and priests were massacred in the Palmiry Forest in east-central Poland. The remainder went to concentration camps. Frank was raised to the rank of SS general in recognition of his efforts.

Like so many other Nazi officials, Frank was an educated person who was seduced by the gangster culture of the Party. The risks were high, but so were the rewards. After serving in the army and the *Freikorps*, Frank joined the DAP in 1919 and became one of the Nazi Party's first members. He studied law and then became Hitler's legal adviser, defending the Nazis when they were hauled into court.

Elected to the Reichstag in 1930, he became Minister of Justice for Bavaria. However, he was rendered a little uneasy by the extra-judicial killings in Dachau concentration camp and he baulked at the idea of the Night of the Long Knives. As a lawyer, he considered that the opponents of National Socialism could be removed by legal means now the Nazis were in power. Nevertheless, he swallowed his principles and became Reich Minister without Portfolio in 1934.

In October 1939, he was made governor-general of the occupied territories in Poland. He had now come to terms with the Nazi way of doing things, so he was responsible for the atrocities that were committed. However, he claimed right up until 1944 that he did not know about the Jewish extermination camps that had been built in the territories under his control.

Frank fled from Poland in advance of the Red Army and was captured in Bavaria by the Americans. Once in captivity, he tried to commit suicide. When he appeared at Nuremberg he admitted some of the charges against him, but the full extent of his guilt only emerged after he had surrendered 43 volumes of his diaries.

While awaiting execution, Frank wrote his memoirs, which included a piece about Hitler. He related that Hitler's nephew had tried to blackmail Hitler over his ancestry. The nephew claimed to have evidence that when Hitler's grandmother, Maria, had worked as a housekeeper for a Jewish family, she had been made pregnant by the family's 19-year-old son. The result of the union had been Hitler's father.

It is clear that Frank did not believe the story, however, when he wrote: 'From his entire demeanour, the fact that Adolf Hitler had no Jewish blood coursing through his veins seems so clearly evident that nothing more need be said on this.'

Apart from Hitler's architect and munitions minister Albert Speer, Frank was the only one of the defendants at Nuremberg to express any kind of remorse.

'A thousand years will pass and still this guilt of Germany will not have been erased,' he said in testimony.

During his captivity, he reconciled himself with Roman Catholicism and went to the gallows with a smile.

Fully reconciled to the fact that Germany desperately needed labour, Himmler started importing any Poles who looked as if they had Nordic ancestry. He told Hitler that he would wring 'every valuable trace of

German blood from Poledom', a policy he called *Wiedereindeutschung*. Young Polish women of Nordic looks were taken as maids for German households and Himmler's race examiners were sent to orphanages, looking for children of Aryan heritage. They were taken to the *Lebensborn* homes that had been opened in Poland and were adopted by SS couples. More than 200,000 Polish children were taken this way.

The business interests of the SS, one of Himmler's hobby-horses, had already spread outside Germany. In the Sudetenland, for instance, the SS took over the mineral water business and began manufacturing furniture. Unlike conventional businesses, the concentration camps provided the SS with a ready source of labour. In Austria, the inmates of the Mauthausen camp were used to quarry stone, while slave labourers from other concentration camps were producing building materials, sewing SS uniforms and testing the medicinal qualities of certain herbs. The commandant of Sachsenhausen concentration camp even got the inmates to build him a yacht, an offence that earned him a posting to Norway.

In June 1939, the SS Economic and Administrative Main Office (WVHA) had been set up under Oswald Pohl. Its Polish interests included over 313 brickworks as well as iron works and cement factories. Himmler planned a huge building programme in the east after the end of the war, where German colonists would settle. Big companies such as Krupp and IG Farben funded new ventures in return for cheap labour from the concentration camps. Meanwhile, the quest for *Lebensraum* continued.

Like Himmler, Pohl was an able administrator who was not too squeamish, so he was just what the Party needed. After serving in the Imperial Navy during the First World War, Pohl first joined the *Freikorps* and was then accepted into the new *Reichsmarine*. Five years later, in

—ϟϟ—————————————————————

1925, he joined the SA and he entered the Nazi Party a year later. In 1933 he met Himmler, who recognized a like mind. Pohl began his SS career in the concentration camps. After working his way through the ranks, he founded the movement to restore Wewelsburg Castle as Himmler's medieval headquarters. His next career move was in June 1939, when he became chief of the WVHA. In 1942, he became an SS lieutenant-general and a full general in the *Waffen-SS*.

At the end of the war he went into hiding, but he was captured by the British in 1946. He was tried in Nuremberg and sentenced to be hanged.

Invasion of the Soviet Union

The occupation of Poland was merely a prelude to the invasion of the Soviet Union. The SS Race and Resettlement Office had already drawn up Master Plan East. This involved deporting some 14 million people from the steppes and forests of western Russia to Siberia. They would be replaced by 2.4 million Germans. Another 14 million inhabitants would be allowed to stay after they had been Germanized. Perhaps 'compelled' is nearer the mark. The majority of the population would be confined in towns of around 20,000 inhabitants, which would be surrounded by villages containing 30 or 40 armed farmers.

At last, Himmler would have his German peasant aristocracy. He even ordered scientists to breed a hardy horse that could survive the harsh winters of the steppes. It was not just to be a mount and a beast of burden, it would also supply milk, cheese and meat. Unfortunately for Himmler, this Utopia in the east would remain a 'sublime idea' in his head, because Göring had plans of his own. In order to avoid a clash of personalities, Hitler put Alfred Rosenberg in charge.

THE BLACK BOOK

The Black Book was the name that was given to the *Sonderfahndungsliste* G.B. (Special Search List G.B.) after the war. Compiled by Walter Schellenberg, it was a list of prominent people that were to be arrested by the SS *Einsatzgruppen* following a successful invasion of Britain by Nazi Germany in the summer of 1940. It included:

Robert Baden-Powell – *founder and leader of the Boy Scouts, which was regarded as a spy organization*

Edvard Beneš – *president of the Czechoslovak government in exile*

Violet Bonham Carter – *anti-fascist liberal politician*

Vera Brittain – *feminist writer and pacifist*

Neville Chamberlain – *former prime minister*

Winston Churchill – *prime minister*

Noël Coward – *actor, playwright and singer-songwriter, a homosexual with connections to MI6*

Anthony Eden – *secretary of state for war*

E.M. Forster – *author*

Sigmund Freud – *founder of psychoanalysis and a Jew, exiled from Vienna but died in 1939*

J.B.S. Haldane – *geneticist and evolutionary biologist*

Ernst Hanfstaengl – *former financial backer of Hitler who fled Germany in 1937*

Aldous Huxley – *author who emigrated to the United States in 1936*

Harold Laski – *political theorist, economist and author*

David Low – *cartoonist*

Jan Masaryk – *foreign minister of the Czechoslovak government in exile*

Ignacy Jan Paderewski – *former prime minister of Poland*

J.B. Priestley – *writer who made popular anti-Nazi broadcasts*

Hermann Rauschning – *former personal friend of Hitler who had turned against him*

Paul Robeson – *African-American singer, writer and communist who had returned to the United States in 1939*

Bertrand Russell – *philosopher and pacifist*

C.P. Snow – *physicist and novelist*

Stephen Spender – *poet*

Beatrice Webb – *socialist and economist*

Chaim Weizmann – *Zionist leader*

H.G. Wells – *author and socialist*

Rebecca West – *suffragist and writer*

Virginia Woolf – *novelist and essayist*

Einsatzgruppen

During the German invasion of western Europe in 1940, the *Einsatzgruppen* once again followed the *Wehrmacht*, but this time their task was only to secure government offices and papers. The *Einsatzgruppen* were even prepared for Hitler's invasion of Britain, if it had taken place. Walter Schellenberg had provided them with a list of 2,820 people who were to be arrested immediately. As it happened, though, the *Einsatzgruppen* were fully employed in a different direction. In June 1940 they were right behind the *Wehrmacht* when Germany invaded the Soviet Union. Heydrich ordered the summary execution of all Soviet officials, members of the Comintern, 'extremist' Communist Party members, members of the central, provincial and district committees of the Communist Party, Red Army political commissars and all Communist Party members of Jewish origin. Pogroms against gypsies and Jews were also to be promoted.

'No steps will be taken to interfere with any purges that may be initiated by anti-Bolshevik or anti-Jewish elements in the newly occupied territories,' he ordered. 'On the contrary, these are to be secretly encouraged.'

In fact, the *Einsatzgruppen* soon exceeded their orders by killing Jewish civilians on their own account. At first, they limited themselves to killing adult males, but as the summer drew on they began killing all Jews, regardless of age or sex. SS Major-General Otto Ohlendorf, commander of *Einsatzgruppe D*, described a typical operation.

> *The unit would enter a village or city and order the prominent Jewish citizens to call together all Jews for the purpose of resettlement. They were requested to hand over their valuables and, shortly before execution, to surrender their outer clothing. The men, women and children were led to a place of execution, which in most cases was located next to a deeply excavated anti-tank ditch. Then they were shot, kneeling or standing, and the corpses thrown into the ditch.*

Meanwhile, *Einsatzgruppe B* reported that 'about five hundred Jews, among other saboteurs, are currently being liquidated every day'.

Otto Ohlendorf was one of the few people who managed to criticize the Party and get away with it. An early member of the Nazi Party, he was arrested by the Gestapo when he complained about what he perceived as the Party's socialist tendencies. He feared that his Party career was over, but he was then recruited by the SD. When he continued his

—⚡⚡——————————————————————————

criticism, Himmler warned him that his reports were both unwanted and illegal. Neverthless, he continued to be promoted.

Perhaps it was Ohlendorf's reputation as a ruthless killer that kept him in the Party's good books. In 1941 Heydrich placed him in command of *Einsatzgruppe D*, which operated in the southern Ukraine and the Crimea. By the winter of 1941–2 his unit had killed more than 92,000 Jews. In 1943, he became deputy director of the Reich Ministry of Economics, where he was to co-ordinate plans to rebuild the German economy after the war.

Ohlendorf was with Himmler when they were both captured by the British. Although Himmler committed suicide, Ohlendorf thought he could justify his actions. But it seems that he was not convincing enough. He was sentenced to death after being tried at Nuremberg. Optimistic to the end, he kept on making appeals, but he was eventually hanged at Landsberg Prison.

The German killing squads rarely needed an excuse, but they were provided with one in Kiev, a few days after the invasion of Ukraine in September 1941. When a series of explosions rocked the city, including the German command post, the German leaders declared that all of the Jews in Kiev would be executed in retaliation. Some 34,000 Jews were then rounded up and marched to a ravine on the outskirts of the city, which was known as Babi Yar. There they were forced to strip before being machine-gunned. They were then covered over, even though some of the victims were still alive. During the occupation, thousands more were executed. After the war it was learned that the explosions had been the work of an NKVD detachment.

When the German armies began retreating from Ukraine, it was felt that the massacre should be concealed, so bone-crushing machinery was brought in and the graves were opened. Prisoners from a nearby concentration camp were then forced to place the bodies on pyres, after which they were doused with petrol and ignited. The prisoners who had done the work were then killed.

Operating in the Baltic states, the troops of *Einsatzgruppe A* adopted a policy of systematically exterminating all of the Jews in their area of operation. It was a chilling indication of things to come. In all, over half a million people were murdered by the *Einsatzgruppen*, the *Wehrmacht* units under their direction and local anti-Semites.

In 1941 Himmler visited Minsk in Belarus to see the killing for himself. He was accompanied by his chief of staff, Karl Wolff. A hundred Jewish men and women were lined up and the troops of *Einsatzgruppe B* were ordered to shoot them. According to Wolff, someone's brains splattered on Himmler's coat.

> *Himmler began to feel ill. He reeled, almost fell to the ground, and then pulled himself together. Then he hurled abuse at the firing-squad members because of their poor marksmanship. Some of the women were still alive, for the bullets had simply wounded them…*

It was clear that the mastermind behind this mass murder was shaken by its reality. Fearing that such experiences would sap the morale of his men – let alone the cost of providing one bullet per corpse – Himmler gave orders that a more efficient way of killing must be found. Soon the *Einsatzgruppen* were experimenting with sealed trucks, or gas vans, which were about the size of furniture vans. Carbon monoxide was fed in, poisoning the prisoners. But the trucks only held from 50 to 70 people at a time – hardly the industrial-scale killing method that Himmler was looking for.

Karl Wolff matches Himmler stride for stride in Salzburg as they inspect the latest Austrian recruits to the SS

Karl Wolff might have got away with his wartime exploits if he had kept quiet after Nuremberg. As it was, he got off lightly. While serving on the Western Front in the First World War, he was awarded the Iron Cross for bravery. After the war, he joined the Hessian *Freikorps*, then in 1931 he enrolled in the Nazi Party and the SS. After being spotted by Himmler, Wolff became his adjutant, chief of staff and liaison officer with Hitler. He also shared Himmler's passion for Teutonic mysticism. However, he was dismissed in 1943 when he divorced his wife against Himmler's wishes.

He was then sent to Italy as military governor of the north, where he helped the deposed Mussolini set up a puppet regime. Right at the end, when all seemed lost, he tried to make peace in Italy. He signed the surrender on the day Hitler committed suicide.

Wolff appeared as a witness for the prosecution at Nuremberg.

Later, he was tried by a German court and sentenced to four years' imprisonment with hard labour, but he was released a week later. He was in the clear at that point, but he made the mistake of giving an interview to a German magazine when former SS officer Adolf Eichmann was being tried in Israel, thereby drawing attention to himself. In 1962, he was arrested and charged with the deportation of 300,000 Jews to Treblinka death camp. He was sentenced to 15 years' imprisonment, but he was released in 1971.

By 1942 the main Nazi extermination camps had been built, which reduced the need for the Nazi killing squads. Nevertheless, another *Einsatzgruppe* was formed in 1942 under SS Lieutenant-Colonel Walter Rauff, when it was thought that the German army would reach the British Mandate of Palestine, where another half a million Jews awaited them. Thanks to the British victory at El Alamein that July, the *Einsatzgruppe* never left Greece.

Rauff was introduced to the Nazi Party by Heydrich, whom he met in the navy. When Rauff left the *Reichsmarine* in 1937, Heydrich gave him the job of putting the SD on a solid war footing.

Between 1940 and 1941, he returned to the navy, serving on minesweepers. Between 1941 and 1942 Rauff embraced the Nazis' killing philosophy wholeheartedly by helping with the development of mobile gas chambers to kill Jews, the disabled, communists and anyone else who was considered an enemy of the state. In 1942 and 1943 he led an *Einsatzgruppe* that was sent to kill Jews in North Africa. When plans to move on to Palestine were thwarted, he continued his activities in Italy.

After the war, he served as a military adviser in Syria, before escaping to Ecuador. He eventually found refuge in Chile. The German government requested his extradition in 1962, but he was freed by Chile's Supreme Court. He died of lung cancer in Santiago in 1984.

Chapter Five

THE *WAFFEN-SS*

The *Waffen-SS* – literally the 'Weapons SS' – was the combat arm of the SS. At first, its members were selected on an 'Aryans-only' basis, but foreign volunteers and conscripts eventually made up a large proportion. Answerable only to Heinrich Himmler and Hitler himself, *Waffen-SS* troops wore the *Totenkopf,* or 'death's head' insignia, of the SS and their bravery was matched only by the scale of the atrocities they committed.

──── ⚡⚡ ────────────────────────────────────

The first officially armed SS unit was the *Leibstandarte SS Adolf Hitler*. Formed in 1933, the force originally numbered just 100 men. Its troops were paid by the Prussian provincial police force and trained by the elite Ninth Regiment of the *Reichswehr*, the defence force of the Weimar Republic that became the *Wehrmacht* when conscription was reintroduced in 1935. At first, the *Leibstandarte* was dismissed as a unit of 'asphalt soldiers' – ceremonial guards who also acted as waiters and musicians on state occasions.

This was not good enough for Himmler. He wanted to turn the SS into a fully fledged military formation that would be completely under his control. In September 1934, he prevailed upon war minister Werner von Blomberg to allow him to set up an SS 'rapid-reaction force' known as the *SS-Verfügungstruppe* (Disposition Troops or SS-VT). This would have the strength of three regiments, along with an intelligence section. Only months after the destruction of the SA in the Night of the Long Knives, the army had another rival.

Junkerschulen

While the *Wehrmacht* recruited its officers from among Prussian aristocrats – the Junkers – would-be SS officers were drawn from a broader social background. As a result, special officer training schools had to be set up for them, where they could learn the social graces as well as military tactics. These were called *Junkerschulen*, or schools for young noblemen. Candidates came from the SS, the SA and the Gestapo. They had to be recommended by their commanding officers and be over 5ft 10in (1.78m) tall.

The educational programme of the schools was extremely varied. Trainee officers were first of all given basic military training, which included playing war games on sand tables. They also studied *Mein Kampf* and were given lessons in etiquette – 'Cutlery is held only with the fingers and not with the whole hand' – and letters were to be ended with 'Heil Hitler, Yours sincerely…' There was an initial emphasis on racial purity, but this requirement had to be dropped during the war when recruits were accepted from the occupied countries. At that point, lectures on the sanctity of Nordic blood were replaced by talks on the evils of Bolshevism.

There was also a stress on physical fitness, which prepared the men for the mobile fighting that characterized the very end of the Second World War. The *SS-Junkerschule* at Bad Tölz was built with slave labour from Dachau. It had a soccer stadium surrounded by an athletics track, a heated swimming pool, a sauna and buildings dedicated to boxing, gymnastics and indoor ball games. At one time eight of the twelve coaches were the German national champions in their fields. Duels using swords or pistols were also allowed. Himmler decreed that 'every SS man has the right and duty to defend his honour by force of arms'.

Military training was given by ex-*Reichswehr* men. Not everyone came up to scratch. Only one recruit in three made it to the end of the five-month course. Graduates were known for their bravery – or recklessness. Alumni of Bad Tölz suffered a fatality rate of 70 per cent on the battlefield.

A second *Junkerschule* at Brunswick was run by Paul Hausser, who became an inspector of the SS-VT with the rank of brigadier. Under his leadership the SS-VT was fashioned into an effective fighting force. In the autumn of 1937, Himmler was able to remark with pride: 'The *SS-Verfügungstruppe* is, according to the present standards of the *Wehrmacht*, prepared for war.'

However, the *Wehrmacht* still had a monopoly of heavy armaments.

———44———————————————————————————————

And through the *Wehrbezirkskommandos* (local recruitment offices or WBKs) the army could restrict the growth of the SS-VT by assigning it a relatively low quota of men. This ended with the reorganization of the army following the sacking of Fritsch and Blomberg. Hitler was now in control. On 17 August 1938 he decreed that the *Verfügungstruppe* was to be expanded to full divisional strength. It would then be used for 'special internal political tasks' and front-line fighting in the event of war.

Himmler's private army

Himmler now had his own private army. It comprised two SS regiments, *Deutschland* and *Germania*, a communications detachment and the *Leibstandarte*, which had already seen action in the march into the Ruhr in 1936 and now numbered 800 troops. A key figure was Felix Steiner, commander of the Munich-based SS regiment *Deutschland*, who armed some of his men with machine guns and grenades, instead of rifles, for greater killing power. He also adopted the newly designed camouflage battledress and bred in his men a distinctive *esprit de corps*. Hausser complained that the *Deutschland* troops were Himmler's 'favourite babies'.

Unlike many of his peers, who used their positions to pursue their private fantasies, Steiner was a simple, straightforward career officer. He won the Iron Cross in the First World War and when the hostilities ended he led a unit of the *Freikorps*. In 1922, he rejoined the *Reichswehr*. When the Nazis came to power Steiner was involved in army training, when he became impressed by the methods used by the SS-VT. In 1935, he took command of a battalion of *SS-Verfügungstruppen* and was subsequently promoted to SS colonel before being given the command of the *SS-Deutschland* Regiment.

He led the regiment during the invasion of Poland and France, earning the Knight's Cross. Himmler then employed him to oversee the creation of the 5th SS Panzer Division *Wiking*, which was mainly composed of volunteers from the Netherlands, Belgium and Scandinavia. With the addition of a number of Latvian volunteers, he formed the III (Germanic) SS Panzer Corps, which fought in Russia. Less bloodthirsty than many of his peers, Steiner refused to obey the order to summarily execute all of the Soviet commissars, though some of his *Wikings* are known to have committed documented massacres.

Despite his loyalty to Hitler, he also disobeyed the order to break the encirclement of Berlin. Instead, he saved his men from certain annihilation by moving west to avoid capture by the Soviets. Hitler had ceased to think or act rationally at this point, 22 April 1945, but he launched into a weak tirade all the same.

> *Steiner will not attack? Steiner is disobeying a direct order from your* Führer, *your Chancellor, and your Party head? I suppose that such insults to my person were taught to him by others among this upper-class, snobbish, rude, and idiotic group of Prussian Generals and Princes! Because of them, the Empire is fallen! Because of one man's fear of glory, we are to lose this war? No, I shall not leave Berlin. I shall stay here until the communists bust down the door to the bunker, and then I shall kill myself, gentlemen.*

Steiner was captured by the British at Lüneburg. He faced charges at Nuremberg, but they were dropped and he was released in 1948.

Hitler decreed that the *SS-Totenkopfverbände* (SS-TV) was to join the SS-VT. The SS-VT had been established by Theodor Eicke in 1936,

—𝕊𝕊—

using concentration camp guards. By and large, it was an army of thugs. In 1937, Eicke declared that it belonged 'neither to the army nor the police nor to the *Verfügungstruppe*'. The SS-VT was now growing apace. By April 1938, it consisted of four regiments which comprised three storm battalions with three infantry companies, one machine-gun company and medical, communication and transportation units. While the *Leibstandarte* had marched alongside the *Wehrmacht* during the *Anschluss*, two battalions of the *SS-Totenkopfverbände* had been stationed with three battalions of the SS-VT during the occupation of the Sudetenland.

On 19 August 1939, the 8,000 men of the SS-TV were mobilized alongside 18,000 of the SS-VT. Himmler bade farewell to his troops with the words: 'SS men, I expect you to do more than your duty.' In other words, do or die.

Even in action the SS-VT remained a political arm of the Nazi Party, funded by the Ministry of the Interior. However, in Poland the SS-VT was under the authority of the army, who were less than impressed. Its members were poorly trained and they recklessly exposed themselves to danger on the battlefield, sustaining proportionally higher casualties than the *Wehrmacht*. One army general complained that the *Leibstandarte SS Adolf Hitler* fired aimlessly in all directions and routinely set fire to Polish villages. At one point Sepp Dietrich had to be rescued by an infantry regiment when his SS men were surrounded by the Poles near Pabianice. Unsurprisingly, the army recommended that the SS-VT be disbanded.

But Himmler argued that the SS-VT had not been properly equipped by the *Wehrmacht* to carry out its objectives. Moreover, it had been hampered by being parcelled out piecemeal to army units rather than being kept together as a single formation. For once he was right. Hitler showed that he agreed with Himmler by reorganizing the *Germania*, *Deutschland* and *Der Führer* regiments into the *SS-Verfügungs* Division, which would fight under the command of the army. But he held back the now motorized *Leibstandarte* and other elements of the SS-VT to form the nucleus of a new division. The SS-TV would become the *SS-Totenkopf* Division and the *SS Polizei* Division would be formed by drafting in members of the uniformed national police force.

Almost overnight, the formation that the army had wanted to disband had increased in numbers from 26,000 to over 100,000. Hitler also ordered the formation of a motorized artillery battalion to support the new divisions, though the army was slow to supply them with guns. In an effort to keep his troops out of the hands of the *Wehrmacht*, Himmler persuaded Hitler to institute special SS courts, so that SS men would not be subject to the jurisdiction of the army. An SS man had already been court-martialled for shooting 50 Polish Jews. A totally trivial offence, in Himmler's eyes.

The *Waffen-SS* gets its name

Himmler then called on the organizational abilities of Gottlob Berger. While serving as an officer in the First World War, Berger had been seriously wounded and had been awarded the Iron Cross. He then joined the *Freikorps* and the Nazi Party in 1922. After serving in the SA, he joined the SS in 1936 and was a co-author of Himmler's pamphlet *Der Untermensch* ('subhumans'), which purported to explain why Jews, gypsies, Poles and Slavs were less than human. However, Himmler was happy enough to recruit non-ethnic Germans for the *Waffen-SS*. Berger was sent to put down an uprising in Slovakia in August 1944 and was then put in charge of a prisoner-of-war camp. He was acquitted of ordering death marches at the end of the war, but was sentenced to 25 years' imprisonment for his part in the Holocaust. This was reduced to ten years because he had refused to kill the VIP prisoners who were held in Colditz Castle despite direct orders from Hitler. He was released in 1951.

Berger began recruiting support formations to be manned by the SS and Himmler remained in command of the reserves, who could then be used for 'police activities' and other 'special duties'. Himmler had problems equipping his new formations because the *Wehrmacht* was more concerned with supplying its own men, so he set up his own SS Procurement Office under Heinrich Gärtner. Gärtner presented a shopping list containing hundreds of artillery pieces, thousands of small arms and millions of rounds of ammunition direct to armaments minister Fritz Todt. Todt was happy to comply if the SS would provide 25,000 Polish workers for the Reich's munitions factories. Gärtner even went direct to the manufacturers in his search for supplies. This was one step too far for the *Wehrmacht*, who tried to put a stop to Gärtner's private supply system. Although Himmler had been thwarted in his ambition to make his growing army totally independent, he began calling it the *Waffen-SS*, or 'Weapons SS'. It was certainly that. Adolf Hitler confirmed the name in a speech made in 1940.

The Battle of France

The three SS divisions – *SS-Verfügungs*, *SS-Totenkopf* and *SS-Polizei* – and the *Leibstandarte SS Adolf Hitler* spent the winter of 1939 and the spring of 1940 training and preparing for the invasion of France. They were to be part of *Fall Gelb* (Case Yellow), one of the two main German operations. Their aim was to cut off and surround the Allied units that had advanced into Belgium.

In May the SS divisions moved up to their starting positions. The *Leibstandarte*, under the overall command of General Sepp Dietrich, was attached to the army's 227th Infantry Division. Its task was to form the vanguard of the ground advance into the Netherlands. The target of the *SS-Verfügungs* Division was the Dutch central front and Rotterdam, while the *SS-Totenkopf* and *SS-Polizei* divisions were held in reserve.

First of all the *Der Führer* regiment moved up to the Dutch border, while the remainder of the *SS-Verfügungs* division – that is, the *Deutschland* and *Germania* regiments – stayed behind the line in Münster, awaiting the order to invade the Netherlands.

On 10 May the *Leibstandarte* overwhelmed the Dutch border guards and spearheaded the German advance into the Netherlands, while *Der Führer* advanced towards Utrecht. The following day, the rest of the *SS-Verfügungs* Division crossed into the Netherlands and headed towards Rotterdam. Stiff resistance stalled the advance and Hitler ordered the terror bombing of the city. Within 15 minutes the city centre was demolished and 800 inhabitants were dead. Two hours later, the city's defence force surrendered.

When the *Leibstandarte* marched into the city, General Kurt Student, commander of the Paratroop Division, was setting up his command post in the former Dutch military headquarters. The Dutch troops were disarming in accordance with the surrender agreement, but the *Leibstandarte* still turned its machine guns on them. Surprised, General Student rushed to his window to find out what was happening, but a stray bullet hit him in the head, putting him out of action for eight months.

Having almost killed one of Germany's finest generals, the

Leibstandarte swept on through Delft, even though the Dutch commander-in-chief had already capitulated. They captured 3,500 Dutch prisoners of war and reached The Hague before they heard the news of the Netherlands' formal surrender.

Meanwhile, the British armoured forces were fighting back. On 21 May units of the British 1st Army Tank Brigade, supported by the 50th (Northumbrian) Infantry Division, counter-attacked in the Battle of Arras, the only tank battle in France. SS-Totenkopf had underestimated the opposition to its cost. Its standard anti-tank gun, the 3.7cm (1.5in) PaK 36, was found to be no match for the British Matilda tank.

After the Dutch surrender, the Leibstandarte moved south to France. As part of the XIX Panzer Corps under the command of General Heinz Guderian, it took up a position 15 miles (24km) southwest of Dunkirk along the line of the Aa canal. On the evening of 24 May, Hitler ordered the advance to halt. It was one of his most inexplicable decisions. The Allied defeat would have been complete if Guderian had not stopped. As it was, the British Expeditionary Force was trapped. The Leibstandarte Division paused for the night, as Hitler had ordered, but across the canal Allied observers on top of the 230ft (70m) heights could rain down shells on Dietrich's men. So on the following morning Dietrich defied Hitler's orders and continued the advance. III Battalion crossed the canal and took the height beyond, driving off the British artillery observers. Instead of being censured for disobeying Hitler's orders, Dietrich was awarded the Knight's Cross.

The same day the British attacked the German bridgehead at St Venant, forcing the SS-Verfügungs Division to retreat. It was the first time any SS unit had been forced to give up the ground it had captured. But nothing was going to stop the Germans' relentless advance. On 27 May the Deutschland Regiment commanded by Felix Steiner reached the defensive line on the Lys Canal at Merville. Its tanks forced a bridgehead across the river and waited for the *SS-Totenkopf* Division to cover their flank and provide support. However, a unit of British tanks arrived first. The *Deutschland* Regiment was almost overrun, but it managed to hold on until the anti-tank guns of the *Totenkopf Panzerjäger* platoon drove the British armour away. Meanwhile the troops of the 14th Company of the *SS-Totenkopf* Division were committing an atrocity at Le Paradis (see box p.148).

On 28 May Dietrich's staff car was raked with fire from an isolated British outpost. Dietrich and his adjutant scrambled for the safety of a ditch when the bullets ignited the fuel tank. However, the burning petrol ran into the ditch and they had to smear their bodies with mud to protect themselves from the heat. They remained in the ditch, under fire, for five hours until III Battalion arrived to rescue them. The *Leibstandarte* had just taken Wormhoudt, only 10 miles (16km) from Dunkirk, where it had been responsible for the Wormhoudt massacre.

By 30 May the British were cornered at Dunkirk, leaving the SS divisions free to continue their advance into France. The *Leibstandarte* soon reached Saint-Étienne, 250 miles (400km) south of Paris, which meant that it had advanced further into France than any other unit. On the following day the French surrendered. Hitler was particularly pleased with the performance of the *Leibstandarte*, telling its men: 'Henceforth it will be an honour for you, who bear my name, to lead every German attack.' And during a speech to the Reichstag on 19 July 1940, he praised 'the valiant divisions and regiments of the *Waffen-SS*'. They were, he said, 'superiority personified, inspired by a fierce will'. Excerpts of the speech were printed as a propaganda leaflet under the headline 'A last appeal to reason' and were dropped over England.

Hitler gave his permission for the *Waffen-SS* to form its own high command, the Command Office of the *Waffen-SS*, within the SS-Leadership Main Office (SS-FHA), Himmler's own high command. It was put in charge of the SS-VT (the *Leibstandarte* and the *Verfügungs* Division, renamed *Reich*) and the armed SS-TV regiments (the *Totenkopf* Division together with several independent *Totenkopf-Standarten*).

PARADIS MASSACRE

On 27 May 1940, soldiers of the 2nd Battalion of the Royal Norfolk Regiment became detached from their regiment. They occupied a farmhouse outside the village of Le Paradis in the Pas-de-Calais and defended it against the men of the *SS-Totenkopf* Division. When they ran out of ammunition the 99 survivors surrendered to the 14th Company of the *SS-Totenkopf* Division under the command of SS Captain Fritz Knöchlein. Instead of being taken prisoner they were machine-gunned and any survivors were finished off with bayonets. A group of French civilians was forced to bury the bodies the next day. But two men of the regiment, Private William O'Callaghan and Private Albert Pooley, escaped by hiding in a pigsty. They were later captured by the *Wehrmacht*, but they survived the war, and so were able to testify against Knöchlein at his trial in 1948. He was sentenced to death and was hanged in Hamburg on 28 January 1949. No other German soldiers or officers were prosecuted for their roles in the massacre. It was later discovered that 21 soldiers from the Royal Scots Regiment were also massacred in Le Paradis at around the same time.

WORMHOUDT MASSACRE

After fighting a rearguard action during the retreat towards Dunkirk, men from the 2nd Battalion Royal Warwickshire Regiment, the Cheshire Regiment and the Royal Artillery, together with a group of French soldiers, were overrun by the advancing Germans. They surrendered on 28 May 1940, expecting to be dealt with according to the Geneva Convention. Instead, they were taken to a barn near Wormhoudt. When there were almost 100 men inside, 12 soldiers from the *SS-Leibstandarte Adolf Hitler* threw stick-grenades into the building, killing many of the prisoners. Ten survivors, in two groups of five, were then taken outside and shot in the back. Eighty men were killed in all. Fifteen survivors were eventually found by a regular German army unit and their wounds were treated before they were sent to prisoner-of-war camps. Postwar testimony revealed that soldiers of II Battalion under the command of Captain Wilhelm Mohnke had carried out the atrocity, but Mohnke never faced a trial for the massacre. The case was re-examined in 1988 and 1993, but the German prosecutor decided that there was insufficient evidence to bring charges. Mohnke died in August 2001.

Foreigners in the *Waffen-SS*

Despite Hitler's words of praise, the recruiting offices held up the processing of 15,000 SS recruits. Gottlob Berger then came up with an idea. Why not set up recruiting offices in the territories they had already occupied where they could tap into a reserve of 'the German and Germanic population not available to the *Wehrmacht*'? The SS had already accepted foreign recruits with 'Nordic' ancestry, including five

——*ss*—————————————————————————

from the United States, three from Sweden and 45 from Switzerland, so the concept was not so outlandish. Even so, Hitler had reservations about recruiting foreigners. He had envisaged the SS as an elite formation pulsing with the best German blood. However, he was planning to attack the Soviet Union and recruiting foreigners was a good way of expanding the SS without taking men from the *Wehrmacht*. Himmler and Berger also argued that it would be better for young radicals in occupied territories to join the SS than the resistance. Hitler eventually gave his permission to form a new SS division of foreign nationals under the command of German officers.

By June 1941, Danish and Norwegian volunteers had formed the *SS-Nordland* Regiment, with Dutch and Flemish volunteers constituting the *SS-Westland* Regiment. Together with *Germania*, transferred from the *Reich* Division, they became the *SS-Wiking* Division. Volunteers came forward in such numbers that the SS had to open a new training camp solely for foreign recruits at Sennheim in Alsace-Lorraine.

Not all of the recruits were happy. They had signed up as anti-Bolshevik patriots and had been told that their native traditions would be respected. But the Flemish Catholics who had signed up in Belgium found that they were not allowed to celebrate Mass in camp. They were also shocked to be derided by their sergeants as a 'nation of idiots' and a 'race of gypsies'. But Himmler sought to mollify them by exchanging their old captured arms with new weapons manufactured in Germany.

The Brits who fought for Hitler

The British Free Corps was perhaps the most bizarre *Waffen-SS* unit. It was made up of a number of British and Dominion prisoners of war, who had been recruited by the Nazis. The force seems to have attracted about 60 members during the period of its existence, though some only served for a few days. However, its strength never seems to have risen above 27 at any one time.

The BFC was the brainchild of John Amery, the son of Leo Amery, Winston Churchill's secretary of state for India. Amery was a fan of National Socialism who saw Jewish-Soviet plotters round every corner. In France after the armistice, he made a number of pro-Nazi speeches in Paris before going off to Berlin, where he put forward his British anti-Bolshevik legion idea. He called it the 'British Legion of St George'. The Nazis were understandably keen on the idea, so Amery staged a recruiting drive in the prisoner-of-war camps. He claimed that he could recruit a brigade of 1,500 fighting men, but the Germans were not so sure.

Months later, he had only come up with four volunteers: an elderly academic named Logio, Maurice Tanner, Oswald Job and Kenneth Berry, a 17-year-old deckhand on the *SS Cymbeline*, which had sunk. Logio was released and Job was recruited by German intelligence and trained as a spy. He was caught while trying to get into England. Only Berry would actually join.

The *Waffen-SS* decided that they could do better themselves, so they dropped Amery and came up with a new recruitment plan. They created two 'holiday camps' near Berlin, where English-speaking guards would gather information about likely recruits once they were relaxed and off their guard. Quartermaster Sergeant John Brown was put in charge of the operation. A former member of the British Union of Fascists, he had been captured at Dunkirk. The Nazis did not know that he was a double agent.

Also in the camp were two genuine pro-Nazi recruits, Thomas Haller Cooper and Roy Courlander.

Few army units anywhere can have been as unpopular as the British Free Corps, who were desperate to recruit anyone that they could

Cooper was also a member of the BUF. He called himself Boettcher, the German equivalent of his name. He had been visiting Germany, his mother's birthplace, when war was declared in 1939. At that point, joining the *Waffen-SS* had been the line of least resistance. After being injured in battle, he had received the Wounded Badge in silver, the only Briton to be awarded a German combat decoration.

Courlander had been captured while serving with the New Zealand army in Greece. His mother was English and his father was a Lithuanian Jew.

Two hundred British prisoners of war then turned up at the camp. Delighted at their windfall, Cooper and Courlander attempted to make as many converts as possible, while Brown tried to subvert the exercise. But out of the first batch they only managed to recruit one man, Alfred Vivian Minchin, a merchant seaman from the SS *Empire Ranger* that had been sunk off the coast of Norway.

Meanwhile two more recruits arrived – Francis George MacLardy of the Royal Army Medical Corps, who had been captured in Belgium, and Edwin Martin of the Canadian Essex Scottish Regiment, who had been captured at Dieppe in 1942 – bringing the strength of the Legion of St George to seven.

Weary of waiting, the Germans decided to try a different tack. A new camp was set up at Luckenwalde, where freshly captured, disorientated prisoners were brought, rather than men who had spent months or years in captivity. First they were maltreated and then they were interviewed by Germans pretending to be Americans, or other British prisoners of war. If that failed, they were threatened with solitary confinement. This approach brought in a further 14 recruits, including Trooper John Wilson of 3 Commando and some members of the Argyll and Sutherland Highlanders. The volunteers were told that they were going to join thousands of their countrymen. Some were fascists but the others were just pretending in order to gain their freedom.

Like Brown, Edwin Martin had also joined to disrupt the operation. Thanks to his efforts the number of men in the Legion of St George had fallen to eight by December 1943. SS Captain Walter Roepke, formerly with the *SS-Allgemeine* and the *SS-Wiking* Division, was then put in charge. He felt that the Legion of St George sounded too religious. Himmler suggested the British Legion but that name had already been taken, so Roepke came up with the name 'British Free Corps'. If he managed to attract 30 recruits, the unit would be commissioned as an infantry platoon, so that was his primary aim.

Under pressure from the recruits, Roepke then made certain concessions. The BFC would be under British command; its members would not be branded with the SS blood-group tattoo; they did not have to swear an oath of loyalty to Hitler; they were not subject to German military law; and they would not be used in any action against British or Commonwealth forces or used for intelligence gathering. However, they would receive pay equal to German soldiers of their rank.

Meanwhile, Roepke put in an optimistic order for 800 SS uniforms with BFC insignia. There were three lions on the collar patches and there was a cuff band with 'British Free Corps' on it and a Union Flag arm badge. The Union Flag badge was attached to the left sleeve, just under the German eagle. 'Look, the eagle is sh***ing on the flag,' said one recruit. Eventually, permission to switch the Union Flag to the right sleeve had to be sought from Himmler.

Another potential saboteur then arrived in the form of Private Thomas Freeman of No. 7 Commando of Layforce. At this stage Roepke surveyed his pitiful force and came up with a new recruiting plan. All of the members of the BFC were sent back to their original camps on a recruiting mission, but they only managed to come back with six further volunteers. Two of these were John Leister, son of a German whose family had Nazi ties, and Eric Pleasants, a former member of the BUF. Both of them were pacifists who had been sent as agricultural workers to Jersey. Having failed to escape when the islands were occupied, they had joined the BFC in the hope of getting access to better food, alcohol and women.

Successive recruiting drives dragged the unit's strength up to 23. Fearing that their numbers might reach the crucial 30, which would propel them into action, Freeman and a like-minded comrade persuaded 14 other members to request a transfer back to their prisoner-of-war camps. The two troublemakers were charged with mutiny and sent to a penal *Stalag*. Freeman escaped and was repatriated by the Soviets in March 1945.

Wilson talked the Germans into making him senior NCO, while Cooper tried to instil SS-style discipline into his men. This did not go down well with the lackadaisical Brits. At that stage, four more recruits arrived. Three had been coerced into joining and one had made his German girlfriend pregnant, which was a capital offence. Getting girls pregnant was an SS monopoly!

The Germans thought they were making headway when they hooked Lieutenant William Shearer, the only officer to join the BFC. Although he had been recruited from a mental hospital, he seemed to know what the BFC was all about. His captors were quickly disillusioned. Not only did he refuse to put on the BFC uniform, he would not even leave his room. After a few weeks, he was returned to the mental hospital, before being repatriated on medical grounds.

The D-Day landings had been a success but there was no let-up for the BFC recruits. SS Major Vivian Stranders joined as second in command.

Originally British, he took German nationality when he joined the Nazi Party in 1932. After the war began, he was posted to the *Waffen-SS*, who used him as an expert on British affairs. At that point, MacLardy left the BFC to join the *Waffen-SS* medical unit and Courlander joined the war correspondent unit *SS-Standarte Kurt Eggers*. BFC men Walter Purdy, John Leister and Francis Maton also joined. Courlander could see the sense in getting out while the going was good, so he took a companion and jumped on to a railway train that was bound for Brussels. Once there, they handed themselves over to the British. As soon as they had gone, two more men took their places. Once again they had been caught *in flagrante* with a couple of German women.

In October 1944, the straggling band of recruits was sent to the *Waffen-SS* Pioneer School in Dresden to be trained as combat engineers. However, all attempts to fashion the BFC into a fighting unit were abandoned when Stranders successfully ousted Roepke, replacing him with SS First Lieutenant Walther Kuhlich, who had been wounded on the front line.

Cooper had been accused of anti-Nazi acts by the other BFC men so he was returned to the *Leibstandarte SS Adolf Hitler* as a military policeman. Wilson was now in charge of recruiting. Although he was more interested in womanizing, he tried to get men who had left the BFC to return. Meanwhile, Pleasants wooed Annelise, Kuhlich's secretary, marrying her in February 1945. Morale slumped when training for the Eastern Front resumed, with men getting drunk and going AWOL. Five more recruits joined, including two South Africans, taking the force's strength up to 27. Two had wanted to join the *SS-Totenkopf* Division until they were swayed by Kuhlich. Then six Maoris volunteered, which would have put the unit's numbers over the magic 30, but they were rejected because the SS was a 'whites-only' organization.

While Wilson was away, Hugh Cowie, a Gordon Highlander, took over as senior NCO. During the bombing of Dresden in February 1945, a few members of the BFC tried to escape, but they were given away by someone's girlfriend. The entire BFC was arrested, but two of them managed to make their escape. Everyone else was taken to Berlin. As the Allies closed in, a sympathetic officer provided three BFC members with British uniforms. Another managed to get transferred, because his girlfriend was connected with *SS-Standarte Kurt Eggers*.

Kuhlich gave the rest of the BFC a choice – fight or be sent to an isolation camp. They all chose to fight, so they were sent to join the III (Germanic) SS Panzer Corps, taking off their BFC insignia on the way. They spent a month on the front line. Cooper was then serving with the III (Germanic) SS Panzer Corps. He took SS Lieutenant-General Felix Steiner to inspect the BFC, but they were found to be of such dubious combat value that they were pulled from the line. Steiner was also concerned about the postwar legal consequences of using prisoners of war in action, because it was a clear violation of the Geneva Convention.

The relieved group of recruits then returned to Berlin, where they tried to locate their Red Cross parcels – they were still technically prisoners of war. At that point the colourful, if dubious, SS Captain Douglas Berneville-Claye appeared. Having been drummed out of the RAF, he had talked his way into the SAS. He was captured in North Africa and sent to Oflag 79 (a prison camp for Allied officers), but he had been released after switching sides. Cooper was not impressed by Berneville-Claye's credentials. Rightly so. He soon commandeered a car and went off to surrender to the Allies.

A couple of the BFC men saw action at the end of the war. Wilhelm 'Bob' Rossler was with the *Nordland* Division during the Battle of Berlin and Roy Courlander also seems to have been there. He is said to have put a Soviet tank out of action. The rest of the group accompanied Steiner when he sallied forth to surrender to the British.

Meanwhile, Hugh Cowie and his fellow would-be escapees seized control of their isolation camp. Heavily armed, they made their way west and surrendered to the United States Ninth Army at Schwerin.

Amery, Cooper and Walter Purdy stood trial for high treason alongside the propagandist William Joyce ('Lord Haw-Haw'). Amery and Joyce were hanged while Cooper and Purdy's sentences were commuted to life imprisonment. Cooper was released in 1953 and Purdy was freed in the following year. The rest were dealt with under military law. MacLardy was sentenced to life imprisonment, reduced on appeal to fifteen years, Cowie was sentenced to fifteen years' imprisonment but was released after seven years, Wilson was sent to prison for ten years and Berry, the very first recruit, served just nine months. Courland was court-martialled by the New Zealand forces, who sentenced him to fifteen years in prison, but he served only seven of them. Freeman successfully defended himself on all charges, and was acquitted. Berneville-Claye was as slippery as ever. After he was acquitted due to lack of evidence he served another year in the army before being discharged for theft.

In mid-1946, MI5 discovered that three former BFC members, who had been demobilized, had escaped punishment. It was too late to court-martial them, so they were summoned to MI5 headquarters and told not to do it again. No doubt they gladly agreed.

Pleasants and his wife Annelise escaped from Berlin through the sewers. He claimed to have killed two Russian soldiers with his bare hands along the way. The couple made their way to Annelise's parents in Dresden, where Pleasants joined a circus as a strong man, but they were arrested in 1946. Although Pleasants confessed to being a member of the SS, the Cold War was under way and he was forced to admit to a charge of spying for the United Kingdom. He was sentenced to 25 years in a labour camp in Arctic Russia, but he was released in 1953, after the death of Stalin. His wife was never heard of again.

Americans in the *Waffen-SS*

Although there was a British Free Corps there was no corresponding American unit. True enough, there was the American Free Corps, also known as the George Washington Brigade, but it was a fictitious unit of the *Waffen-SS* made up for propaganda purposes. But that did not mean that there were no Americans in the *Waffen-SS*. A number of Americans fought alongside the Germans, but they were spread out among different units. However, most of them died and little was done to investigate their cases. A selection of American *Waffen-SS* recruits follows:

Andy Beneschan
Born 1 September 1918 in New York, he was an SS sergeant before being killed in action in Bosnia on 16 April 1945.

Charles Braschwitz
Born 17 August 1911 in New Jersey, he became a sergeant in the *SS-Polizei* before being killed in action on 7 May 1945 at Laibach, Slovenia.

Peter Delaney (aka Pierre de la Ney du Vair)
Born in Louisiana, he is believed to have served in the French collaborationist *Légion des Volontaires Français* and as an SS captain in the *SS-Standarte Kurt Eggers* before being killed in 1945.

―――𝟒𝟒――――――――――――――――――――――――――――――――――――

Lucas Diel

Born 28 December 1912 in New York, he was an SS corporal before dying in Hungary on 9 December 1944.

Andreas Hauser

Born 30 August 1893 in Los Angeles, he was an SS lance corporal until he was killed in action on 18 January 1945 at Welikij in Ukraine.

Charles MacDonald

Born 7 May 1922 in Buffalo, New York, he reportedly rose to become an SS second lieutenant before being killed in action in Estonia on 14 March 1944.

Martin James Monti

Born 1910 in St Louis of an Italian-Swiss father and a German mother, he was a second lieutenant in the US Army Air Corps before he went AWOL in October 1944. He flew to Milan in a stolen plane and worked as a propaganda broadcaster under the pseudonym Martin Wiethaupt. Later he met Peter Delaney, who probably arranged for him to enter the *Waffen-SS* as an SS second lieutenant in the *SS-Standarte Kurt Eggers*. At the end of the war he returned to Italy where he surrendered to the United States forces, claiming that the SS uniform he was wearing had been given to him by partisans. He was charged only with desertion and was sentenced to 15 years' hard labour. His other crimes had not come to light. His sentence was commuted and he rejoined the United States Air Corps, but in 1948 he was discharged and picked up by the FBI. He was charged with treason and sentenced to 25 years' imprisonment, but he was paroled in 1960.

Edwin or Erwin Peter

Born 12 March 1918 in New York, he rose to become an SS company sergeant major before being killed in action on 2 July 1941 in Latvia.

Raymond George Rommelspacher

Born 30 May 1926 in Chicago, he was an SS-Grenadier and was killed in action on 6 October 1944 in Normandy.

Going to Mussolini's aid

At the beginning of 1941, the *Polizei* division had been brought under SS Leadership Main Office (FHA) control, although it would not be formally merged into the *Waffen-SS* until 1942. At the same time the *Totenkopfstandarten* – apart from the three regiments constituting the *Totenkopf* Division – lost their death's head designation and insignia and were reclassified as *SS-Infanterie* or *SS-Kavallerie* regiments. The 11th Regiment was transferred into the *Reich* Division to replace the *Germania* and the remainder were grouped into three independent brigades and a battle group in Norway.

By the spring, the *Waffen-SS* had grown to be the equivalent of six or seven divisions. It comprised the *Reich, Totenkopf, Wiking* and *Polizei* divisions, the battle group (later division) *Nord* and the *Leibstandarte*, along with the 1 SS Infantry, 2 SS Infantry and SS Cavalry brigades. They were being prepared for the attack on the Soviet Union when events took an unexpected turn after Mussolini's invasion of Greece went horribly wrong. 'Il Duce' was now in deep trouble, so Hitler had no choice but to go to his aid.

Reich was ordered to leave France for Romania, and the *Leibstandarte*, reinforced to full brigade strength, was sent to Bulgaria. There was

—ᛋᛋ————————————————————————————

little love lost between the SS and the *Wehrmacht* as they jostled on the traffic-choked roads. On one occasion, an SS officer threatened to open fire on an army convoy if it tried to overtake his column and on another the lead vehicle of an army column was held up at gunpoint to clear the road for the SS.

The fighting started on the morning of 6 April. Attached to the XL Panzer Corps, the *Leibstandarte* advanced west and then south from Bulgaria into the mountains. By 9 April it had reached Prilep, 30 miles (48km) from the Greek border. Further north the *SS-Reich*, with the XLI Panzer Corps, crossed the Romanian border and advanced on Belgrade, the Yugoslav capital. On 12 April the shattered city surrendered. The Yugoslav army followed suit a few days later.

Then on 10 April the *Leibstandarte* crossed into Greece and came face to face with the 6th Australian Division at the Klidi Pass. For 48 hours the two sides fought for control of the heights, often engaging in bloody hand-to-hand combat. Eventually the *Leibstandarte* captured the pass, which allowed the German army to advance into the Greek interior. The victory finally elicited grudging praise from the *Wehrmacht*. The order of the day from General Georg Stumme, commander of XL Panzer Corps, commended the *Leibstandarte* for its 'unshakable offensive spirit'.

'The present victory signifies for the *Leibstandarte* a new and imperishable page of honour in its history,' Stumme went on. 'Forward for *Führer, Volk und Reich*.'

The *Leibstandarte* continued its advance on 13 May, but the reconnaissance battalion under the command of Kurt Meyer faltered when it came under heavy machine-gun fire from the Greek army defending the Klisura Pass. Meyer ordered his men forward. When there was no response he grabbed a hand grenade and waved it in the air.

'Everyone looked thunderstruck at me as I brandished the grenade, pulled the pin and rolled it precisely behind the last man,' he recalled. 'Never again did I witness such a concerted leap forward as at that second. As if bitten by tarantulas, we dived around the rock spur and into a fresh crater.'

Thus emboldened, the *Leibstandarte* routed the defenders and captured 1,000 prisoners of war at the cost of six dead and nine wounded. On the following day, Meyer captured the town of Kastoria and bagged another 11,000 prisoners of war. By 20 May the *Leibstandarte* had cut off the retreating divisions of the Greek Epirus–Macedonian army. The Greeks surrendered to Sepp Dietrich while shouting 'Heil Germania!' and 'Heil Hitler!'. Three days later Greece capitulated and the British fled. As a reward the *Leibstandarte* was promoted to a full motorized

Concentration camps like Auschwitz lay at the end of the line for many who survived their encounters with the SS, including POWs

division. But while a few additional elements had been added at the start of the Russian campaign, it remained effectively a reinforced brigade.

Operation Barbarossa

With the southern flank secured, Hitler could go ahead with Operation Barbarossa, the invasion of the Soviet Union. At 0530 hours on 22 June 1941, the German ambassador in Moscow went to see foreign minister Molotov. He delivered a declaration of war. The reason – or excuse – was 'gross and repeated violations' of the Molotov–Ribbentrop Pact. If Stalin had read *Mein Kampf* he might have been prepared. Hitler had announced his intention to invade the Soviet Union back in 1926: 'Germany's future has to lie in the acquisition of land in the east at the expense of Russia.'

The German ambassador's words were a mere formality, because a huge German army was already pouring across the Russian border on a 900-mile (1,450km) front from the Baltic to the Black Sea.

The *Wehrmacht* attacked in three army groups. The *SS-Totenkopf* and *SS-Polizei* divisions were attached to Army Group North. They advanced through the Baltic states and on to Leningrad. The *SS-Reich* division, which became *2 SS-Das Reich* that autumn, was with Army Group Centre when it headed towards Moscow and the *SS-Wiking* Division and the *Leibstandarte* were with Army Group South. Their targets were Ukraine and the city of Kiev.

A week later the *SS-Nord* Division joined XXXVI Corps, which consisted of both German and Finnish troops. Confident of success they poured across the border into Finland, which the Red Army had taken the previous year under the Molotov–Ribbentrop Pact.

The advance came to a juddering halt when they came up against a powerful Soviet force at Salla, near the Russian border with Finland. Disorientated by the thick forests and the heavy smoke from forest fires, the division's units disintegrated. Three hundred of the invading troops were killed and 400 were wounded in the first two days of the invasion. However, over the winter of 1941–2 the division was reinforced from the general pool of *Waffen-SS* recruits. The replacements were younger and better trained than the SS men of the original formation, who had been largely drawn from the *Totenkopfstandarten* of concentration camp guards.

The war in the Soviet Union proceeded well for Germany at first, but then came the *rasputitza*, the autumn rains that turned the roads into quagmires. In the south, a Soviet counter-attack forced the Germans out of Rostov, Germany's first major reverse on the Eastern Front. By late October, the *Leibstandarte* was at half strength because of enemy action and the dysentery that swept through its ranks. *Das Reich* had lost 60 per cent of its strength, but the struggle had barely begun. Hanging low over the invaders was the bloody spectre of the Battle of Moscow. On 1 December, Hitler ordered an all-out attack on the capital, but the Germans ground to a halt in sub-zero temperatures, within sight of the city's onion domes. On 6 December, the Red Army counter-attacked, driving the Germans back 40 miles (64km). *Das Reich* suffered crushing losses. Of the 2,000 soldiers that had started out with *Der Führer* Regiment, only 35 men were still standing. The *Waffen-SS* had suffered 43,000 casualties, which meant that around one out of every four of the German troops had been killed or wounded. This time the *Wehrmacht* heaped unstinted praise on the *Waffen-SS*. Writing to Himmler, Eberhard von Mackensen, the general commanding III Panzer Corps, commended the *Leibstandarte* for 'its inner discipline, its cool daredevilry, its cheerful enterprise, its unshakable firmness in a crisis, its exemplary toughness, its camaraderie...' and assured the *Reichsführer* 'that the *Leibstandarte* enjoys an outstanding reputation not only with its superiors but also among its army comrades'. The *Waffen-SS* was also praised by the Russians. A captured Soviet officer said that they had been relieved when the *SS-Wiking* Division had been replaced in the line with a regular army division.

However, it was not just a picture of reckless bravery. The *Waffen-SS* had committed its share of atrocities in Russia, just as it had done in France when it had murdered a number of helpless British prisoners of war. Soviet prisoners of war had been shot too. And when the people of Ukraine had greeted the Germans as liberators, the *Waffen-SS* had rewarded them with rape and murder.

The 1 SS Infantry and 2 SS Infantry brigades, which had been formed from surplus concentration camp guards from the SS-TV, had joined up with the SS Cavalry Brigade and had moved into the Soviet Union behind the advancing armies. At first they fought Soviet partisans and the isolated units of the Red Army, capturing 7,000 prisoners of war. Then from mid-August 1941 until late 1942 they were assigned to the Reich Main Security Office under Heydrich. The brigades were now used for rear area security and policing and, most importantly, they were not under army or *Waffen-SS* command. In the autumn of 1941 they left the anti-partisan role to other units and began assisting the *Einsatzgruppen*. They formed firing parties and participated in the wholesale extermination of the Jewish population of the Soviet Union. By the end of 1941, these three brigades were responsible for the murders of tens of thousands of Jews and other selected victims.

The SS Cavalry Brigade, being more mobile, was particularly

culpable. It had first gone into action on 27 July. By 1 August the force was responsible for the deaths of 800 people.

That day, Himmler had a meeting with Erich von dem Bach-Zelewski and the Reich Commissioner for *Ostland* (Germany's eastern territories), Hinrich Lohse. The three men came to a chilling decision, after which Himmler issued a brutal order: 'All Jews must be shot. Drive the female Jews into the swamps.'

On receiving Himmler's command, SS Major Gustav Lombard advised his battalion that 'in future not one male Jew is to remain alive, not one family in the villages'. Five days later, his force's body count had reached 3,000 'Jews and Partisans'. Over the next weeks, soldiers of 1 SS Cavalry Regiment under Lombard's command murdered an estimated 11,000 Jews and more than 400 Red Army stragglers.

As a youth Lombard often went to stay with his family in America – he was related to the movie actress Carole Lombard, who severed relations with her German family after Hitler's rise to power. After studying modern languages at the University of Missouri, he returned to Germany in 1919, where he worked for American Express and the Chrysler Motor Company in Berlin.

When Hitler came to power in 1933, Lombard joined the Nazi Party and the SS. As a dedicated horseman he was attracted to the *SS-Totenkopf* Cavalry Brigade, which was serving in Poland. He was soon attacking citizens, rather than the enemy, when his unit was ordered to hunt down and kill any non-German males between the ages of 17 and 60. It seems that the exercise was to everyone's liking, because Lombard's colleagues proudly reported that they had executed 250 people during their deployment.

This would prove to be only a fraction of Lombard's eventual killing tally. A grateful Himmler awarded him the Knight's Cross for his services. Accompanied by the remnants of his last command, the 31st Volunteer Grenadier Division, Lombard went into Soviet captivity at the end of the war. He was released in 1955.

Although he had been a mass murderer of the first degree, Lombard escaped with his life and a relatively light sentence. Other *Waffen-SS* killers faced the gallows when the enormity of their crimes came to light. And as we shall see later, those with the right contacts were spirited abroad at the end of the war, where they would often become respected members of their adopted communities.

Chapter Six

THE
SS-ALLGEMEINE

The SS was reorganized after the creation of the *SS-Verfügungstruppe* (the combat arm) in 1934. The *SS-Totenkopfverbände*, which ran the concentration camps, stayed a separate unit. Opportunists, alcoholics, homosexuals and those of uncertain racial status were purged. Those that remained became the *SS-Allgemeine* (General SS), which soon thrust its claws into every part of German life.

——𝓢𝓢————————————————————

Following its reorganization in 1934, the SS comprised three separate forces: the *SS-Allgemeine*, the *SS-Verfügungstruppe* (SS-VT) and the *SS-Totenkopfverbände*. By 1938, *SS-Allgemeine* numbers had risen to 485,000. That figure was boosted by 50,000 when the *SS-Totenkopfverbände*, with the exception of the *SS-Totenkopf* Division, was merged into the *SS-Allgemeine* in May 1939.

In 1935, the *SS-Hauptamt* (SS Head Office or SS-HA) controlled the concentration camps and the SS-VT, as well as the *SS-Allgemeine*. But the SS-VT expanded rapidly, becoming the *Waffen-SS* in 1940. The SS then needed an operational headquarters, so the SS-HA became an administrative office and the SS Leadership Main Office (SS-FHA) was created. Reporting directly to Himmler, it controlled the Command Department of the *Waffen-SS* and the Command Department of the *SS-Allgemeine*.

Although the *SS-Allgemeine* could be described as the 'General SS', or the political wing of the SS, many of its members were called up into the *Wehrmacht* or the *Waffen-SS* as the war progressed.

Only around 100,000 of its members, such as full-time officers and members of the various domestic departments of the SS, were exempt from military service. Part-time voluntary units were organized by region and district, each district containing a number of *Standarten* or regiments. Some districts even had *Reiterstandarten* – cavalry units.

Diverse roles

The departments of the *SS-Allgemeine* were as various as they were numerous, but the innocuous-sounding Reich Security Head Office (RSHA) perhaps struck terror into the most hearts. It had been created by Himmler through the merger of the Security Service (SD) and the Security Police (SiPo) and its first chief was Reinhard Heydrich.

The SiPo was split into two sections: the secret state police (Gestapo) and the criminal police (Kripo). After the death of Heydrich, Himmler took over until January 1943. At that point, SS lieutenant-general and general of police Ernst Kaltenbrunner was appointed to fill Heydrich's shoes.

The job of the RSHA was to fight the enemies of the Third Reich – which could be anyone and everyone. However, its main targets included Jews, Roma (gypsies) and other 'racial undesirables', communists, Freemasons, pacifists and Christian activists. Its numerous prisoners would first be sent to the concentration camps, before going on to extermination camps in Poland and the Ukraine. The RSHA also oversaw the *Einsatzgruppen* death squads who murdered their way across eastern Europe.

Nazi racial policies were administered by the *SS-Allgemeine*'s Race and Settlement Office (RuSHA). Under its aegis, more than 300 men were expelled from the SS in 1937 for contravening Nazi race laws, but in 1940 Himmler reinstated those who had been expelled for marriages that had failed to match Nazi criteria. Perhaps it was because his own marriage had also fallen short of his high ideals. RuSHA shared the task of organizing the Germanization of captured territory with the VoMi (Main Welfare Office for Ethnic Germans) and the office of the RKFDV (Reich Commissioner for the Strengthening of Germanism).

The somewhat bizarre *Ahnenerbe*, the Nazi think tank for investigating ancient history, was also administered by the *SS-Allgemeine*. It was one of Himmler's favourite toys. In June 1941, the organization removed the 900-year-old Bayeux Tapestry so that its Nordic symbolism could be decoded. According to them, it showed the Germanic Franks overwhelming their English enemies. There were also plans to make expeditions to Bolivia, Behistun in Iran and Iceland so that inscriptions, customs and folklore could be examined. It was thought that the Germans' Aryan past could be tracked down to those places. Mummies were studied in the Canary Islands for the same purpose. But the *Ahnenerbe*'s main project was the Aryanization of the conquered territories in eastern Europe, which Himmler considered would take 20 years.

The *Ahnenerbe* also commissioned medical experiments at Dachau. Because *Luftwaffe* pilots were reaching new heights, some of the camp's inmates were locked in vacuum chambers to see how the human body would react. As well as flying higher, German airmen were crash-landing in icy waters, so prisoners were subjected to similar conditions in a bid to find out if the pilots could survive. Some subjects were stripped and immersed in tanks of icy water, while others were kept outside in freezing weather for up to 14 hours. Attempts were then made to revive them, either by thrusting them into baths of hot water or by using women to stimulate them sexually, a method suggested by Himmler. *Ahnenerbe* scientists also measured Jewish facial features and collected Jewish skulls in an attempt to demonstrate their racial theories.

Less quirky, but even more sinister, was the SS Economic and Administrative Main Office (WVHA), which was responsible for managing finances, supplies and business projects for the *SS-Allgemeine*. It also ran the concentration camps and oversaw the Holocaust. Valuables such as gold watches, rings, currency, gold fillings and glasses were taken from victims when they arrived at the death camps. These items were then sent back to Berlin in WVHA-marked crates, for processing at the Reichsbank. Between August 1942 and January 1945, a total of 76 WVHA consignments had arrived in Berlin, providing hundreds of millions of Reichsmarks for the war effort. The WVHA also aided the economy by providing seemingly limitless amounts of slave labour. These unfortunates were used in the armaments industry and on construction projects such as the building of the Atlantic Wall that fortified the coast from the Arctic to the border of Spain.

After the invasion of the Soviet Union, the SS took operational control of manufacturing and mining in the territories it occupied. It controlled land and forestry, stone quarries, cement works, brick and building materials factories, porcelain and pottery factories, mineral water extraction and bottling, meat processing, bakeries, small arms manufacturing and repair, wooden furniture design and production, herbal medicines, fish processing, the publication of books and magazines on Germanic culture and history, art acquisition and restoration, the forging of ceremonial swords and daggers and the production of military clothing and accessories for the *Wehrmacht* as well as the SS.

The WVHA's economics office controlled the entire production cycle, from the extraction of raw materials to manufacture and distribution, either directly or through a complex network of shell companies that had been set up by WVHA chief SS Lieutenant-General Oswald Pohl.

Himmler's personal headquarters, under Karl Wolff, was also part of the *SS-Allgemeine*, as was the *SS-Personalhauptamt*, the central recording office for the SS (SS-PHA). Its records largely concerned themselves with officers. The Nazis' administrative diligence proved an invaluable resource for the Nuremberg prosecutors. Then there was the SS Leadership Main Office (SS-FHA), which was the operational headquarters of the SS. It was responsible for the administration of *Junkerschulen* officer schools, medical services, logistics and rates of pay, as well as being the administrative and operational headquarters of the *Waffen-SS*. The SS-FHA had priority over all of the other branches of the German armed forces when it came to the selection of recruits. When Himmler stepped down as SS-FHA chief in 1943, SS Lieutenant-General Hans Jüttner managed the department until the end of the war.

After serving as a lieutenant in the German army during the First World War, Jüttner worked as a salesman. In 1933, he became a university sports teacher in Breslau and then he joined the SA collegiate office. He switched to the SS-VT in 1935, joining the inspection department in Berlin.

Promotion was rapid. By 1939, he had become the inspector of reserve troops of the SS-VT Division and from early 1940 he was leading the SS-VT command office. That summer he was appointed chief of staff of the newly created SS-FHA. From 1943, he was in command of all *Waffen-SS* field troops, training and reserve units, schools, command garrisons and headquarters.

On 17 May 1945 Jüttner was taken prisoner by the British and three years later he was sentenced to ten years' imprisonment in a labour camp. This was reduced to four years on appeal. In 1961 he testified for the prosecution in the trial of Holocaust architect Adolf Eichmann and he later became the proprietor of a sanatorium in Bad Tölz, where he died.

Foreign branches

As the Nazi empire spread across Europe, the *SS-Allgemeine* set up the *Germanische SS* (Germanic SS) to oversee the external branches and collaborationist organizations that modelled themselves on the SS. Individuals would apply for membership of the SS and after fulfilling all of the physical and racial requirements they would receive an SS number. Then they would join part-time SS units that performed voluntary drills, undertook ideological instruction, marched in parades and provided security at Party rallies.

The Netherlands

Foreign branches enforced Nazi racial doctrines in occupied countries and served as local security police alongside the Gestapo and the SD. On 9 June 1940 Hitler ordered Anton Mussert, leader of the Dutch National Socialist Movement, to recruit men for the *Wiking* Division of the *Waffen-SS*. He refused, but the *Wiking* Division was set up anyway. When *Reichskommissar* Arthur Seyss-Inquart threatened to replace Mussert with Dutch fascist politician Meinoud Rost van Tonningen, Mussert was forced to agree to the establishment of the *Nederlandsche SS* under Johannes Hendrik 'Henk' Feldmeijer.

While doing national service in 1931, Feldmeijer met a leader of the recently formed Stormtroopers of the National Socialist Movement in the Netherlands (NSB), which fired his interest in the organization. One of the first 1,000 members, he supported NSB leader Anton Mussert in his bid to be dictator of the Netherlands. He then became a paid member of the party's propaganda department, travelling to Germany, Italy and Scandinavia.

Henk Feldmeijer belonged to the *Völkisch* section of the NSB, which developed ideas about the Germanic heritage of the Dutch and cultivated anti-Semitism. As a result, he had contacts with the German SS behind the back of the NSB. Nevertheless, he was appointed commander of Mussert's bodyguard and he trained them as a paramilitary group. In May 1940 he was arrested by the Dutch government, who took him as a prisoner into France when the Nazis invaded. Released when the

German army overtook his captors he returned to The Hague, where he met Himmler and Seyss-Inquart. They all held discussions about the Nazification of the Netherlands and the formation of a Dutch SS, the *Nederlandsche SS*.

As the commander of the *Nederlandsche SS*, Feldmeijer reported directly to Himmler. After exhorting his members to make a direct contribution to the war effort he led by example, serving at the front twice: first as a gunner with the *Leibstandarte SS Adolf Hitler* in Yugoslavia and Greece, and then as flak commander in *SS-Division Wiking* in southern Russia.

In March 1943, he was promoted to the rank of colonel in the *SS-Allgemeine* and a year later he became a captain in the *Waffen-SS*. He also won the Iron Cross Second Class.

Feldmeijer then took part in the reprisals for the liquidations committed by the Dutch resistance. In September 1943, *Sonderkommando-Feldmeijer* killed at least 20 resistance members. However, on 22 February 1945 Feldmeijer met his own end when Allied aircraft strafed his car.

The *Nederlandsche SS* was the Dutch version of the *SS-Allgemeine*. It had the same age, fitness, height, genealogy and character requirements as its German equivalent. Recruits were to have no dishonourable criminal convictions and they had to pledge their unconditional loyalty to all of their superiors. Their uniforms were black, like those of the German SS. The *Nederlandsche SS* was divided into five regional *standaarden* or regiments, with headquarters at Groningen, Arnhem, Amsterdam, The Hague and Eindhoven. There was also a separate police regiment. The regiments were intended to contain 500 men plus staff but the average *standaard* numbered only 130 men – the rest were siphoned off by the *Waffen-SS*.

The *Nederlandsche SS* was an important recruiting ground, as well as being a reserve. It was also used as a propaganda tool and it helped advance the idea of 'Greater Germany', which would embrace all northern European peoples. This concept was reinforced when the name was changed to *Germaansche SS in Nederland* (Germanic SS in the Netherlands) in November 1942.

As a political formation, the *Germaansche SS in Nederland* helped expand Himmler's empire, but at its peak it only boasted around 7,000 members. However, there was also a Dutch version of the German *SS-Fördernde Mitglieder* (SS-FM), an association of SS supporters who paid a monthly fee. It had a membership of around 4,000. By the end of 1944, with the tide turning against Germany, the *Germaansche SS in Nederland* became an organization that existed only on paper.

Flanders
There was a similar formation in Flanders, the Flemish-speaking region of Belgium. Originally called the *Algemeene-SS Vlaanderen*, it was renamed the *Germaansche SS in Vlaanderen* (Germanic SS in Flanders) in 1942. It provided military drill and ideological education, and ran its own newspaper, *De SS-Man*. There was only one *standaard*, or unit, which was divided into four regional *stormbans* (storm units), but there was also a Flemish version of the SS-FM, called the *Beschermde Leden* (BL). The BL had around 4,200 members, who were equally divided between women and men.

During the German occupation of Belgium, opinion regarding the future of Flanders was more or less split between the followers of *DeVlag*, a pro-Nazi organization, and the Flemish National Union (VNV), the largest nationalist movement in Flanders.

DeVlag had been set up by Dr Jef van de Wiele in 1935. Its symbol was the Nazi eagle and swastika combined with the black lion of Flanders. In May 1941, after the German invasion of Belgium, *DeVlag* started to receive support from the SS and was reorganized into a National Socialist organization. This caused a rift with the VNV.

The VNV wanted Flanders to be an independent state within the German union, while *DeVlag* proclaimed unconditional loyalty to the *Führer* and the Reich – its 50,000 members were in favour of the annexation of Flanders by Germany. Naturally, Himmler supported *DeVlag*. Every leading member of *DeVlag* was obliged to join the German SS in Flanders, while members of the German SS in Flanders were ordered to join *DeVlag*, moulding the two organizations together.

In recognition of his efforts van de Wiele was promoted to SS major, thereby becoming the highest-ranking Flemish official. He enjoyed a good relationship with Léon Degrelle, the leader of the Walloons (French-speaking Belgians), to the extent that he accompanied him on public engagements. Meanwhile, van de Wiele worked enthusiastically with the Nazis, advocating the full mobilization of the region. In 1943 he turned the entire country's youth movement over to the Hitler Youth.

On 4 December 1942, SS Second Lieutenant August Schollen, the leader of *Stormban III/1*, was shot in Brussels. His friend, First Lieutenant Robert Verbelen, the leader of *Stormban IV/1*, then began a reign of terror against the resistance and leading figures in Belgian society.

The son of a Belgian policeman, Verbelen was educated in French. He became a journalist and general secretary of the Flemish football league and he was also a member of the VNV. Although one of his brothers had joined the resistance, Verbelen was one of the first to join the *Algemeene SS Vlaanderen*. He later became leader of the Security Corps of *DeVlag*.

Once he was a member of *DeVlag*, Verbelen raised the *DeVlag-Veiligheidskorps/DeVlag-Sicherheitskorps* in 1944, to protect its supporters. Together with the Gestapo and the SD, he cracked down on any armed resistance. As the Allies advanced into Belgium in September 1944, many members of the *Germaansche SS* fled to Germany, where they joined the *Waffen-SS*, serving with the *SS-Jagdverband 'Nordwest'*.

Shortly after that, Flanders was annexed by the Nazis and van der Wiele was appointed *Gauleiter* of the Region of Flanders. He fled to Germany to set up a government in exile.

Robert Verbelen went off to join him as part of this short-lived government, but then he moved to Austria, where he became a police informer and worked for American intelligence. In 1947 he was sentenced to death *in absentia* for the murder of 101 Belgian citizens. Although he was using his real name, along with a number of aliases, Verbelen was granted Austrian citizenship. However, in 1962, the Nazi-hunter Simon Wiesenthal alerted the public prosecutor in Vienna. As an Austrian citizen, Verbelen contested his extradition to Belgium, so in 1965 the public prosecutor instituted proceedings against him in a Vienna court. He was charged with five counts of murder and instigation of murder. Although the Austrian jury found Verbelen guilty of instigating the murders of two people, it ruled that he had only been carrying out his superiors' orders and thus he was acquitted of committing war crimes. This acquittal was later overturned by the Austrian Supreme Court, but the case was never retried.

Verbelen continued living in Austria, where he published articles in a number of far-right publications and wrote espionage novels.

Van de Wiele enjoyed a short moment of glory, but it was all too late because the Allies had already invaded Belgium. He was tried as a traitor and sentenced to death. This punishment was later commuted

— 🙰🙰——————————————————————————

to life imprisonment and he was released after 17 years. He settled in West Germany.

Norway

The Norwegian *Norges SS* was formed in May 1941, despite fierce opposition from Vidkun Quisling, the former defence minister who had invited Hitler to invade. Although the *Norges SS* was technically a formation within Quisling's National Union party, he had no control over it. Its leader was Norway's police chief, Jonas Lie. The *Norges SS* was backed by *Reichskommisar* Josef Terboven and Himmler flew in to administer the oath. Having sworn an oath of allegiance to both Hitler and Quisling, the new SS men were sent on a six-week induction course.

Lie was the son of a famous Norwegian literary family. He followed in the family tradition by becoming a war correspondent during the Second World War and he later became a policeman. Even though his uncle was a passionate anti-Semite, one of his duties had been to accompany Leon Trotsky when he travelled on a freighter from Norway to Mexico in 1936. He also produced a series of detective novels under the name of Max Mauser. After leaving the National Union party in 1935 he rejoined it in 1940.

Lie became one of the first Norwegian SS volunteers in the *Waffen-SS* when he served briefly as a war correspondent in *Leibstandarte SS Adolf Hitler* during the Balkans campaign of 1940. With him was Sverre Riisnæs, who later became Minister of Justice in the Quisling government. After forming the *Norges SS*, Lie commanded the 1st Police Company of the Norwegian Legion of the *Waffen-SS* in 1942–3, when he won the Iron Cross First Class.

Himmler mistrusted Lie, in spite of his bravery on the field, so he replaced him with Riisnæs, who was a willing servant of the Nazis. In his capacity as Minister of Justice, Riisnæs had adjusted the Norwegian legal system to legitimize the Nazis' actions and he had authorized the persecution of those who would not co-operate with the German invaders.

Lie was found dead on the day of Norway's liberation. It is thought that he had suffered a heart attack after overindulging in akvavit, a potent Norwegian drink. Riisnæs was still around, so he was arrested and charged with treason, but his mental state made him unfit to stand trial.

When war was declared on the Soviet Union in June 1941, 85 per cent of the *Norges SS*, around 130 men, joined the Norwegian SS Volunteer Legion. Five months later Quisling became president and the *Norges SS* was renamed *Germanske SS Norge* (GSN). In May 1943, most Norwegian volunteers were transferred into the *SS-Panzergrenadier Norge* and soon afterwards the GSN formed a full company of its own to fight on the Eastern Front.

The total strength of the Norwegian SS in September 1944 was 1,247, with 330 at the front, 245 in the police force and 511 in emergency units. That meant that only 161 members were available to run the organization in Norway. Meanwhile, its supporters, the *Støttende Medlemmer*, numbered 3,422, while 9,137 subscribed to its newspaper, *Germaneren – Kamporgan for Germanske SS Norge*.

When Norway was liberated by the Allies in May 1945, Quisling stood trial for treason and was executed.

Denmark

King Christian X had accepted the 'protection of the Reich' as far back as 9 April 1940, when Denmark had been threatened by aerial bombing,

——*SS*————————————————————

but the *Frikorps Danmark* only came into existence on 29 June 1941, after being formed at the instigation of the SS and the DNSAP. It is estimated that between 6,000 and 10,000 Danes served in the *Frikorps Danmark*, which saw action on the Eastern Front in 1942.

In June 1943, the *Frikorps* was disbanded and some of its men were transferred to a Danish regiment in the *SS-Freiwilligen Panzergrenadier Division Nordland*, a division of the *Waffen-SS*. Others joined the Danish auxiliary police corps (HIPO corps) or the Schalburg Corps, a branch of the *Germanic-SS*. The Schalburg Corps was named in honour of the former leader of the *Frikorps*, Christian Frederik von Schalburg, who had been killed in action on 2 June 1942. Unlike the *Germanic-SS* units in Norway and the Netherlands, this particular detachment was not a part of the local Nazi Party. Instead it was a separate organization, whose leader was Knud Børge Martinsen.

After joining the Danish army in 1928, Martinsen was on the general staff when Germany occupied Denmark in 1940. Two weeks later, he joined the National Socialist Workers' Party of Denmark (DNSAP). He then resigned in order to join the *Waffen-SS*, serving with *Frikorps Danmark* under Christian Frederik von Schalburg. After Schalburg's death, Martinsen took command of the *Frikorps*. When it was disbanded, he was transferred to the *SS-Freiwilligen Panzergrenadier Division Nordland*.

After two months, Martinsen returned to Denmark to take command of the Schalburg Corps, which had become a recruitment unit for the *Waffen-SS*. In October 1944, he was arrested by the Gestapo and imprisoned in Berlin. He eventually escaped and made his way back to Denmark, where he was arrested. After a trial he was sentenced to death and executed by firing squad in Copenhagen.

Members of the Schalburg Corps who had not had any combat

experience on the Eastern Front had to endure six weeks of political indoctrination and combat training. The corps was divided into two groups: one consisted of regular soldiers and the other, the Danish People's Defence, was made up of civilians. Some of them were expected to provide financial backing. Members of the corps were used as a guard battalion to protect railroads and crossroads from sabotage.

In July 1944, the Schalburg Corps was incorporated into the SS as the SS Training Battalion Schalburg, first under SS Major Poul Neergaard-Jacobsen and then under SS First Lieutenant Egill Poulsen. After six months, it was renamed the SS Guard Battalion Zealand. It was officially disbanded on 28 February 1945.

France

While the French had the *Légion des Volontaires Français* (LVF), they did not have an *SS-Allgemeine* group. However, the SS formed close links with Vichy France's paramilitary *Milice* (Militia), whose job it was to round up the Jews and summarily execute members of the resistance. The force later merged with the LVF to form the *SS-Charlemagne Division*. Few were prosecuted after the war.

Switzerland

There was even support for the Nazis in neutral Switzerland. That is, if Switzerland merited the description. The Germans had the power to flatten Switzerland whenever they chose, but with so many factories churning out precision components, not to mention the fact that Switzerland was a ready market for Nazi gold, the 'neutral' arrangement suited both sides very well.

Swiss doctor Franz Riedweg was one of the Nazi Party's most ardent Swiss supporters. After studying medicine in Berne, Rostock and Berlin, he became a member of the Swiss National Front. In 1936, he became a political adviser to Jean-Marie Musy, a member of the Federal Council of Switzerland, and a year later he joined the ranks of Action Against Communism, which produced the propaganda film *The Red Plague*.

His next move was to marry the daughter of war minister Werner von Blomberg, which he did in 1938. It was a good tactic for a would-be Nazi, because he was soon rubbing shoulders with Goebbels, Himmler and Heydrich. No wonder he was seen as the most influential Swiss citizen in Nazi Germany during the Second World War. He was then made a lieutenant-colonel in the SS, which propelled him into the *Leibstandarte SS Adolf Hitler*, where he served as a doctor during the invasion of Poland, before going to France.

In 1941, he became the medical officer of the *SS-Hauptamt* in Berlin and in the same year he started the 'Panorama House' in Stuttgart, which served as a detention centre for Swiss nationals. He also became the director of non-German volunteers to the *Waffen-SS*. A couple of years later he headed the Germanic control centre in the SS headquarters and was awarded the Iron Cross. A year after that, in 1944, he received orders to form the *Schweizer Sportbund*, or the *Germanische SS Schweiz*, but the war was nearing its end and the Swiss SS was never formed. The Swiss then withdrew his citizenship.

Undaunted, he went off to war with *III Germanisches Panzer Korps*, but he was captured in Mecklenburg-Vorpommem. In his absence, he was tried by a Swiss court for attempting to destroy the independence of Switzerland by military means and was sentenced to 16 years' imprisonment. However, he continued working as a doctor in Munich, where he died at the age of 98. His way of life had obviously suited him.

Karl Otto Koch (seen above with his wife Ilse, their dog and son) killed the doctor who had treated him for syphilis so the secret never got out (see pp. 187-8)

Policing the SS

The SS was a law unto itself. After three top SS men at Dachau concentration camp had been charged with incitement to murder in 1934, Himmler decided that it would be a good idea to place the SS above German law and make it answerable only to the *Hauptamt SS Gericht* (Head Office SS Court). Led by SS Lieutenant-Colonel Franz Breihaupt, some 600 lawyers investigated and prosecuted cases against people who had been charged with violating the SS code of honour, though Himmler often intervened and altered the sentences. By 1944, there were 12 offices throughout Germany and 38 courts across the Reich.

—ϟϟ—

After winning an Iron Cross in the First World War, Breihaupt joined the Nazi Party in 1931 and the SS in the following year. In 1933, he was elected to the Reichstag, serving on Himmler's staff from 1934 onwards. Rising effortlessly through the ranks, he had become an SS lieutenant-general by the time he took over the *Hauptamt SS Gericht*. He died on 28 April 1945, apparently murdered by his aide, SS Second Lieutenant Karl Lang.

While the *Hauptamt SS Gericht* was intended to be a convenient way of making SS members immune from prosecution in the ordinary course of events, some of its staff took their jobs seriously. Too seriously for some. One of them was SS First Lieutenant Konrad Morgen, who became known as the 'Bloodhound Judge'. Morgen was regarded as a pacifist, even more so when he published *War Propaganda and the Prevention of War* in 1936. As a lawyer, his belief in the primacy of law in Hitler's increasingly dictatorial regime had brought him into conflict with a provincial magistrate. In order to save his career, he had accepted a post as an assistant judge with the *Hauptamt SS Gericht*. When he was posted to Krakow, he began investigating cases of corruption, but his scrupulous regard for the law irritated the police chief, SS Lieutenant-General Friedrich Krüger. As a punishment, he was sent to join the *SS-Wiking* Division, which was stationed on the Eastern Front at the time.

Morgen should have expected that sort of treatment at the hands of Krüger. The son of a military family, Krüger served as an officer during the First World War, when he was wounded three times and won the Iron Cross First and Second Class. After serving in the *Freikorps*, he joined the Nazi Party in 1929 and the SS in 1931, but after two months he quit to join the SA, where he served on Röhm's personal staff. He was spared on the Night of the Long Knives because his switch to the SA was seen as a purely pragmatic move. After Röhm's death he switched back to the SS again.

In October 1939, he was appointed High SS and police leader in occupied Poland. As such, he was responsible for crushing rebellions in the extermination camps. He was obviously unpopular because two bombs were thrown at his car at one point, though he survived. However, he was dismissed in November 1943 after falling out with the governor-general, Hans Frank.

He was then sent off to Nazi-occupied Yugoslavia with the 7th SS Mountain Infantry 'Prince Eugen' Division, where he fought with the partisans.

His unit became infamous for its civilian atrocities. After going on to fight in Finland he committed suicide in Austria in May 1945. Hitler was already dead by then.

His older brother was SS Lieutenant-General Walter Krüger (1890–1945), who formed the *SS-Standarte Germania* and took part in the siege of Leningrad, among other things. Like his brother, he committed suicide at the end of the war. There was nothing left to live for now the Nazi dream was shattered.

Although Friedrich Krüger had sent Morgen off to the Eastern Front, the lawyer's investigative skills were seen as a more valuable asset than his fighting abilities, so he was dragged back and posted to the SS Criminal Police Division (RKPA), where he would deal with financial crimes.

Running an eye over the death list for Buchenwald concentration camp, the Higher SS and police leader for Weimar, SS Lieutenant-General Josias, Prince of Waldeck and Pyrmont, stopped short when he reached the name of Dr Walter Krämmer, who had once treated him. Investigating, Josias discovered that the camp commandant, SS Colonel

Karl Otto Koch, had killed Krämmer and a medical orderly named Karl Peixof because they had treated him for syphilis, something that Koch wanted covered up. Another prisoner had been 'shot while trying to escape' when he had been sent to fetch water some distance from the camp. Josias asked Morgen to investigate.

Perhaps the grandest member of the SS, Josias was a cousin of Queen Wilhelmina of the Netherlands and a relative of the British royal family. He was born in the family castle at Bad Arolsen. After being injured in the First World War, he joined the Nazi Party in 1929 and the SS in the following year. Elected as the Reichstag member for Düsseldorf-West in 1933, he was promoted to the rank of SS lieutenant-general. In 1939, he became the Higher SS and police leader for Weimar and consequently had authority over Buchenwald concentration camp which was situated nearby.

Two years later he was promoted to the position of high commissioner of police in occupied France. One of his first acts was to announce that French hostages would be placed on German troop trains in order to discourage sabotage attempts on them. He was made a full general in the *Waffen-SS* in July 1944.

Arrested on 13 April 1945, he was accused of running Buchenwald and being involved in the execution of Karl Otto Koch. Found guilty, he was sentenced to life imprisonment in the very camp that he claimed to know little about. His sentence was commuted to 20 years, but he was released after just three years on medical grounds.

Morgen was already investigating another case at Buchenwald at the time. Working in collusion with Koch, a Nazi provisions merchant named Bornschein had been profiteering while supplying the camp. In order to avoid prosecution by the local police, Bornschein had joined the *Waffen-SS*, so only the RKPA had jurisdiction. Morgen moved into the Hotel Elephant in Weimar, one of Hitler's favourite hostelries. After prosecuting Bornschein, Morgen amassed evidence showing that Koch had been hiring out camp labourers to civilians, racketeering in food supplies, murdering unco-operative inmates and generally running the camp for his own profit.

By this time Koch had been moved to Majdanek concentration camp in Lublin, eastern Poland, but his wife, Ilse, was still living at the commandant's house in Buchenwald. Morgen intercepted the couple's letters and examined their bank accounts. It was like lifting the lid from a can of worms. He soon discovered that Koch had embezzled at least 100,000 marks and he also found proof of the murders of Dr Krämmer and Karl Peixof. It appeared that witnesses to the murders had been slain as well, while camp officials such as Dr Waldemar Houst, the camp doctor, were also involved in the murders and in acts of sadism.

Josias filed charges of incitement to murder against Koch, and Morgen added allegations of embezzlement. He also arraigned other members of the camp staff. The charges were passed to the chief of the criminal police, SS Major-General Artur Nebe, who relayed them to Gestapo chief SS Major-General Heinrich Müller. Next they went to Ernst Kaltenbrunner, head of the RSHA. The chief of the SS legal department took one look at the charges and passed them on to Himmler. Fearing that the file might be overlooked or ignored, Morgen sent a carefully worded telegram to Himmler outlining the case. Himmler was ever anxious that nothing should besmirch the honour of the SS – except mass murder, of course – so he gave Morgen full authority to proceed against Koch.

After winning the Iron Cross Second Class, Koch was captured by the British on the Western Front, returning to Germany in 1919. In 1931, he joined the Nazi Party and the SS and four years later he became commandant of Columbia-Haus concentration camp in Berlin-Tempelhof, before taking over at Sachsenhausen in 1937. He moved to Buchenwald in 1941 and was then transferred to Majdanek following allegations of corruption, fraud, embezzlement, drunkenness, sexual offences and murder.

After a year, he was relieved of duty when 86 Soviet prisoners of war escaped. Accused of criminal negligence, he was returned to Berlin, where he faced the charges drawn up by Josias, Prince of Waldeck and Pyrmont, and Konrad Morgen. At his trial, Koch was sentenced to death for disgracing both himself and the SS. He was executed by firing squad on 5 April 1945, one week before American troops arrived to liberate the camp.

Koch was certainly a criminal of the first order, yet the dual standards of the SS were such that someone like Nebe, who had arguably committed even greater crimes, could be the police chief who first brought him to justice. Nebe had walked a curious tightrope during his SS career. He was often appalled by the atrocities he was asked to commit, yet he went along with them just the same. He was involved in several plots against Hitler and others, but he experimented with a new method for gassing Jews.

Gassed twice himself in the First World War, Nebe joined the criminal police (Kripo) in 1920. By 1924, he had become a commissioner. In 1931, he joined the Nazi Party and the SS on the same day.

Then came his first killing. In 1933, Rudolf Diels, then head of the Gestapo, ordered Nebe to dispose of Gregor Strasser. After that, various reorganizations of the police force resulted in Nebe becoming head of the national criminal police under the RSHA, reporting directly to Heydrich. He regularly dined with Heydrich and Himmler.

In order to test Nebe's loyalty, Himmler gave him command of

Einsatzgruppe B. Nebe was so appalled by Heydrich's murderous orders that he reported them to the group surrounding Colonel Hans Oster, who opposed Hitler's war aims. Trying to wriggle out of the job, Nebe asked to be made head of the International Police Commission, but Oster and some others persuaded him to take the *Einsatzgruppe* job so that he could give them up-to-date information from inside the SS and the Gestapo. Nebe's group killed 46,000 people but that was only a fraction of the 221,000 murders that had been racked up by *Einsatzgruppe A*, which was led by SS Major-General Franz-Walter Stahlecker. Stahlecker was killed by Soviet partisans in March 1942.

Nebe was sickened by the murders but he found himself on the verge of a nervous breakdown when his driver killed himself over what he had witnessed. Nevertheless, Himmler ordered him to arrange the execution of 100 Jews during his visit to Minsk. As if killing innocent people were not enough, Nebe was ordered to have sex with two of his female victims. This was the execution at which Himmler nearly fainted because someone's brains splattered on his coat. Afterwards Nebe was ordered to find a method of killing that would not be so distressing for the executioners. He experimented with gassing his victims by pumping the exhaust gases from a truck into the sealed rear compartment.

After the war, movie footage of his hideous research was found in his Berlin apartment.

Yet Nebe still appeared to see himself as a concerned observer. When he attended the Wannsee Conference in 1942, he leaked the details of the 'Final Solution' to Hans Oster, his fellow conspirator. However, he did not demur when Gestapo chief Heinrich Müller ordered him to select 50 out of the 73 recaptured prisoners for execution after the 'Great Escape' from Stalag Luft III in March 1944. He always did what was asked of him.

Nebe's involvement in several plots against the Nazi hierarchy proved to be his final undoing. He was involved in a 1938 plot to overthrow Hitler, for instance, and he also conspired to ruin Himmler's attempt to smear General Werner von Fritsch. All of that apparently escaped detection, but his association with the 'Valkyrie' plot to kill Hitler on 20 July 1944 did not pass unnoticed. He was supposed to have led a team of 12 policemen to kill Himmler, but the message never reached him. Nevertheless, he went into hiding, but he was betrayed by a girlfriend. Sentenced to death by the *Volksgerichtshof* (People's Court), he was hanged.

Heinrich Müller was far less complicated than Nebe. He despised Hitler and yet he rounded up those who plotted against him, because that was his job.

After serving as a pilot in the First World War and winning the Iron Cross, Müller witnessed the shooting of hostages in the short-lived Bavarian Soviet Republic, which was said to have given him a lifelong hatred of communism. Then in 1919 he joined the political department of the Bavarian police force. In 1931 he was the investigating officer when Hitler's niece, Geli Raubal, was shot, and it was said that he took a bribe to ensure the scandal would not taint Hitler, who was thought to have killed Geli in a fit of jealousy.

A bribe sounds about right. He would not have been motivated by goodwill, because he once referred to Hitler as 'an immigrant unemployed house painter' and 'an Austrian draft-dodger'. Perhaps that is why he did not become a member of the Nazi Party until 1939. Nevertheless, Heydrich chose him to replace Diels as head of the Gestapo, because Diels was Göring's man. Müller became Adolf Eichmann's boss and he also received reports on the operations of the *Einsatzgruppen*. Eichmann ran the Gestapo's Office of Resettlement and then its Office of Jewish Affairs.

After the 20 July plot, Müller was in charge of the investigating committee that rounded up the conspirators. He was awarded the Knight's Cross for his efforts. Then on 29 April 1945, with the Red Army fighting its way into Berlin, Müller was put in charge of the interrogation and execution of Hermann Fegelein, who was Himmler's liaison officer with Hitler and Eva Braun's brother-in-law. Himmler had tried to negotiate with the Western Allies. Two days later Müller disappeared to no one knows where.

Like Müller, Kaltenbrunner was a man who did his duty. He made sure that nothing stood in the way of the German nation, no matter what the human cost.

Born in Ried im Innkreis, Austria, not far from Braunau am Inn, Hitler's birthplace, Kaltenbrunner studied law at the University of Graz. He acquired a deep scar on his face during his student days, which he attributed to duelling, though some said it was caused by a drink-related car accident.

In 1932 he joined the Nazi Party in Austria and then he formed an *SS-Sturmbann* with Adolf Eichmann. Following the murder of Engelbert Dollfuss, he was jailed for six months for conspiracy. As leader of the Austrian SS, he assisted in the *Anschluss*, was promoted to SS major-general and became a member of the Reichstag in 1938.

After Heydrich's death, Kaltenbrunner was appointed as his successor – when Himmler had done the job himself for eight months – even though Himmler complained of his drinking. Kaltenbrunner headed Operation Long Jump – a failed attempt to assassinate Churchill, Roosevelt and Stalin at their meeting in Tehran in 1943 – and he was awarded the Knight's Cross after preparing the case against *Abwehr* chief Wilhelm Canaris, following the 20 July plot. As the war drew to a close, he moved his headquarters to Altaussee in Austria, the so-

——*ᚦᚦ*————————————————————

called 'Alpine redoubt' where hardliners aimed to continue the war.

At Nuremberg, Kaltenbrunner was found guilty of war crimes and crimes against humanity and was sentenced to death. He went to the gallows denying he knew anything of the crimes of which he was accused. The three children he had with his wife, and the two he had with his mistress, all survived the war.

Morgen takes on Himmler

While investigating Koch, Morgen began to look into what was happening at Majdanek. In early November 1943, he became an accidental eyewitness to part of Operation Harvest Festival – the liquidation of three large and several smaller Jewish labour camps in the Lublin district of eastern Poland and the murder of their 50,000 inmates. At the Poniatowa labour camp Morgen watched as more than 15,000 inmates of all ages and both sexes reported to the execution site, where they handed over their personal effects and clothing and then went naked into the trenches, where they were shot. But as all of this had been personally authorized by Himmler, there was nothing Morgen could do about it.

Camp commandant *SS-Oberführer* Christian Wirth gave Morgen a tour of the extermination camps at Treblinka, Sobibor and Belzec, where he saw the gas chambers, the crematoria and the mass graves. Believing this to be evidence of localized crime, he began to investigate. Then he discovered that the orders for the mass murders at these camps had come directly from Hitler's chancellery and could not be stopped by the SS legal department. However, he began to prosecute individual SS officers for the 'arbitrary killings' that took place outside the directives of the 'Final Solution'. He also investigated cases of cruelty, corruption and other comparatively minor crimes. Eventually Himmler had to tell him to back off.

Christian Wirth was a former Stuttgart policeman who had been recommended to Himmler by Nebe. He headed the T-4 Euthanasia Programme that eliminated disabled people and mental patients, as well as others who were considered incurable, and he also oversaw mass sterilization projects.

Franz Stangl, the commandant of the Sobibor and Treblinka death camps, described Wirth as

> *a gross and florid man ... When he spoke about the necessity of this euthanasia operation, he wasn't speaking in humane or scientific terms, the way Dr Werner at T-4 had described it to me. He laughed. He spoke of 'doing away with useless mouths', and that 'sentimental slobber' about such people made him 'puke'.*

Born in Austria, Stangl joined the police force and became a member of the Nazi Party in 1931, when it was illegal. After the *Anschluss*, he was promoted quickly up the ranks. Himmler appointed him superintendent of the T-4 Programme at the Euthanasia Institute at Schloss Hartheim. It was there that he first met Christian Wirth, who was later involved in gassing Jews at Chelmno and Belzec.

In 1942, he was transferred to Poland where he worked under Odilo Globocnik (see pp.217-19) and he became the commandant of Sobibor extermination camp. Around 10,000 Jews were killed before Stangl became the commandant of Treblinka.

'I remember Wirth standing there, next to the pits full of black-blue corpses,' said Stangl. 'Wirth said: "What shall we do with rotting garbage?" I think unconsciously that started me thinking of them as cargo' – which is what Stangl began calling his victims.

Stangl oversaw the murder of 700,000 people at Treblinka. The camp was second only to Auschwitz in the numbers that were gassed. During this barbarous operation, the victims were robbed of large amounts of money in different currencies – £400,000, $2,800,000 and 12,000,000 roubles – as well as 145 kilograms of gold from rings and teeth and 4,000 carats of diamonds. The criminals even took hair, clothing and spectacles.

As the Red Army advanced the camp was destroyed, leaving only 40 surviving inmates. The guards were sent to fight the Yugoslav partisans, which was a virtual death sentence. Stangl was arrested after the war, but he escaped to Brazil where he worked in the Volkswagen factory in São Paulo under his own name. However, a disaffected relative reported his whereabouts to Simon Wiesenthal and in 1969 he was extradited to Germany, where he stood trial for the murder of around 900,000 people.

He admitted to these killings but like a true psychopath he said: 'My conscience is clear. I was simply doing my duty.'

He was sentenced to life imprisonment and he died in jail.

Because of opposition from the Church, T-4 was cancelled and Wirth was transferred to Poland to oversee the gassing of the gypsies and the Jews. He had no time for the mobile units being used at Chelmno extermination camp. At Belzec, Sobibor and Treblinka he constructed three special 'shower rooms', believing that the victims would be pacified by the idea that they were going to have a shower, though an eyewitness recalled Wirth striking a hesitating woman across the face with the whip he always carried. Exhaust gas from a diesel engine was then pumped in through the shower heads.

Geraniums were planted outside, the grass was trimmed and a sign was hung over the gate, saying: 'Entrance to the Jewish state.' Over the entrance to the gas chamber itself hung a banner made from a synagogue curtain which said, in Hebrew: 'This is the gate of the Lord into which the righteous shall enter.'

After killing 1.7 million Polish Jews and thousands of gypsies, Wirth was transferred to San Sabba concentration camp in Trieste where he was also responsible for suppressing the partisans in occupied Yugoslavia. Those who had been on the extermination programme often found themselves being given dangerous assignments to get rid of them. Wirth was killed by partisans in May 1944, while travelling in an open-topped car.

In 1944, Morgen began investigating the commandant of Auschwitz extermination camp, Rudolf Höss. Needless to say, his enquiries were not welcomed. One of Morgen's aides, SS Battalion Sergeant Major Gerhard Putsch, vanished without a trace and the hut where Morgen kept his files was burnt to the ground. However, he managed to prosecute several high-ranking Nazis such as Maximilian Grabner, the Gestapo chief and head torturer at Auschwitz, who was arraigned for theft and corruption, and the commandant of Dachau, Alex Piorkowski, who was also convicted of corruption. Koch's successor at Majdanek, Hermann Florstedt, was another criminal who was successfully put on trial. He was executed by the SS for corruption and arbitrary killing on 15 April 1945.

Like many SS monsters, the character and behaviour of Rudolf Höss is riddled with paradox. As a child he had hoped to become a Catholic priest and during the First World War he became the youngest NCO to serve in the German army. He was wounded several times and he won the Iron Cross. After the war he joined the *Freikorps*, then in 1922 he renounced his Catholic faith and joined the Nazi Party. In the following year Höss and Martin Bormann, later Hitler's private secretary, were sentenced to life imprisonment for the murder of schoolteacher Walter Kadow, whom they suspected of reporting *Freikorps* members to the French authorities in the occupied Ruhr.

Released in 1928 as part of a general amnesty, Höss joined the Artaman League, which promoted a clean-living, rural lifestyle. In 1929 he married Hedwig Hensel, who bore him five children, then in 1934 he joined the *SS-Totenkopfverbände*. He served as an administrator at Dachau for four years. According to his autobiography, he was squeamish about the corporal punishment that was inflicted on the inmates but he was unconcerned when he witnessed executions.

After a period at Sachsenhausen he became the first commandant of Auschwitz, which was then only a detention camp. However, he greatly expanded its facilities. In June 1941 he received orders that Hitler had decreed the physical extermination of all European Jews, which would take place at Auschwitz. Höss's camp had been chosen because it had good rail links and it was isolated, so it would be easier to maintain secrecy. The only person he told was his wife, who lived at the camp with their children. After he told her, she was reluctant to sleep with him. It is said that he then had an affair with an inmate, who was disposed of by being sent to the gas chamber. A complex man, he also appears to have written poetry about the beauty of the place.

Following a fact-finding visit to Treblinka, Höss decided that he could do better. Treblinka's gas chambers only accommodated 200 people, but Höss made his chambers ten times larger, so that they had a capacity of 2,000. Engine exhaust fumes were used to murder the inmates at Treblinka, but that did not look very efficient to Höss, so he experimented with sulphuric acid and then with Zyklon B. This was quicker, taking between three and 15 minutes – 'We knew when the people were dead because they stopped screaming,' he said.

Höss prided himself on his ability to conceal the truth from his victims. He thought that they would go willingly into the gas chambers if they were told that they were going to be deloused. The only problem was that the crematoria could not keep up with the number of bodies coming out of the gas chambers. Consequently some of the bodies had to be burnt in pits, so the victims were alerted by the reek of burning flesh.

Höss claimed to have worried about murdering children – all children were sent to the gas chambers because they were of no use as forced labour. But Eichmann assured him that if the children were killed first there would not be a new generation to wreak revenge on them. Despite his professed concern, Höss had no qualms about the hideous experiments that the doctors were performing on inmates, nor did he care that the Gestapo were torturing some of the prisoners. Promoted to the position of deputy inspector of concentration camps in December 1943, Höss returned to Auschwitz to oversee the murder of 430,000 Hungarian Jews in May 1944. In the last days of the war he fled ahead of the Red Army and hid in Germany under the name of Fritz Lang. He might well have remained anonymous, but his wife gave him away. She could not come to terms with the fact that she had married a monster. After appearing at Nuremberg as a witness, he was handed over to the Polish authorities.

At his trial he was accused of murdering three-and-a-half million people.

'No. Only two-and-a-half million,' Höss replied. 'The rest died from disease and starvation.'

Sentenced to death, he was hanged at Auschwitz, on the very gallows he had constructed himself.

If he was to have any chance of stopping the Holocaust, Morgen knew that he would have to take the matter up with Himmler himself. He arranged a meeting, but Himmler cancelled the appointment at the last minute. Morgen was preparing a full investigation of Auschwitz when he received direct orders from Hitler's office commanding him to cease his activities. Nevertheless, he brought 800 cases of corruption and obtained at least 200 convictions. It is also thought that he was at least partly responsible for the closure of the extermination camps at Treblinka, Sobibor and Belzec in 1943 and 1944.

After the war, the Allies made use of the evidence Morgen had amassed when they prosecuted the Nazi war criminals and he appeared as a witness for the prosecution in several cases. Grabner and Piorkowski were hanged as a result. However, he refused to testify against Ilse Koch because he did not have any concrete proof that she had committed any of the crimes that she was charged with – though he did believe that she was guilty. Attempts were made by the Allied authorities to intimidate him – he was even threatened with extradition to the Soviet Union. But this was a man who had stood up to the Nazis. Eventually, they let him go. He continued practising law in West Germany, where he died in 1976.

Morgen might not have been sure of Ilse Koch's guilt, but many others were. Known as the 'Witch of Buchenwald' – or sometimes the 'Bitch of Buchenwald' – she met the camp's commandant, Karl Otto Koch, when he was a guard at Sachsenhausen. It was alleged that she sadistically tortured inmates and forced them to rape one another for her own amusement.

Arrested alongside her husband for murder and embezzlement,

she was acquitted by an SS court, but in June 1945 she was arrested by the Americans. It was alleged that she had ordered the murder of certain people so that she could have their tattooed skin made into lampshades. However, Konrad Morgen could find no evidence for this story. Nevertheless, she was found guilty of aiding and abetting her husband and participating in some of the murders at Buchenwald. She was sentenced to life imprisonment. Released after two years by the military governor of the American zone of occupation in Germany, she was arrested again. This time she stood trial before a West German court for the instigation of some 135 murders. Sentenced to life imprisonment again, she hanged herself in prison.

Despite Konrad Morgen's efforts, around six million Jews would lose their lives in the Nazi camps.

Chapter Seven

THE HOLOCAUST

'It wasn't Hitler, Göring, Goebbels, Himmler or any of that lot who dragged me off and beat me up,' said Viennese gypsy, Karl Stojka, who was deported to Auschwitz in 1943. 'No, it was the local shoemaker, the milkman or a neighbour. As soon as they got a uniform, an armband and a steel helmet, suddenly they were the master race.'

n 1922, journalist Joseph Hell asked Hitler what he would do about the Jews. After falling into 'a kind of paroxysm', Hitler gradually worked himself up into a frenzy.

> *Once I really am in power, my first and foremost task will be the annihilation of the Jews. As soon as I have the power to do so, I will have gallows built in rows – at the Marienplatz in Munich, for example – as many as traffic allows. Then the Jews will be hanged indiscriminately, and they will remain hanging until they stink; they will hang there as long as the principles of hygiene permit. As soon as they have been untied, the next batch will be strung up, and so on down the line, until the last Jew in Munich has been exterminated. Other cities will follow suit, precisely in this fashion, until all Germany has been completely cleansed of Jews.*

These views were reiterated in *Mein Kampf*, published in 1926:

> *The personification of the devil as the symbol of all evil assumes the living shape of the Jew ... by defending myself against the Jew, I am fighting for the work of the Lord.*

As Hitler's most loyal disciple, Heinrich Himmler also spoke venomously about the 'extermination' of the Jews. So far it had all been talk, but the Enabling Act of 23 March 1933 changed everything. The Nazis could now pass laws without recourse to the Reichstag. Just over a week later, on 1 April 1933, a boycott of Jewish businesses began. Jewish shops and professional offices were encircled by SA troops, who attempted to deter potential clients with words and posters. Anti-Semitic slogans were scrawled or painted on some of the buildings.

Then on 7 April the Law of the Restoration of the Professional Civil Service was passed, which prevented Jews from working for the state. Other laws restricted the number of Jewish students in German schools and universities, prohibited Jews from owning farms and forbade 'Jewish activities' in the medical and legal professions. In other words, Jews were having their livelihoods taken from them.

Things soon got worse. Hitler declared that anyone who was considered to be an 'enemy of the state', or a communist, could be arrested and imprisoned without trial. Himmler's bully-boys were then turned loose into the streets, where they wrought havoc amongst the terrified citizens. Dachau, the first concentration camp in Germany, had been opened in March 1933 and thousands of innocent detainees soon began to pour through its gates. Other camps quickly followed. It was not long before the political prisoners under Himmler's control could be counted in millions.

In 1935, the Nuremberg Laws prevented Jews from marrying non-Jews, annulled existing marriages and deprived Jews of citizenship and civil rights. If these laws did not solve the 'Jewish problem', Hitler told the Reichstag, it 'must then be handed over by law to the National Socialist Party for a final solution'.

Many Jews had already left Germany. After being told that the Berlin Philharmonic's concert hall would be burnt down if he did not stop conducting, Bruno Walter fled to Austria. He took French citizenship in 1938 and headed to the United States in 1939, which would become his permanent home. The conductor and composer Otto Klemperer followed suit by heading for Los Angeles, while playwright Bertolt Brecht went to Scandinavia in 1933 and then moved on to the United

—*ϟϟ*———————————————————————

States. Albert Einstein renounced his German citizenship and found a home in Princeton. Nazi stormtroopers retaliated by ransacking his summer home at Caputh, near Berlin, and confiscating his yacht. Following the *Anschluss*, Sigmund Freud left Austria for England, where he died the following year.

In Hanover, a young Polish Jew named Herschel Grynszpan had suffered persecution at school, so he decided to emigrate to Palestine. When he was told that he would have to wait for a year, he went to Paris. He entered France illegally because he had no means of support – Jews were not permitted to take money out of Germany at that time. Unable to work, he fell on hard times. Meanwhile, his parents were begging him for help. The Germans had stripped 12,000 Polish Jews of their property and deported them to Poland, but the Polish authorities had revoked their citizenship and refused them entry. Overnight they had become stateless refugees. By 7 November 1938 Grynszpan could not take any more so he bought a gun and walked to the German embassy, where he shot junior official Ernst vom Rath. He claimed that he was acting on behalf of 12,000 persecuted Jews. Vom Rath died on 9 November, the 15th anniversary of the Beer Hall Putsch. Grynszpan's action had provided the very excuse that the Nazis had been looking for.

Goebbels made an inflammatory speech, urging 'spontaneous demonstrations' against the Jews. Telephone orders then went out, after which the SS joined the SA on the streets of Germany and Austria. The gleeful troops indulged themselves in an orgy of destruction. More than 7,000 Jewish shops were smashed up and looted in what became known as *Kristallnacht* (Night of Broken Glass). Jewish homes, hospitals, schools and cemeteries were attacked and more than 1,000 synagogues were burnt down or otherwise vandalized. The official death toll was

91, but it is thought that many more people died in the attacks. In Berlin, fashionably dressed women clapped and laughed to see the Jews being savagely beaten by youths armed with lead piping. Some even held their babies up high, so they could witness the spectacle. The cost of broken windows alone came to millions of Reichsmarks. When Göring heard that the broken glass would have to be replaced by imported glass, bought with scarce foreign currency, he said: 'They should have killed more Jews and broken less glass.'

Some 30,000 Jewish men between the ages of 16 and 60 were arrested and handed over to the SS. The concentration camps at Dachau, Buchenwald and Sachsenhausen were expanded to meet the demand. Inmates were only released if they could show that they intended to emigrate, leaving behind whatever wealth they had. The Jews were forced to clear the rubble from their destroyed synagogues and the proceeds of any insurance claims were confiscated. On top of that, the Nazi government imposed a fine on the Jewish community of one billion Reichsmarks – around £100 million or $400 million in 1938. Jewish children were forbidden to go to school from 15 November onwards and the local authorities imposed curfews. By December, Jews were barred from theatres and other public places. They had to travel in separate compartments in railway trains and their property was seized as part of a programme of 'Aryanization'.

Those who had been delivered into the hands of the SS could expect no mercy.

'Forget your wives and children,' one SS camp commandant told the new arrivals. 'Here you will die like dogs.'

And die they did. They died because of the insanitary conditions, the starvation rations and the heavy work. Prisoners worked at least eleven hours a day, six days a week and punishments were brutal.

—ϟϟ————————————————————————

Inmates would be subjected to 25 lashes for stealing a cigarette and the punishment for being late for roll-call was a long period in solitary confinement. Some victims went insane. Anyone who talked politics was summarily executed.

Between 1933 and 1939, Hitler occasionally issued broad amnesties. Those who were released were forced to sign affidavits which declared that they had been well treated. But for many the only release was death. SS guards were ordered to shoot anyone who tried to escape, refused to obey an order or was guilty of any form of mutiny. Guards were told: 'Any pity whatever for the enemies of the state is unworthy of an SS man.'

At first, releases and fresh arrests were kept more or less in balance, so the prison population hovered around the 25,000 mark. However, the *Anschluss* and the occupation of Czechoslovakia resulted in a further 75,000 arrests. More victims would be rounded up in Poland and the other occupied territories.

And many German citizens were arrested too. In October 1941 alone, 15,160 ordinary people were detained by the Gestapo. Some were thought to be hindering the war effort, while others had just been grumbling about it. With all of these seizures the number of concentration camp inmates climbed to 220,000. Some camps were so overcrowded that a fifth of the prisoners died every six months. The slogan *Arbeit Macht Frei* ('work will make you free') was placed at the entrances to a number of camps. It can only have been meant as a cruel insult.

As well as Jews, the camps were occupied by trade unionists and Social Democrats – in fact, anyone who was seen as a political dissident. Stormtroopers had begun raiding Berlin's famous gay bars during the Weimar Republic. Later, male homosexuals were sent to concentration camps, where the SS made them wear yellow armbands, then pink triangles. Some 20,000 Jehovah's Witnesses were imprisoned when they failed to swear allegiance to the state or refused to register for the draft or omitted to say 'Heil Hitler', while all Roma people (gypsies) were persecuted on racial grounds.

T-4 Euthanasia Programme

In October 1939, Hitler authorized the T-4 Euthanasia Programme. He slyly backdated the order to 1 September, so that it would appear to be a wartime measure.

'War is the best time for the elimination of the incurably ill,' said Hitler. They were a burden on the *Volk*, he thought, and an embarrassment to those claiming to be a 'master race'.

In fact, the murder of the physically and mentally disabled, the incurably ill and the elderly had started long before. Soon after Hitler came to power, the Minister of Health in Bavaria proposed sending anyone he considered 'inferior' to the concentration camps, including the mentally retarded. Then medical institutions began withholding medical treatment and food from selected individuals.

The T-4 Programme – so called because the chancellery offices that ran it were based at Tiergartenstrasse 4 in Berlin – became systematized under Dr Karl Brandt, one of Hitler's personal physicians, and Philipp Bouhler, the head of the chancellery. They were charged with expanding the 'authority of physicians… so that patients considered incurable, according to the best available human judgment of their state of health, can be granted mercy killing'. The two leaders of the programme began by ordering a survey of psychiatric institutions, hospitals and homes for the chronically ill, thereby effectively co-opting the entire medical establishment.

The programme's administrators did not bother to examine anyone, or read their medical records. Instead, they decided whose lives were 'unworthy of living' by reading the forms that had been sent to them by institutions throughout Germany.

Those who believed in eugenics, a fashionable view at the time even in Britain and the United States, became enthusiastic about the programme. Nazism was seen as Darwinism in action. However, many people were put to death just because they were seen to be economically unproductive. The Nazis referred to them as 'useless eaters'.

Karl Brandt was an enthusiastic proponent of the Nazis' euthanasia programme from the very start. After completing his training as a doctor in 1928, he joined the Nazi Party in 1932 and the SA in the following year. Under the 1933 Law for the Prevention of Hereditarily Diseased Offspring he began performing abortions on numerous women who were considered to be genetically disordered, mentally or physically handicapped or racially deficient. It was thought that their children could inherit their conditions.

His career took a leap forward when he treated Hitler's adjutant, SA Lieutenant-General Wilhelm Brüchner, after a car accident. His grateful patient introduced him to Hitler's inner circle. In 1939, he was appointed co-director of the T-4 Euthanasia Programme and three years later he became Reich Commissioner for Sanitation and Health, and an SS major-general.

As the war drew to a close, Hitler was furious when he discovered that Brandt had sent his wife and children towards the American lines so they would not be captured by the Soviets. Brandt was arrested, tried and sentenced to death. Only the intervention of Himmler and Speer stopped the sentence being carried out. Captured by the Allies, Brandt was again sentenced to death when an American court found him guilty of having approved medical experiments in the concentration camps. His defence was that 'any personal code of ethics must give way to the character of total war'. Unfortunately for him, the court did not see things his way. His speech from the scaffold was cut short by the black hood that was placed over his head.

Philipp Bouhler was a skilled administrator who could organize Hitler's correspondence or the killing of people with the same consummate ease. Wounded in the First World War, Bouhler joined the Nazi Party in 1921. His first job was with the *Völkischer Beobachter*, the Party newspaper. Then in 1933 he became a member of the Reichstag, before succeeding Himmler as police chief in Munich. After making a success of his time in Munich he was called to Berlin, where he became head of Hitler's chancellery and chairman of the censorship committee. During that time he published *Fight for Germany* and *Napoleon: A Genius's Cometary Path*, one of Hitler's favourite books.

Finally, in 1939, he became co-director of the T-4 Euthanasia Programme. He and his wife committed suicide after being captured by the Americans at the end of the war. The game was up and they knew it.

At first, the victims of the T-4 Programme were killed by starvation and lethal injection but later they were gassed. Chambers disguised as showers were built at six killing centres in Germany and Austria – Bernburg, Brandenburg, Grafeneck, Hadamar, Hartheim and Sonnenstein. SS personnel in charge of the transport of the prisoners donned white coats in order to maintain the illusion that it was a medical procedure. Relatives were informed when the 'patients' were transferred, but they were not allowed to visit them. They were later furnished with a death certificate, a letter of condolence and an urn containing the ashes.

Doctors and psychiatrists were able to save a few of their patients –

but only if they co-operated by sending replacements. While the Church had remained silent on the 'Jewish question', the bishop of Münster, Count Clemens August von Galen, vehemently protested about the 'mercy killings', arguing that all life was sacred. Opposition grew so strong that Hitler was jeered by an angry crowd for the only time in his 12-year reign. This incident resulted in the official cancellation of the T-4 Programme on 24 August 1941. By then, at least 70,000 people had been killed. But the programme continued as part of the escalating Holocaust. In all, some 200,000 people lost their lives because of the T-4 Programme.

Targeting the Jews

While the Nazis had done their utmost to rid Germany of its Jews, the rapid expansion of the Third Reich had brought another two million Jews under the control of the SS. There were so many of them that the *Einsatzgruppen* could not cope, so on 21 September 1939 Heydrich ordered the establishment of the *Judenräte* – councils made up of leading Jewish citizens and rabbis. The *Judenräte* were made personally responsible for carrying out German orders. There was little choice because failure meant death.

Two months later, Jews were forced to identify themselves by wearing the Star of David. Jewish schools were closed, Jewish organizations were dissolved, property was seized and men were conscripted into forced labour.

The Jews were then forced into ghettos. There were around 400 ghettos in Poland alone, the largest of them being the Warsaw Ghetto. Thirty per cent of the city's population was forced into 2.4 per cent of its area. The population density of the ghetto reached over 200,000 per square mile, with an average of 9.2 people to a room. As if this were not enough, the ghetto was sealed off from the rest of the city in the autumn of 1940. Food was supplied but it was not enough to sustain life, so starvation and disease took their inevitable toll before the systematic extermination of the Jews began. Following the invasion of the Soviet Union in June 1941, the *Einsatzgruppen* began the methodical task of murdering all of the Jews in the newly conquered territories. By the end of the year, 80 per cent of the Jews in Lithuania had been killed. The mass murder of around a million Jews, including virtually all Jewish males of arms-bearing age, was also occurring in Belarus, Estonia, Latvia, Ukraine, Moldova and most of the Russian territory west of the line that ran from Leningrad to Rostov. Hitler made Himmler responsible for 'security' behind the lines and he also gave the SS the authority to implement settlement plans in the occupied Soviet Union. It was a project that was dear to Himmler's heart.

The Final Solution

On 31 July 1941 Göring authorized Heydrich, then chief of the RSHA, to co-ordinate the resources of the Reich 'for a total solution of the Jewish Question in the area of German influence in Europe'. In the following six months, the first trainloads of German, Austrian and Czech Jews rolled eastwards to killing sites in the so-called Reich Commissariat, Ostland. The Soviet Jews were already being systematically annihilated.

Department IV B4 of the RSHA, led by Adolf Eichmann, directed local police agencies to round up all Jews inside the Reich. It then organized the required railway trains through the director of German State Railroads and the Reich Ministry of Transport. The shooting

Adolf Eichmann joined the SS in 1932 and went on to play a major role in organizing the deaths of millions of Jews

of the Jews was handled by regional security police forces and SD commanders.

Adolf Eichmann was yet another casualty of the Great Depression who had found steady employment with the Party, even if it was the chief executioner's job. Born in Solingen, Germany, he moved with his family to Linz in Austria, Hitler's favourite city, during the First World War. In 1932, he joined the Nazi Party and the SS and in the following year he joined the terrorist school of the Austrian Legion in Lechfeld.

Two years later he was attached to the SS unit at Dachau and then he joined the SD's Berlin office as an expert on Jewish affairs.

His first plan was to rid Europe of its Jews by sending them to Palestine. He even went so far as to attempt to meet the Arab leaders in Palestine, but his efforts were blocked by the British authorities. With Palestine out of the running he went off to Vienna in 1939. Within a short time the whole of the city's Jewish population had been transported to Poland. Large numbers died on the rail journey and when the survivors arrived, they discovered that no food or housing had been provided for them.

Eichmann performed a similar task in Prague in the following year. When the RSHA was established, he was rewarded by being made head of the Jewish affairs section. It was rumoured that he had Jewish relatives and had even kept a Jewish mistress when he had lived in Vienna. Whether this was true or not, such a thing would have fitted in well with the Nazis' double standards.

In 1945, he was captured by United States troops, but he escaped from his prison camp. He managed to get to Argentina, where he settled in 1958, but two years later he was kidnapped by Israeli secret service agents and smuggled out of the country. At his trial in Tel Aviv, he denied responsibility for the mass killings.

'I had orders,' he said, 'but I had nothing to do with that business.'

He was only responsible for the transportation, he maintained.

'I never claimed not to know about the liquidation,' he said. 'I only said that department IV B4 had nothing to do with it.'

He was squeamish about the gassing, he said, after observing a gassing van in operation at Chelmno.

'I didn't look inside. I couldn't. Couldn't! What I saw and heard was enough. The screaming and … I was much too shaken.'

After that he kept his distance.

'I was horrified. My nerves aren't strong enough. I can't listen to such things … without them affecting me.' Eichmann was sentenced to death all the same.

On 20 January 1942 Heydrich invited 15 key officials from various Reich ministries, including Adolf Eichmann, to a conference at a lakeside villa in the Berlin suburb of Wannsee. At the Wannsee Conference, as it became known, he presented plans 'to implement the desired final solution of the Jewish Question'. He informed the delegates that Hitler had authorized the operation and had designated the SS to co-ordinate a European-wide 'Final Solution policy'. He impressed upon them that the success of such an unprecedented operation depended on the active participation of their agencies.

The word extermination was never used during the conference, but the intention was clear. An earlier plan of deporting the Jews to Madagascar was dismissed as impractical during wartime. Instead, all of the Jews in Europe would be rounded up and sent east, where they would be used as forced labour. Their working and living conditions would be so hard that a large number of them would die of 'natural diminution'. Those who survived this harsh regime would be 'treated accordingly'.

Heydrich summed up the situation:

> *Another possible solution of the problem has now taken the place of emigration – that is, the evacuation of the Jews to the east... Such activities are, however, to be considered provisional actions, but practical experience is already being collected which is of the greatest importance in relation to the future final solution of the Jewish problem.*

Indeed, practical experience had been gathered by SS men during the gassing of innocent victims in the T-4 Programme. At Chelmno in western Poland, the systematic gassing of prisoners using gassing vans had begun on 8 December 1941, just hours after the Japanese had attacked Pearl Harbor. But while the suffering of the victims was of little concern to the SS guards, there were more practical considerations. The vans only had a limited capacity, the process was slow and unloading them was 'unpleasant'.

Extermination camps

In October 1941, SS and police leader Odilo Globocnik received a verbal order from Himmler to start work on the construction of an extermination camp at Belzec. Others would follow at Sobibor and Treblinka. Permanent gas chambers would be installed in the camps.

When they arrived, victims would be separated by sex before being stripped of their clothing. They would then be herded into the gas chambers, where they would be killed by exhaust gas from diesel engines, which would be pumped through pipes in the ceiling. The bodies would then be removed by parties of camp inmates, the

The SS-Sturmbrigade Dirlewanger, *whose members were largely ex-convicts
and psychopaths, trains its sights on the Warsaw Ghetto*

Sonderkommando, who would plunder gold teeth, dentures and other
valuables from the corpses and then take the bodies to the crematoria
or dump them in mass graves. Members of the *Sonderkommando* were
murdered and replaced periodically in order to remove any potential
witnesses to the scale of the mass murders.

In 1943, there were uprisings at Sobibor and Treblinka and the
gassings stopped. The extermination of the Polish Jews, known as
Operation Reinhard, was almost complete, so Himmler ordered that
the remaining prisoners be shot and the camps closed down. Forty-
two thousand Jewish forced labourers at the Trawniki, Poniatowa and
Majdanek camps were also shot. Globocnik wrote to Himmler: 'I have
completed Operation Reinhard, and have dissolved all the camps.'

Born in Trieste, Globocnik moved to Austria with his family during the First World War. He joined the Nazi Party in 1930 and the SS in 1933. It was around that time that he was thought to have been involved in a jewel robbery, during which a Jewish jeweller was murdered. Soon afterwards, he became deputy *Gauleiter* of Austria.

After the *Anschluss* Hitler appointed him *Gauleiter* of Vienna, but he was dismissed for illegal currency speculation in 1939. After that, he was made to serve as a member of the *Waffen-SS* during the invasion of Poland. However, Himmler did not like to see talent going to waste so he promoted Globocnik to SS and police leader of the Lublin district, with the added responsibility of annihilating the Polish Jews. Globocnik was responsible for the liquidation of the Warsaw Ghetto, which contained around half a million Jews, and the Bialystok Ghetto, where another 15,000 Jews were being held. As head of the death camp organization, he was responsible for the deaths of at least another 1.5 million innocent people from other parts of Europe.

Globocnik oversaw forced relocations, exploited slave labour and stole the property of those he murdered in the extermination camps. In September 1943, he transferred to Trieste as SS and police leader for the Adriatic coast, where he persecuted the Italian Jews and the Yugoslav partisans. He was captured by the British in Austria in 1945, when he committed suicide.

While Globocnik and the other SS men were clearing the Polish ghettos and transporting their inmates to the death camps, Eichmann was shipping the Jews out of western Europe. The most notorious camp was Auschwitz. It was, in fact, three camps. Auschwitz I was the original camp, which served as an administrative centre for the whole complex. Established on the orders of Himmler in April 1940, Poles, Jews and Soviet prisoners of war were held there. They had to work in the associated arms factory and were ruled over by brutal *Kapos,* usually German criminals. The camp also contained a punishment block, which dispensed various kinds of torture. Sometimes four men would be made to stand all night in a tiny cell or prisoners would be kept without food or water in the basement until they died. There were also sealed cells, where prisoners would gradually suffocate. Other victims would be left hanging with their arms behind their backs for hours, or days, which dislocated their shoulders.

On 3 September 1941, deputy camp commandant SS Captain Fritzsch experimented on 600 Russian prisoners of war and 250 Polish inmates by cramming them into the basement of Block 11 and gassing them with Zyklon B, a highly lethal cyanide-based pesticide. After that, Zyklon B was used in the gas chambers of Auschwitz II, the extermination camp that was also known as Birkenau.

Having joined the Nazi Party and the SS in 1930, Fritzsch became a guard at Dachau in 1934. In May 1940, he became the first deputy commandant of Auschwitz, which was then just a concentration camp. Fritzsch was sadistic, even by SS standards. Each time an inmate escaped he made sure that ten prisoners were starved to death in the basement of the punishment block. He also enjoyed psychological torture. On one occasion he set up a Christmas tree in the roll-call square. It was hung with lights and there were 'presents' under it – but the presents were the bodies of prisoners who had died while working or who had frozen to death during roll-call.

After being transferred to Flossenbürg in 1942, Fritzsch was arrested and charged with corruption and murder. His sentence was to be sent to the front line with *SS-Panzergrenadier-Ersatzbatallion 18.* Nothing more was heard of him.

Begun in October 1941, Auschwitz II played a major part in the

'Final Solution'. The SS built 300 wooden barracks, four large bath houses where prisoners were gassed, 'corpse cellars' for storing bodies and cremating ovens where the bodies were burnt.

Another camp called Buna-Monowitz, later Auschwitz III, was built nearby in May 1942. This housed slave labour for a chemical and synthetic rubber works which had been built by IG Farben at a cost of 700 million Reichsmarks. Other German corporations built factories with a similar forced labour requirement. Forty-five subcamps were built to house these workers.

It was at Auschwitz that one of the most callous and evil medical practitioners of all time conducted his hideous experiments. While studying philosophy in Munich in the 1920s, Josef Mengele came under the influence of the racial ideology of Alfred Rosenberg. He went on to take a medical degree and then joined the SA in 1933. In the following year he joined the research staff of the newly founded Institute for Hereditary Biology and Racial Hygiene.

From November 1940 to early 1941, Dr Josef Mengele worked for RuSHA in Department II of its Family Office, where he was responsible for the 'care of genetic health' and 'genetic health tests'. When the war started Mengele served as a medical officer with the *Waffen-SS* in France and Russia, but in 1943 Himmler appointed him chief doctor at Birkenau, the extermination camp at Auschwitz.

When new batches of prisoners arrived at Auschwitz, Mengele first of all selected a number of likely victims for his cruel experiments. It was then his task to decide who was to live and who was to die. He was known as the 'Angel of Death', or sometimes the 'White Angel', because he wore a white coat and stood on a platform with his arms outstretched, overlooking the new arrivals. After giving them a cursory glance, he directed them to go left to the gas chambers or right to join the forced labour squads, where they at least had a slim prospect of survival. Young children, their mothers and the old and infirm would be sent directly to the gas chambers, while the young and able-bodied would be sent to work. But inadequate food, poor shelter and minimal sanitation soon destroyed the health of those who had been sent into slavery. Once they were unfit for employment, they would be sent back to Birkenau to be gassed.

On one occasion, a mother did not want to be separated from her 13-year-old daughter, so she bit and scratched the face of the SS man who tried to force her to her assigned line. Mengele drew his gun and shot both the woman and the child.

As a blanket punishment he sent everyone to be gassed, including those who had been selected for work, with the comment: 'Away with this shit!'

When it was reported that one block was infested with lice, Mengele sent every one of its 750 female occupants to be executed. He also performed hideous medical experiments on some of the inmates. His favourite subjects were twins. He injected blood taken from one twin into another twin of a different blood type and then recorded the reaction. The recipient of the blood invariably suffered a searingly painful headache and a high fever that lasted for several days. His experiments were as diverse as they were evil. In order to determine if eye colour could be genetically altered, Mengele had dye injected into the eyes of several subjects. This resulted in painful infections and blindness. If his victims died, Mengele would harvest their eyes and pin them to the wall of his office. Young children were placed in isolation cages, and subjected to a variety of stimuli to see how they would react. Several twins were castrated or sterilized. Many twins had limbs and organs removed in macabre surgical procedures performed without an anaesthetic. Other twins were injected with infectious agents to see how long it took to succumb to various diseases. These and other gruesome procedures had no medical purpose, other than to show the supposed superiority of 'Aryans'.

Strangely enough, some child survivors remember him as a kind man, even though he had killed their parents. He gave them sweets and he was their protector, because he wanted to ensure that the prison guards did not maltreat his medical subjects.

In 1945, Mengele surrendered to the Americans, initially using his own name. Treated as a normal prisoner of war, he was given papers in the name of Fritz Hollmann before being released. He then worked as a farmhand before escaping to Argentina in 1949, taking with him his 'research notes' from Auschwitz. After Adolf Eichmann was captured by Israeli agents in 1960, Mengele fled to Paraguay. He then moved to Brazil where he took the name Wolfgang Gerhard. In 1979, he suffered a stroke while swimming and he drowned. His body was exhumed in 1985 and identified as that of Mengele.

Curiously, there was an unusually high incidence of twins in a village named Cândido Godói in Brazil, which Mengele visited repeatedly. Many of them had blond hair and blue eyes. Brazilian scientists have discounted the theory that Mengele had been continuing his experiments there, but others are not so sure.

Between 1.1 and 1.5 million people died at the hands of the SS at Auschwitz. Ninety per cent of them were Jews. Some 83,000 Poles died there too, along with 19,000 Roma (gypsies).

As the Soviet armies advanced into Poland, the camp was abandoned. In January 1945, 60,000 prisoners were marched to Wodzislaw, where they were put on freight trains – some in open cars – and moved west. Many were shot, or died of hunger or exposure, along the way. When the Red Army arrived, only 7,650 were still alive.

Chapter Eight

THE SS IN RETREAT

The SS rose to power on the coat-tails of the Nazi Party. But as Germany's star began to fade, the SS had more to lose than any other Nazi organization. Defeat would uncover the murderous crimes of the Holocaust. So the *Waffen-SS* threw itself back into battle. Better to die fighting than die on the gallows.

────✠✠────────────────────────────────────

A hough the German army had failed to take Moscow in 1941, the *Waffen-SS* had covered itself in glory, both in the Balkans and in the Soviet Union. From March 1942 onwards it was further expanded by the creation of two new divisions.

The first of them was the 7th *SS-Freiwilligen Gebirgs* (Mountain) *Division Prinz Eugen*. Formed from conscripted ethnic Germans in occupied Serbia, Croatia, Hungary and Romania, its purpose was to undertake anti-partisan operations in the Balkans.

After that the *SS-Kavallerie* Brigade was expanded to form the *SS-Kavallerie Division Florian Geyer*. The new division was commanded by SS Major-General Wilhelm Bittrich, but a year later he was supplanted by SS colonel, later major-general, Hermann Fegelein.

Wilhelm Bittrich managed to be a dedicated SS soldier and a critic of the Nazi Party at the same time. What's more, he lived to tell the tale.

During the First World War, he fought as an officer and trained as a pilot. Eager to take advantage of his training, he joined the SS in 1932 so that he could fly with SS Flying Echelon 'East'. He continued flying under an agreement with the Soviets, which circumvented the aviation ban imposed by the Treaty of Versailles.

Bittrich joined the SS-VT in 1934 and the *Leibstandarte* in 1939, commanding the *Deutschland* regiment in Poland and France. In January 1942, he fell ill and was forced to step down but he had recovered by May, when he took command of the *SS-Kavallerie* Brigade, expanding it into a division. He went on to command the *Das Reich* and *Hohenstaufen* divisions. As commander of *II SS-Panzer Korps* he was responsible for the defeat of the Allies at Arnhem in 1944, the last victory that the *Waffen-SS* would see. He was then decorated, even though he had been implicated in the July Plot to assassinate Hitler and had been marked for death by Himmler because of his unflattering comments about the Nazi regime. His last wartime task was the defence of Vienna. Arrested in 1945, he was tried by the French for war crimes, but he was acquitted in 1954.

Hermann Fegelein, a playboy and a womanizer, was the complete opposite of the steady Bittrich. After serving as a stable boy for Christian Weber, one of the original members of the Nazi Party, he enlisted in the 17th Cavalry Regiment in 1927. He went on to join the SA in 1930 and the SS in 1931.

It might have been Fegelein's boyish good looks that made Himmler favour him, or it could have been his smooth, ingratiating manner. Whatever it was, the *Reichsführer* made sure that Fegelein's career moved onwards and upwards. In 1937, he became head of the SS Main Riding School that Himmler had established in Munich and while serving in the Polish campaign he formed the first *Waffen-SS* cavalry unit from the *SS-Totenkopfverbände*. After being wounded three times in action behind the lines in Russia he was awarded the Knight's Cross. Later, Himmler gave him command of the *SS-Kavallerie Division Florian Geyer*.

In June 1944 he married the sister of Hitler's mistress and short-lived wife, Eva Braun, which enabled him to move yet deeper into Hitler's charmed circle. Then as Himmler's personal adjutant to Hitler, he was wounded in the July Plot, which raised his status even further. But by April 1945 he could see that Germany was going to lose the war. Charmed circle or not, he did not intend to go down with the sinking ship. One day, Hitler suddenly noticed that Fegelein had left the *Führerbunker*. He was found at his home in civilian clothes, carrying a large amount of foreign currency and some of Eva Braun's jewellery. It was obvious that he was preparing to escape with his Hungarian mistress.

—ϟϟ———————————————————————

When he was taken back to the bunker, Eva Braun begged for his life on the grounds that her sister was pregnant. Nevertheless, a court-martial was ordered. Although the evidence of his desertion was clear, Fegelein was drunk and raving, and was considered unfit to stand trial. However, he suffered a stroke of bad luck when the news came that Himmler was trying to make peace with the Allies. As Himmler's 'golden boy', Fegelein was held responsible for his patron's treachery. According to some reports, he was then shot.

The struggle in the east

Hitler met with more resistance than he had bargained for when he invaded the Soviet Union on 22 June 1941. The Red Army was ill-equipped and unprepared but it had two allies. One was the Russian autumn rains and the other was a civilian population that would fight to the bitter end. By the end of 1941 the Soviet Union was bloodied but unbowed. The bitter fighting between the two nations would last until 1945.

Stalingrad might have been lost, but the SS still managed to make its presence felt in other areas. In one famous incident, the Red Army attempted to bottle up the German 16th Army at Demyansk, south of Leningrad.

The intention was to cut the Germans off from the Staray Russa railway, so that they had no lines of supply. Beginning in January 1942, the Red Army devoted every available man and machine to the encirclement of the *SS-Totenkopf* Division, five *Wehrmacht* infantry divisions and numerous German auxiliary divisions. But SS men were trained to fight to the death if need be. After months of bloody fighting the *SS-Totenkopf* Division finally managed to hack its way through the opposing armour. The *Totenkopf's* commander, SS Lieutenant-General Theodor Eicke, was awarded the Oak Leaves to the Knight's Cross. The *SS-Totenkopf* Division was then withdrawn to France, where it underwent reorganization and retraining along with *Das Reich* and the *Leibstandarte*.

When they had been honed into battle-readiness, the three divisions were formed into *I SS Panzer Korps*, which was rushed to the Eastern Front in January 1943, just as the *Wehrmacht* was being crushed at Stalingrad. SS Lieutenant-Colonel Joachim Peiper formed a battalion from the *Leibstandarte* and rescued the *Wehrmacht's* 320th Infantry Division at Kharkov, earning the Knight's Cross.

The son of an army officer, Peiper volunteered for duty with the *Leibstandarte* in 1934 and then attended *Junkerschule* at Brunswick. He was Himmler's adjutant from 1938 to 1939. When war broke out, he served in the *Leibstandarte*, a motorized regiment, during the campaign in western Europe.

The Soviets bitterly denounced Peiper's 'blowtorch battalion'. The force had acquired its name by attacking enemy-held villages at night, when its troops fired indiscriminately and set the straw roofs alight. Peiper was accused of similar tactics in Italy. When he returned to the Eastern Front as commander of the 1st SS Panzer Regiment, he won the Oak Leaves to his Knight's Cross, but he was again accused of burning villages and killing prisoners.

His savagery was even-handed though. In Belgium, he executed five young German recruits for looting, making the others march past the corpses.

The 1st SS Panzer Regiment also saw action in Normandy, when Peiper suffered a nervous breakdown. However, he was back in action for the Battle of the Bulge, when men of his unit murdered over 100 American prisoners of war. After the war, Peiper and 73 others were tried for the massacre. Forty-three of them, including Peiper, were condemned to death. Fortunately for him, his sentence was commuted to life imprisonment and he was released in 1956. But fate eventually caught up with him. Twenty years later, he was murdered when his home was set on fire. It is thought that the perpetrator was a former member of the French resistance.

Battle of Kharkov

Following the surrender of the German Sixth Army at Stalingrad, the SS Panzer Corps was in full retreat. Hitler ordered it to 'stand fast and fight to the death' at Kharkov, but SS Lieutenant-General Paul Hausser was convinced that his tanks would be annihilated if they were trapped in the city. Disobeying Hitler's order, he pulled his unit out and turned it round to face the enemy. Another order came to encircle Kharkov from the north, but only a direct attack was going to save the day. Without any support from the *Luftwaffe*, the Panzer Corps smashed through the Soviet line.

After four days of savage house-to-house fighting, Kharkov was recaptured by the *Leibstandarte* in March 1943. The offensive cost the Red Army an estimated 70,000 casualties, while the SS Panzer Corps lost around 44 per cent of its strength. Hausser was eventually pardoned for his disobedience and was awarded the Oak Leaves to his Knight's Cross.

Paul Hausser never wanted to be anything other than a soldier. He was a military cadet at the age of 12. Commissioned in 1899, he served as a staff officer during the First World War. He stayed on in the *Reichswehr* at the end of the conflict, rising to become a colonel. After retiring in 1932 he joined Stahlhelm, a right-wing veterans' organization, which was incorporated into the SA and then the SS. Hausser transferred to the SS-VT in 1934, becoming an inspector of *SS-Junkerschule* in 1935 and a brigadier in 1936.

Known as 'Papa' to his men, Hausser fought in Poland and France, commanding the Second SS Division *Das Reich*. During the advance into Russia he lost an eye – a black eye patch became his trademark – and won the Knight's Cross. In Normandy, in 1944, he was injured again when he led the break-out from the Falaise Gap, winning the Oak Leaves with Swords. Promoted to general and colonel-general (a special rank) of the *Waffen-SS*, he commanded Army Group G, ending the war on Field Marshal Kesselring's staff. At the Nuremberg trials, he vigorously defended the military role of the *Waffen-SS* and denied any involvement in wartime atrocities. When he was released in 1948, he attempted to re-establish the reputation of the SS, claiming that the foreign units of the SS were really the precursors of the NATO army.

The Third Battle of Kharkov, as it was called, ended on 15 March 1943 and two days later Joachim Peiper's 'blowtorch battalion' raced to take control of Belgorod. Now was the time to eliminate the Kursk salient – that is, the point at which the Soviet line jutted westwards for some 80 miles. The plan was to cut off the Soviet forces in the salient by making two pincer attacks at its neck. II SS Panzer Corps, part of 4 Panzer Army, was chosen to spearhead the northward offensive. The attack penetrated to a depth of 22 miles (35km) before it was stopped by the Soviet 1st Tank Army. Despite appalling losses, the Soviet tank armies held the line. This was the prelude to the Battle of Kursk, the largest tank battle in history. Despite all of its efforts, the II SS Panzer

—𝓈𝓈——————————————————————

Corps was prevented from making its expected breakthrough and by 13 July the Soviets had won a decisive victory.

The *Leibstandarte* Division was still in fighting trim after Kharkov, so when the Allies invaded Italy in September 1943, the *Leibstandarte* was pulled out of Russia and sent to Italy to join the *16 SS-Panzergrenadier Division Reichsführer-SS*. When the Italians surrendered, the *Leibstandarte* began disarming Italian units. On 19 September, the German High Command heard reports that elements of the Italian Fourth Army were regrouping in Piedmont, near the French border, so Peiper's 3rd Battalion was sent to demilitarize them. Arriving in the province of Cuneo, Peiper was met by an Italian officer who warned him that his forces would attack unless Peiper's unit left the province immediately. Peiper refused, which goaded the Italians into action. The veterans of Peiper's battalion defeated the Italians in a fierce battle and then disarmed the remaining Italian forces in the area.

Clearing the Warsaw Ghetto

The *Waffen-SS* had to do more than face the enemy. Sometimes the force was directed against German citizens. This was the case when the Warsaw Ghetto was ordered to be cleared in 1942. It is estimated that 320,000 Jews, 30 per cent of Warsaw's population, were crammed into this small district. Between 23 July and 21 September the Nazis shipped 265,000 Jews to Treblinka, where they were gassed. That meant 55,000 people were left in the ghetto. On 9 January 1943, Himmler visited Warsaw and ordered the deportation of another 8,000 Jews. However, the people that were selected did not report as ordered. Instead, they concealed themselves in prepared hiding places. The Jewish resistance had managed to obtain some pistols, a few rifles and one machine gun from the Polish Home Army (AK), so they had something to retaliate with. Over the next three days, a large number of heavily armed German troops swarmed into the ghetto. If they thought it was going to be a pushover they were wrong. The Jews had nothing to lose, so they fought fiercely and without personal regard. In the end, the soldiers managed to remove around 5,000 Jews – but at a cost of 20 dead and 50 wounded.

It was Hitler's birthday on 20 April and Himmler had come up with the perfect present. A special ghetto clearance operation was just what his *Führer* wanted. On 19 April, 821 *Waffen-SS* Panzergrenadiers from five reserve and training battalions and one cavalry reserve battalion moved in, along with some *Wehrmacht* units. They were met by a resistance that was now 1,500 strong, who fired at them and threw homemade bombs that even destroyed a couple of tanks. The Germans responded with flame-throwers. The resistance fighters resorted to the sewers, defying all attempts to burn, smoke or flood them out. They kept up their resistance until 16 May, when their ammunition ran out. It had taken 28 days to remove the remaining 40,000 Jews, with some 7,000 shot. Others died in the flames or committed suicide. The Germans reported 16 dead and 85 wounded. After supervising the dynamiting of the Great Synagogue of Warsaw, an exultant SS Major-General Jürgen Stroop wrote a report entitled: 'The Warsaw Ghetto is no more.'

If anyone saw himself as a member of the 'master race' it was Stroop. After volunteering to fight in the First World War, he won the Iron Cross Second Class and was wounded. He joined the Nazi Party and the SS in 1932 and was made an auxiliary policeman. Promoted rapidly, he served in the Sudetenland.

After the invasion of Poland, Stroop was transferred to Poznan as the head of *Selbstschutz*, the notorious 'self-defence' formation of the local ethnic Germans. In 1941, he served on the Eastern Front with the infantry regiment of the 3rd *SS-Totenkopf* Division, where he was awarded a clasp to the Iron Cross and an Infantry Assault Badge in bronze.

In September 1942, he was promoted to SS brigadier and was made inspector of the SiPo and SD in south Russia.

Stroop's hatred of Jews was well known, so on 17 April 1943 he was sent to Warsaw as a replacement for SS and police leader *SS-Oberführer* Ferdinand von Sammern-Frankenegg, who had been court-martialled for 'defending Jews'. Sammern-Frankenegg was sent to Croatia, where he was killed by Yugoslav partisans. Stroop systematically cleared the Warsaw Ghetto against stiff resistance and then sent his lavishly illustrated report to Himmler, who proudly showed it to Hitler. In Himmler's eyes, Stroop's attack on the Jews had been the equal of any military campaign and it deserved to be honoured as such. Accordingly, Stroop was awarded the Iron Cross First Class at a gala reception in Warsaw.

He was then posted to Greece where he directed the deportation of Jews to Auschwitz. Captured in Bavaria in the uniform of an infantry officer, he was found to be carrying false papers. After a short trial he was convicted of the summary execution of Allied airmen in the area of his command and was sentenced to death. He was sent to Poland to be executed. Unrepentant to the last, he sat in his cell and joyfully recalled the destruction of Warsaw's Great Synagogue.

'What a wonderful sight! I yelled out, "Heil Hitler!" and pressed the button. A terrific explosion brought flames right up to the clouds. The colours were unbelievable. An unforgettable allegory of the triumph over Jewry.'

Former adjutant to Himmler, Joachim Peiper; wherever he went, soldiers under his command were accused of terrible war crimes (see pp.229–30 and 253)

Convicted of war crimes, he was executed publicly on the site of the former ghetto.

THE ORADOUR-SUR-GLANE MASSACRE

On 10 June, the 2nd *SS-Division Das Reich* arrived at the town of St Junien, 12 miles (19km) from Oradour, where it encountered the local Maquis. The troops marched on to Oradour, where they surrounded the village and ordered everyone to assemble in the market square.

At about three o'clock, the women and children were locked in the local church while the men were formed into groups before being taken to local garages and barns, where they were shot. Finally, the church was blown up and then set on fire. Those who attempted to escape were shot.

In 1953 a French military court established that 190 men, 245 women and 207 children had been murdered. The SS troops at Oradour were commanded by SS Major Otto Dickman, but he had been killed in action in the Normandy battle area, so the court looked further down the line. Twenty members of his company were convicted and sentenced to death, though only two were executed.

Expanding the *Waffen-SS*

By 1943, Himmler was beginning to realize that the tide was turning against Germany. What the Fatherland needed was more SS troops in the field – and quickly. Whole divisions, not battalions, were added at full speed. This was nothing new, however. Over the course of the

*Jürgen Stroop (in peaked cap) watches the mayhem grow all around him
as the Warsaw Ghetto goes up in flames*

war the *Waffen-SS* grew from three elite divisions of German-born Aryans to an international force that comprised 41 divisions and many other units. *Waffen-SS* numbers never exceeded 10 per cent of the total strength of the German army, but its troops were far more deadly than those of its larger rival.

Foreign nationals had begun to join the ranks of the *Waffen-SS* in 1941, when the *SS-Nordland* Regiment had been formed from Danish and Norwegian volunteers. Building on that earlier success, Himmler pulled *SS-Panzergrenadier-Regiment Nordland* out of the line in February and used it as the basis for the 11th *SS Volunteer Panzergrenadier Division Nordland*. Divisions were also formed in France and later in the year volunteers from the Hitler Youth were brought into the 12th SS Panzer Division *Hitlerjugend*.

Scandinavian and French nationals were one thing, but Himmler's greatest departure from his Aryan ideal came when he managed to persuade Hitler to let him form a Bosnian Muslim division. The 13th *Waffen* Mountain Division of the *SS-Handschar* (1st Croatian) was created to fight Tito's Yugoslav partisans.

After that, a division was formed from volunteers in Galicia – the part of Poland that was absorbed into Ukraine after the Soviet invasion of 1939. But Himmler could not afford to sit around waiting for volunteers. There was a war to fight. Compulsory military service was introduced to the Reich Commissariat of Ostland and the 15th *Waffen* Grenadier Division of the SS (1st Latvian) was raised. By the time the 16th *SS-Panzergrenadier Division Reichsführer-SS* had been created back in Germany, the *Waffen-SS* had expanded from eight divisions to sixteen.

They were sorely needed. By this time the Allies were getting closer. When they landed at Anzio in January 1944 the 16th *SS-Panzergrenadier Division Reichsführer-SS* sent a battle group to meet them. It was followed by the *Brigata d'Assalto, Milizia Armata*, which was known to the Germans as the 1st *Italienische Freiwilligen Sturmbrigade*. The brigade performed so well that a delighted Himmler declared that it was to be fully integrated into the *Waffen-SS*.

Despite a few local successes the war was going badly for Germany, so the *Waffen-SS* was expanded again in 1944. Conscripts and volunteers were pulled from the Germans' occupied territories and a number of *Waffen-SS* divisions were hastily created. Ostland was again plundered for conscripts. First of all, Latvia had to yield up its remaining men of fighting age and then Estonia was forced to supply enough troops for a division. In the Balkans, the 21st *Waffen* Mountain Division of the SS Skanderbeg (1st Albanian) was created from Albanian and Kosovan volunteers.

The speed at which some of these non-German divisions were raised was matched by the length of their basic training. Raw troops were often sent into battle after receiving only two or three weeks' instruction and many units were issued with miscellaneous items of captured equipment. On top of all of that, officers and men shared a mixture of languages in some forces, which sometimes made vital communications difficult. Even so, some divisions managed to perform exceptionally well, even by SS standards.

Then a second *Waffen-SS* cavalry division, the 22nd SS Volunteer Cavalry Division *Maria Theresia*, was formed. The bulk of its men were ethnic German conscripts from the Hungarian army. Another Netherlands division was then created, followed by a polyglot division that was really the size of a brigade. The 24th *Waffen Gebirgs Division der SS* was made up of ethnic German volunteers from Italy, with other volunteers from Slovenia, Croatia, Serbia and Ukraine. Its primary purpose was to fight partisans on the frontiers of Slovenia, Italy and Austria, where the mountainous terrain required specialist troops and equipment.

Himmler then ordered the Hungarian defence minister to form the 25th *Waffen* Grenadier Division of the SS *Hunyadi* (1st Hungarian) and the 26th *Waffen* Grenadier Division of the SS (2nd Hungarian). The divisions consisted mainly of Hungarian and Romanian volunteers, though one regiment from the Hungarian army was ordered to join them. Another division that saw action on the Hungarian Front was the 31st SS Volunteer Grenadier Division, which was formed from conscripted ethnic Germans, mainly from the Batschka region of Hungary.

In Belgium sufficient volunteers were found to create two further divisions, one from the Flemish-speaking north and the other from

—⚡—

the French-speaking south. To add to the cosmopolitan nature of the *Waffen-SS* the 30th *Waffen* Grenadier Division of the SS (2nd Russian) was formed in East Prussia from Ukrainian, Belarusian, Russian and Polish collaborators, while fresh Italian volunteers who wanted to fight for the Germans were formed into the 29th *Waffen* Grenadier Division of the SS (1st Italian).

Plans to convert the Kaminski Brigade into the 29th *Waffen* Grenadier Division of the SS RONA (1st Russian) were dropped after the execution of its commander, Bronislav Kaminski.

Kaminski served in the Red Army during the Russian Civil War (1918–20) and then returned to civilian life. Although he appears to have been leading an ordinary existence in 1937, he became a victim of Stalin's Great Purge. After being arrested as a 'counter-revolutionary' he was exiled to Bryansk Oblast, a Russian province. He harboured an understandable grudge against his homeland at that point, so he joined the anti-partisan militia when the Germans invaded, becoming its head in 1942. As a reward for co-operating with the Germans, he was allowed to establish the autonomous administration of Lokot. His orders were to conscript all able-bodied men, including Russian 'volunteers' from a nearby concentration camp. Kaminski's troops were armed with discarded Soviet equipment, while uniforms were supplied by the Germans.

By January 1943, Kaminski had assembled nearly 1,000 men, together with eight tanks and three armoured cars. His force was called the Russian National Liberation Army (RONA). It took part in the attack on the Kursk salient in July 1943 and it also committed a number of atrocities against civilians. Needless to say, several attempts were made on Kaminski's life.

In February 1944 Kaminski's men were evacuated to Belarus. At that point his second in command tried to defect to the partisans, after being offered an amnesty for his entire regiment. Kaminski displayed his absolute devotion to the Reich by strangling his subordinate in front of his men, followed by eight other mutineers. An admiring Himmler awarded him the Iron Cross. After Kaminski's unit had been renamed the *Volksheer-Brigade Kaminski* in his honour, his troops undertook more anti-partisan operations. The brigade then became part of the *Waffen-SS*. It was renamed as the *Waffen-Sturm-Brigade RONA*, and Kaminski was given the rank of *Waffen-Brigadeführer der SS*, the only man to hold such rank. Himmler was so impressed by the performance of the unit that he decided to turn the brigade into the 29th *Waffen-Grenadier-Division der SS (russische Nr. 1)*. Kaminski was promoted again, this time to *Waffen* brigadier and *Waffen-SS* major-general.

The Warsaw Uprising of August 1944 changed everything for Kaminski. Still called the *Waffen-Sturm-Brigade RONA*, his brigade was sent off to assist in the suppression of the Warsaw rebels. After an orgy of savage killing, 10,000 people lay dead in the Ochota area alone, but Kaminski's men did not leave it there. Himmler received reports that they had indulged in extensive looting and had raped two German women. The *Reichsführer-SS* used this as an excuse to court-martial Kaminski and have him shot. Looted property belonged to the Reich – that is, to Himmler. Kaminski's men were told that their commander had been killed by Polish partisans, but they did not believe the story.

Fighting on two fronts

By 1944 Germany was fighting against Great Britain and the United States in the west and the Soviet Union in the east. Hitler had always been aware that fighting on two fronts was nothing but suicidal. In fact,

—*SS*————————————————————————

the Molotov–Ribbentrop Pact had been designed to avoid that very possibility, back in 1939.

The Eastern Front was a huge theatre of war in its own right. Although the Allies were now involved, Germany's main fight was with the Soviet Union. SS units were sent in all directions, often covering huge distances to get to the point of battle.

In January 1944, six German divisions, including the 5th SS *Wiking*, the 5th SS Volunteer *Sturmbrigade Wallonien* and the Estonian SS Battalion *Narwa*, were encircled by the Red Army in a defensive position along the Dnieper River in Ukraine. Just as the German troops were getting ready to go down fighting, the *1 SS-Leibstandarte* thundered to the rescue, after travelling some distance. The *Leibstandarte* kept the Soviets occupied while the trapped divisions made their escape.

The 500th SS Parachute Battalion and the 7th SS *Prinz Eugen* were deployed far to the south as part of Operation *Rösselsprung* (Knight's Move in chess). Their objective was the capture of partisan leader Josip Broz Tito, who was thought to be hiding in the cave headquarters of the Yugoslav partisans near Dravr. The troops launched an offensive in April and May 1944, but by the time they fought their way into the cave Tito had fled.

Right up in the north III SS (Germanic) Panzer Corps in Army Group North fought along the Narva – a river in Estonia – in July and August 1944, during the retreat from Leningrad. SS Lieutenant-General Felix Steiner commanded volunteer SS units from Norway, Denmark, the Netherlands and Belgium, along with conscript SS units from Latvia and Estonia. Stalin had planned to retake Estonia and use it as a base for attacks on Finland and East Prussia, but the stiff resistance of the German troops delayed the Soviet effort in the Baltic by seven-and-a-half months.

In the meantime, the D-Day landings were one of Hitler's major preoccupations. The Allies' plans were unknown so I SS Panzer Corps *Leibstandarte SS Adolf Hitler* was moved to Septeuil, 25 miles (40km) west of Paris.

From that position it could move quickly to the coast when the invasion began. The corps comprised the 1st *SS-Leibstandarte SS Adolf Hitler*, the 12th *SS-Hitlerjugend*, the 17th *SS-Götz von Berlichingen* and the *Wehrmacht*'s Panzer-Lehr-Division.

Normandy landings

On the day of the Normandy landings, 6 June 1944, many German leaders were taken by surprise. The first *Waffen-SS* unit in action was the 12th *SS-Hitlerjugend*, which arrived in the Caen area on 7 June. SS Brigadier Kurt Meyer made Ardenne Abbey his headquarters. Twenty-seven captured Canadian soldiers of the North Nova Scotia Highlanders and the 27th Canadian Armoured Regiment were taken there and shot. Their bodies were not discovered until the Canadian Regina Rifle Regiment liberated the abbey in the following month.

The massacre would come back to haunt Meyer at the end of the war. After serving with the Mecklenburg police, Meyer joined the *Leibstandarte* in Berlin in 1934. He saw service in the campaigns in Poland and France before going to Greece, where he led his reconnaissance battalion from the front – this earned him the nickname '*Schnelle* (Speedy) Meyer'. Otherwise he was known as 'Panzermeyer', because he was said to be as tough as a battle tank.

While commanding a reconnaissance detachment in the Balkans and Russia, Meyer earned the Knight's Cross and the German Cross. In 1943 he was given command of the 12th SS-Panzer Division *Hitlerjugend*, which he led in an aggressive bid to halt the Allied invasion in June 1944. He was wounded on 6 September and captured at Amiens on 17 November, where he fell into the hands of Belgian partisans. Perhaps fortunately for him, he was rescued by the Americans and handed over to the British.

After the war, he was brought before a Canadian military court where he was charged with the massacre of the Canadian prisoners. Although he was convicted and sentenced to death by firing squad, the sentence was commuted to life imprisonment. After being transferred to West Germany, he was released in 1954.

Other German units arrived in Normandy in the days that followed the landings.

On 11 June, the 17th *SS-Götz von Berlichingen* arrived, coming into contact with the United States 101st Airborne Division. Then the 1st *SS-Leibstandarte* arrived at the end of the month. The division defended the village of Carpiquet and its aerodrome against the Canadian troops who were trying to break out of the beachhead.

The only other *Waffen-SS* unit in France at this time was the 2nd *SS-Das Reich*, which was based at Montauban, north of Toulouse. It was ordered to move north. On its way it passed through Tulle in central France, where the Maquis had killed 139 members of the German garrison. As was often the case, the local population would pay the price. The SS rounded up all men between the ages of 16 and 60. Ninety-nine of them were tortured and hanged and the rest were sent as slave labour to Dachau concentration camp, where most of them died. On the next day *Das Reich* reached Oradour-sur-Glane, where it massacred 642 French civilians.

Over the days that followed the Allied landings further SS units such as II SS Panzer Corps were rushed to Normandy. The force had arrived from the Eastern Front on 26 June, just in time to counter another Allied attempt to break out of the eastern end of the beachhead, but in the absence of further reinforcements the *Waffen-SS* was hard pressed to stop the Allied advance. Its efforts were studded with costly failures such as Operation *Lüttich*, which sought to prevent the American forces from leaving the western end of the beachhead. The 1st *SS-Leibstandarte* and the 2nd *SS-Das Reich* took part in the campaign, losing half of their tanks.

In one bloody incident the Americans managed to trap the 1st *SS-Leibstandarte*, the 10th *SS-Frundsberg*, the 12th *SS-Hitlerjugend* and the 17th *SS-Götz von Berlichingen* in the Falaise pocket, while the 2nd *SS-Das Reich* and the 9th *SS-Hohenstaufen* were on the outside. At this stage there was a gap through which the German forces could make their escape.

The *Das Reich* and the *Hohenstaufen* were ordered to attack Hill 262 in order to keep the Falaise gap open, but despite all of their efforts the gap had been closed by 22 August. All of the German forces inside the pocket were dead or in captivity. The fighting around Hill 262 alone cost 2,000 dead and 5,000 prisoners. The 12th *SS-Hitlerjugend* had started the campaign with almost 20,000 men and 150 tanks but by the end of the battle it was down to 300 men and 10 tanks.

With the German army in full retreat, two more *Waffen-SS* formations were sent to the battle in France – *SS-Panzergrenadier Brigade 49* and *SS-Panzergrenadier Brigade 51*, which had been formed from staff and students at the *SS-Junkerschulen*. At the beginning of August they held the crossings over the Seine southeast of Paris, which allowed the army to retreat. The few survivors were incorporated into the 17th *SS-Götz von Berlichingen*.

—ϟϟ————————————————————————

SS barbarity

While the crucial battles were being fought in France or on the Eastern Front, the 4th *SS-Polizei Panzergrenadier Division* was stationed in Greece. On 10 June its troops went on a bloody two-hour rampage in the village of Distomo. Running from door to door they massacred a large number of Greek civilians, supposedly in revenge for a partisan attack. In all, 218 men, women and children were killed. According to survivors, the SS forces 'bayoneted babies in their cribs, stabbed pregnant women and beheaded the village priest'. An internal enquiry was told that the troops had not been fired on, but it still exonerated their commander, SS Captain Fritz Lautenbach. After the war, no one was prosecuted, but West Germany paid Greece 115 million Deutschmarks in restitution.

The troops of the 16th *SS-Panzergrenadier Division Reichsführer-SS* were no less barbarous when they were conducting anti-partisan operations in Italy. On 12 August 1944, a battalion entered the village of Sant'Anna di Stazzema. All of the able-bodied men fled into the woods while women, children and the elderly were herded into barns and stables, where they were murdered with machine guns and hand grenades. The victims included some 110 children. The youngest, Anna Pardini, was only three weeks old. Eight pregnant women were killed. One of them, Evelina Berretti, had her baby pulled from her womb before she was shot. All of the livestock were also killed and the village was burned. The SS men then unconcernedly ate their lunch nearby. After the war the divisional commander, SS Major-General Max Simon, was the only person to be held to account. However, in 2005, ten former members of the SS were found guilty *in absentia* and sentenced to life imprisonment. The name of the officer in charge, SS Captain Anton Galler, was only discovered in 1999. He had died six years earlier. There was more carnage to come from the 16th *SS Reichsführer-SS*. Between 29 September and 5 October 1944 its men systemically murdered more than 800 people in the vicinity of Marzabotto in the Apennines. The officer in charge, SS Major Walter Reder, reported the 'execution of 728 bandits'. But many of these 'bandits' were children – 45 were less than 2 years old and 110 were under 10. The SS troops had also killed 142 men over 60 years old, 316 women and five Catholic priests. Reder was prosecuted immediately after the war and in 2007 another ten former SS men were convicted *in absentia*.

Max Simon was also accused of being involved in the Marzabotto killings, but how much control he had over the troops in his division is not known.

After winning the Iron Cross in the First World War, Simon joined the *Freikorps* and then the *Reichswehr*. A protégé of Theodor Eicke, he joined the Nazi Party and the SS in 1933. After serving as commandant of the Sachsenburg concentration camp, he raised the 1st *SS-Totenkopfstandarte Oberbayern*, becoming its colonel. The regiment was involved in the *Anschluss* and the occupation of Czechoslovakia and Simon also fought in the Battle of France and the invasion of Russia.

He was given command of the newly formed 16th *SS-Panzergrenadier Division Reichsführer-SS* in October 1943. In July 1944, the division moved into Italy to fight the British in the Arno sector and undertake anti-partisan operations. Simon was awarded the Oak Leaves to the Knight's Cross and the German Cross in Gold at that time. He was then given command of the XII SS Corps, which surrendered to the Americans in Bavaria in May 1945.

After a trial, Simon was sentenced to death by a British court for the murders that had been committed by his troops, including those in Marzabotto, but his punishment was commuted and he was released in 1954. Several further attempts were made to prosecute him in Germany, without success.

However, the officer in charge of the 16th *SS Reichsführer-SS* at the time of the Marzabotto massacre, Major Walter Reder, was certainly guilty of murder. Born in the Sudetenland, Reder was already a member of the Hitler Youth when he joined the SS-VT in 1934. He was then sent to the *SS-Junkerschule* at Brunswick before being put in command of various *Totenkopf* units.

Reder participated in the invasion of Poland and won an Iron Cross. During Operation Barbarossa, he commanded a regiment that spearheaded the advance on Leningrad. Injured during the Third Battle of Kharkov, he lost the lower part of his left arm. When he recovered, he commanded a battalion at the liquidation of the Warsaw Ghetto. He was then posted to northern Italy, where he oversaw the Marzabotto massacre.

Subsequently captured by the Americans, Reder was released because of his war wounds, but he was then re-arrested and transferred to the British lines.

Finally, he was sent to Italy, where he was sentenced to life imprisonment. Following a number of petitions for clemency he was released in 1985, after writing a letter of apology to the citizens of Marzabotto. He was greeted by the Minister of Defence, a member of the far-right Austrian Freedom Party, when he returned to Austria, after which he quickly rescinded his apology.

As 1944 progressed, the German forces were becoming even more stretched, with units scurrying here and there to face constant new challenges.

In Finland, the 6th *SS-Gebirgs Division Nord* held the line during the Soviet summer offensive and then it formed the rearguard for the three German corps in an epic 1,000-mile (1,600km) march to Mo i Rana in Norway.

In early September 1944, the II SS Panzer Corps was pulled out of the line in Belgium for a refit, so it was in the Arnhem area of the Netherlands just as the Allies launched Operation Market Garden. The Training and Reserve Battalion of the 16th *SS Division Reichsführer-SS* was also in the area. Together they ensured that the Allied airborne operation was a failure. The city of Arnhem was not liberated until 14 April 1945.

Warsaw Uprising

Meanwhile, the *Waffen-SS* was dealing with the Warsaw Uprising. Between August and October 1944, the *Waffen-Sturm-Brigade RONA* and the *Dirlewanger Brigade* were sent to Warsaw to put down the mutiny. Hitler had ordered the city to be razed, so the SS troops could be as barbarous as they chose. During the battle, the *RONA* was responsible for the Ochota massacre, but the *Dirlewanger* behaved even more atrociously. Encouraged by their commander *SS-Oberführer* Oskar Dirlewanger, who told them to take no prisoners, the *Dirlewanger* troops looted, gang-raped women and children, played 'bayonet catch' with live babies and tortured captives by hacking off their arms, dousing them with petrol and setting them alight to run flaming down the street. The soldiers' behaviour was so bad that even Himmler became alarmed. He ordered a battalion of SS military policemen to stand by, in case the *Dirlewanger* troops turned on their own leaders or on nearby German units.

The original members of the *Dirlewanger Brigade* were convict poachers (they recruited from jails), so the unit was at first called the

——𝑆𝑆——————————————————————————

Wilddiebkommando Oranienburg (Poacher's Command Oranienburg). At first it carried out anti-partisan duties in Poland. A short time later, Himmler made Oskar Dirlewanger the group's commander. It then became part of the *Waffen-SS*, at which point it began to recruit criminals whose crimes were so serious that they were not allowed to serve in penal battalions. Sensing potential freedom, many inmates from the concentration camps volunteered and patients from mental hospitals were also admitted. By September 1940 the formation numbered about 9,000 men and its name was changed to *SS-Sonderbatallion 'Dirlewanger'*.

The force was involved in so many cases of rape, theft, looting and indiscriminate killing in Poland that the General Government's SS and police leader, Friedrich Krüger, had it transferred to Belarus, where it is estimated that along with the Kaminski Brigade it burned 200 villages and murdered 120,000 people, mostly civilians.

Like many others, Oskar Dirlewanger found a home in the SS when things were going badly for him in the outside world. Much decorated and wounded during the First World War, Dirlewanger joined the *Freikorps* and then fought in the Ruhr and Upper Silesia. In 1922, he graduated with a degree in political science, joining the Nazi Party in the following year. But he had personal failings. After serving two years in prison for paedophilia, he was convicted again of the same offence and sent to a concentration camp. Fortunately for him, his friend Gottlob Berger obtained his release. After a period in the Spanish Foreign Legion, Dirlewanger joined the German Condor Legion, which had been formed to fight for General Franco in the Spanish Civil War.

In 1939, Dirlewanger was finally redeemed when Berger secured him a commission in the SS. Dirlewanger then persuaded Berger to let him set up a special unit that would be recruited from convicted

Oskar Dirlewanger was a convicted paedophile who found a home in the SS.
The men under his command were the lowest of the low

criminals. As befitted a former convict and sexual deviant, Dirlewanger encouraged his men to behave in the most brutal fashion. He did not do badly himself. First of all he gave his troops permission to loot and then he shot them so that he could take their plunder for himself. During the Warsaw Uprising, it is said that he entertained the mess with the death throes of young Jewish girls, whom he had injected with strychnine.

After the uprising had been put down, Dirlewanger's brigade was transferred to Slovakia where there was a national revolt in progress. In the last weeks of 1944, the *Dirlewanger Brigade* was sent to the front in northern Hungary, but so many men deserted to the Russians that the unit had to be withdrawn. However, it was soon reinforced, becoming the 36th *Waffen* Grenadier Division of the SS. The new unit met with no more success than its predecessor, being forced to surrender when it was encircled southeast of Berlin.

By then an *SS-Oberführer*, Dirlewanger was wounded and sent to the rear, where he was captured by the French. His next stop was the Altshausen jail, where he was beaten and tortured. It is unclear whether he died at the hands of the Polish guards or former members of his own brigade.

THE OCHOTA MASSACRE

At 10 am on 4 August 1944 the *Waffen-Sturm Brigade RONA* moved into the Ochota district of Warsaw. Its first target was Opaczewska Street, where it expelled the inhabitants, shooting the elderly or anyone that was reluctant to leave. The flats were then looted and set on fire. As the mayhem spread, the troops of the *RONA* murdered people in allotments and threw grenades into basements where people were hiding. By the following day, thousands of people had been expelled from their homes and herded into a makeshift camp. On the way, the men were beaten and the women were raped and murdered.

There was no water, food or medical aid in the camp. Nevertheless, SS Lieutenant-General Erich von dem Bach-Zelewski had the effrontery to issue a favourable report: 'There was nothing wrong there; everything was in order.' Hundreds died and their fellow inmates were forced to carry the corpses to a nearby gymnasium, where they were burned. Others were buried in a pit. A sadistic German officer shot three captured Boy Scouts as they lowered a body into the mass grave.

The brigade went on to the Radium Institute, which had been founded by Marie Curie for the treatment of cancer. They looted the hospital, gang-raped and murdered the patients and staff and then set fire to the building.

Moving on, the troops threw grenades into a Polish field hospital. Over 10,000 innocent civilians died in the *RONA*'s orgy of killing and destruction.

MASSACRE AT MALMÉDY

Leading the German advance guard in the Ardennes was General Joachim Peiper. At Honsfeld in Belgium his men shot 19 GIs and robbed their dead bodies before moving on to an airfield near Bullingen where they forced a group of captured Americans to refuel their tanks. Afterwards, Peiper shot them in cold blood. Eight more prisoners of war were killed at Ligneuville and 100 American prisoners were machine-gunned in Malmédy. By some miracle 20 Americans managed to escape. They hid in a café but Peiper's men soon found them.

Without further ado the building was set on fire and they were machine-gunned when they ran out. A triumphant Hitler imagined that the news of these massacres would demoralize the American troops, but the opposite was the case. It gave them an incentive to fight back.

The end of the dream

In late August 1944, the 5th SS *Wiking* was ordered back to Modlin on the Vistula. Fighting alongside the *Luftwaffe's Fallschirm-Panzer Division 1 Hermann Göring*, the unit annihilated the Soviet 3rd Tank Corps. Grouped with the 3rd SS *Totenkopf* in the IV SS Panzer Corps, the SS *Wiking* helped force the Red Army back across the Vistula, where the Eastern Front stabilized until January 1945.

Meanwhile, Hitler was planning a counter-offensive action through the Ardennes in Belgium. On 26 October 1944, the Sixth SS Panzer Army was formed under Sepp Dietrich. It incorporated I and II Panzer Corps, along with Otto Skorzeny's SS Panzer Brigade 150. The aim was to split the British–American line in half and then capture Antwerp. The Panzer Army would then go on to encircle and destroy four Allied armies, thereby forcing the Western Allies to negotiate a peace treaty and join the war against the Soviets.

But supplies were short and the Panzer commanders were told that they would have to capture petrol on the way. Due to stout resistance this proved impossible, so with fuel running short the Germans returned to the retreat on 8 January 1945.

Otto Skorzeny was something of a swashbuckling character. Born

Peiper's troops? Remarkable film captured from a German soldier included this image of desperate-looking SS men heading for Malmédy

in Vienna to a military family, he acquired a prominent duelling scar as a student. After his studies he joined the Austrian Nazi Party in 1931, followed by the SA, so his role in the *Anschluss* was almost inevitable. Skorzeny was working as a civil engineer during Hitler's invasion of Poland in 1939, but the event fired him to volunteer for the *Leibstandarte SS Adolf Hitler*. He went on to fight in the Netherlands, France and the Balkans.

Injured fighting with *Das Reich* on the Eastern Front, he was given permission to form *Oranienburg*, a special forces unit, at which point he came into his own. In 1943 he parachuted into Iran to stir up dissident hill tribes and then he was personally selected by Hitler to lead the raid to rescue Mussolini. The Italian leader was being held in the Campo Imperatore Hotel on the Gran Sasso d'Italia, which was only accessible by cable car from the valley below. Skorzeny's men overwhelmed the guard and snatched Mussolini without a shot being fired.

Skorzeny was then involved in two failed operations – Operation Long Jump and Operation *Rösselsprung*. Afterwards, he helped stop a possible mutiny in Berlin after the July 1944 attempt on Hitler's life. Then he kidnapped the son of the Hungarian premier Miklós Horthy, in order to forestall possible peace negotiations with the Soviets.

During the Battle of the Bulge he led a brigade of English-speaking Germans dressed in American uniforms, who created confusion behind the Allied lines. Hitler awarded him the Oak Leaves to the Knight's Cross. He was then put in charge of the Werewolves, a Nazi organization that was formed to engage in guerrilla warfare against the occupying Allies. But Skorzeny soon realized that he had too few men for an effective fighting force so he set up the 'ratlines' – secret routes for smuggling Nazis out of Germany.

On 16 May 1945, he surrendered to the Americans and was tried for his improper use of American uniforms during the Ardennes Offensive. However, he was acquitted when the court was told that the British Special Operations Executive had done a similar thing by dressing in German uniforms. While awaiting 'denazification' he escaped and went to live in Spain, where he continued his clandestine activities.

By late December 1944 the German forces began running out of steam. The Allies were just too numerous and too widespread. The Siege of Budapest was just one indication of the turning tide. IX *Waffen* Mountain Corps of the SS (Croatian) and other Axis forces were encircled in Budapest. In an attempt to rescue them, the IV SS Panzer Corps – the 3rd *SS-Totenkopf* and the 5th *SS-Wiking* – attacked the Soviet 4th Guards Army, but the superior Soviet forces halted them just 17 miles (27km) from Budapest. The city surrendered on 13 February 1945.

Although the war was almost over, the *Waffen-SS* continued to expand. In January the 32nd SS Volunteer Grenadier Division was formed from the remnants of other units and staff from the *SS-Junkerschules* and in February the *Waffen* Grenadier Brigade of the SS Charlemagne (1st French) was upgraded to a division, as was the SS Volunteer Grenadier-Brigade *Landstorm Nederland*. SS police units transferred to the *Waffen-SS* became the 35th SS and Police Grenadier Division, while the *Dirlewanger Brigade* was reformed as the 36th *Waffen* Grenadier Division.

But there were few new volunteers or conscripts for the *Waffen-SS*, so units from the *Wehrmacht* were attached to bring it up to strength. Another ploy was to bring together the remnants of failed divisions. The 37th SS Volunteer Cavalry Division *Lützow* was formed in this way. In the end, the only reasonable sources of recruits were again the *SS-Junkerschules*. The 38th SS Division *Nibelungen* was formed by conscripting the remaining students and staff. Even so, the force contained only around 6,000 men, the strength of a normal brigade.

On 15 January 1945, the XIII SS Army Corps joined the last major counter-attack in the west through Alsace and Lorraine. Ten days later, they were on the retreat again.

Things were going no better on the Eastern Front. In February 1945, the Eleventh SS Panzer Army assembled in Pomerania and then attacked the advancing 1st Belorusian Front, but it was repulsed by the Red Army. III (Germanic) SS Panzer Corps was pulled back to Stargard and then Stettin, which is located on the Oder. From there, joined by the X SS Corps, it launched another offensive. In early March, the force was encircled by the Soviets, who hit them relentlessly with everything at their disposal. By 8 March the last 8,000 men had surrendered.

After the failure of the Ardennes Offensive, Hitler decided to launch a final major offensive on the east, so the 6th SS Panzer Army was refitted. Its numbers were boosted by drafting in raw recruits and men from the now defunct *Luftwaffe* and *Kriegsmarine*. Support would be provided by the IV SS Panzer Corps. For the first time ever, six SS Panzer divisions were taking part in the same offensive. The attack, known as Operation Spring Awakening, took place in the Lake Balaton area in Hungary. It took the Soviets completely by surprise. Fortunately for them, they had been massing 1,000 tanks for an assault along the Danube valley, so they had a large, fully prepared tank force to hand.

It was the Germans' turn to be shocked. The German advance quickly ground to a halt. There was little that the 6th SS Panzer Army could do with less than 50 per cent of its strength and no prospect of reinforcements.

Hitler was furious. The 1st *SS-Leibstandarte* had not fought 'as the situation demanded', he screamed. He then ordered the troops to remove their 'Adolf Hitler' cuff bands, but Sepp Dietrich did not relay the order to his men.

The 6th SS Panzer Army withdrew towards Vienna where the II SS Panzer Corps, under Wilhelm Bittrich, faced the Red Army. Vienna fell on 13 April after Bittrich's II SS Panzer Corps had pulled out to avoid encirclement.

All hope for the Germans had gone as the Red Army closed in on Berlin, but Hitler still believed that the city could be saved and the Nazi dream could yet become reality. However, Hitler's health was deteriorating quickly and he did not realize that he was directing divisions that had long gone. Nevertheless, he managed to muster III (Germanic) SS Panzer Corps, and on 16 April the remnants of the 11th *SS-Nordland*, the 33rd *SS-Charlemagne* and the Spanish Volunteer Company of SS 101 were sent as support.

A week later, Hitler appointed SS Brigadier Wilhelm Mohnke as commander of the central sector of Berlin, which included the Reich chancellery. Mohnke's command post was underneath Hitler's bunker. He had been given the job because he had been injured in an air raid, which meant that the *Leibstandarte* had to leave him behind when it went to Hungary. His first task was to form Battle Group Mohnke from the *Leibstandarte* Flak Company, the *Leibstandarte* Training and Reserve Battalion, the *Führer-Begleit* Company and the 600-strong *Reichsführer-SS Begleit Bataillon*. Its core group, though, was the 800-strong *Leibstandarte* Guard Battalion, which was normally assigned to guard Hitler.

As befits a soldier who defended Berlin to the end, Mohnke was a fervent Nazi. One of Hitler's original *Stabswache*, he became a founder member of the *Leibstandarte* in 1933. He was wounded during the Polish campaign, when he was awarded the Iron Cross.

However, Mohnke had a barbarous side to his character, which emerged when he started to take command. For example, he was the leader of the 2nd Battalion of the *Infanterie-Regiment SS-Leibstandarte* when its troops massacred 80 British prisoners of war at Wormhoudt during the Battle of France. He was wounded again in the Balkans, losing part of his foot on the first day of the campaign, but he rejoined the *Leibstandarte* in Russia. In 1943, he was transferred to the newly formed 12th SS Panzer Division *Hitlerjugend*.

Mohnke was responsible for further atrocities in France. When his regiment was in Normandy, he interrogated three captured Canadians. Afterwards, they were taken into a bomb crater and shot, while Mohnke looked on. He was implicated in four similar incidents, which resulted in the murder of nine other Canadians. By December 1944 Mohnke was commander of the *Leibstandarte*. He was the one who issued the order to take no prisoners at Malmédy.

Mohnke was in Hitler's bunker when he committed suicide on 30 April 1945 and he was seen to weep openly. On the following day he set fire to the bunker and joined an escape group. Captured by the Soviets, he was one of the first German prisoners of war to be released in October 1955. It seems that he got away with his crimes.

Only two weeks before Hitler's suicide, there were plans to escort him in a breakout. On 16 April 1945 the remnants of the 11th *SS-Freiwilligen-Panzergrenadier Division Nordland*, commanded by SS Brigadier Joachim Ziegler, were ordered back into Berlin for that purpose.

Ziegler had served with the Condor Legion in Spain before fighting in Poland, the Low Countries and France, winning the Iron Cross. In June 1943, he was transferred from the *Wehrmacht* to III (Germanic) SS Panzer Corps and was granted permission to wear an SS uniform. Just over a year later, in July 1944, he was given command of the 11th *SS-Freiwilligen-Panzergrenadier Division Nordland*. In September 1944 Ziegler was awarded the Knight's Cross because of the conduct of his division. Then things started to go wrong. In February 1945, his division joined the offensive in Pomerania, but it was forced to withdraw. It then fought a rearguard action into Berlin where Hitler dismissed him and placed him under arrest in the bunker – though strangely enough he presented him with the Oak Leaves to his Knight's Cross two days later.

After Hitler's suicide, Ziegler was freed. He was trying to negotiate a truce when he was killed near Friedrichstrasse railway station.

Ziegler's replacement as commander of the *Nordland*, Gustav Krukenberg, was a career soldier like Ziegler. Krukenberg met with no more success than Ziegler. On 27 April the *Nordland* was pushed back into the central government district, where it fell under Mohnke's overall command.

After serving as an officer in the First World War, Krukenberg became private secretary to the foreign minister. In 1932 he joined the Nazi Party, where he worked in the Propaganda Ministry after Hitler came to power. At that time he was a member of the *Allgemeine-SS*. After the outbreak of war, he rejoined the army and then he transferred to the *Waffen-SS* in 1943.

A fluent French-speaker, Krukenberg commanded the *SS-Charlemagne Division*. He was leading the remnants of the unit in the defence of Berlin when he took over the command of the *Nordland* from Joachim Ziegler. When Hitler killed himself, he gathered up the rest of his command and tried to break out. Still friendly with Ziegler, he was with him when he was killed. Krukenberg finally surrendered to the Soviets after hiding out in an apartment for a week.

Nothing could stop the Red Army now, but the troops of the SS had been conditioned to fight until the end. As the Soviets raced to take the Reichstag and the Reich chancellery, they met with stiff resistance. In bloody street fighting the survivors of the 33rd *SS-Charlemagne* held out against overwhelming odds. But there could be no fight without the *Führer*. After receiving news of Hitler's suicide, Mohnke ordered a breakout. What was left of the 11th *SS-Nordland* headed northwest towards Mecklenburg, but the unit faced fierce fighting around the Weidendammer Bridge. A few very small groups managed to reach the Americans on the Elbe, but most could not make it through the Soviet rings. The lucky ones were killed in action – the Soviets were merciless captors.

On 2 May hostilities were officially ended by order of Helmuth Weidling, the *Wehrmacht*'s commandant of Defence Area Berlin. When news of the surrender reached them, some of the remaining SS men shot themselves rather than surrender to the Soviets. They included

Mohnke's adjutant, SS First Lieutenant Gert Stehr of the *Führer* Escort Detachment, formerly the *Leibstandarte*.

At the victory parade in Red Square on 24 June 1945, captured standards were displayed. The most prized exhibit was the standard of the *Leibstandarte SS Adolf Hitler*.

Chapter Nine

NUREMBERG

Winston Churchill did not think that the captured Nazis should be given the luxury of a trial after the Second World War. He was in favour of immediate execution. However, at the conference held at Yalta in February 1945, Britain, the United States and the Soviet Union agreed to prosecute the Nazi leaders and other war criminals. They did not just have Hitler and Himmler in their sights.

An International Military Tribunal was set up by the London Conference in August 1945. It was given the authority to indict offenders on four counts: crimes against peace – planning and initiating wars of aggression; crimes against humanity – genocide, extermination and deportation; war crimes – violations of the laws of war; and conspiracy to commit any of the first three offences. Britain, the United States, the Soviet Union and France would each provide one judge and one prosecutor.

The International Military Tribunal first sat on 18 October 1945, in the Supreme Court Building in Berlin. The prosecution entered indictments against 24 Nazi leaders and six 'criminal organizations' – Hitler's cabinet, the leadership corps of the Nazi Party, the SS and the SD, the SA, the Gestapo and the General Staff and High Command of the *Wehrmacht*.

However, Heinrich Himmler, the architect of the SS and the man who has been described as 'the greatest mass murderer of all time', could not be charged. On 23 May 1945 he managed to evade justice, at least in this life, by committing suicide.

The main trial

On 20 November 1945, the tribunal moved to the Palace of Justice in Nuremberg. The building contained some 80 courtrooms and around 530 offices, with the added bonus of a large undamaged prison block. The proceedings were conducted under the presidency of Lord Justice Geoffrey Lawrence (later 3rd Baron Trevethin and 1st Baron Oaksey) and the legal procedures followed Anglo-American common law practice. During the 218 days of the trials, testimony from 360 witnesses was introduced, with 236 witnesses appearing in the court itself.

The histories of those called up for trial were many and various. For example:

Fritz Saukel

Originally a merchant seaman, Fritz Saukel was interned in France during the First World War. He joined the Nazi Party in 1923 and became *Gauleiter* of Thüringia in 1927, later becoming the region's Reich Regent. In 1933 he became a Reichstag member and a year later he was made an honorary lieutenant-general in the SA and the SS. As general plenipotentiary for labour deployment, Saukel imported five million workers into Germany. They were treated harshly, to say the least, but when he was questioned at Nuremberg he denied that they had been used as slave labour or that any deliberate attempt had been made to work them to death. Found guilty of war crimes and crimes against humanity, he went to the gallows protesting his innocence.

Rudolf Hess

During the First World War, Hess served in the same infantry regiment as Hitler, before transferring to the Imperial Air Corps. After the war he joined the *Freikorps*. He then studied at Munich University under political theoretician Karl Haushofer. While he was there he joined the Thule Society, a *völkisch* and occultist organization that later sponsored the DAP. All of this made him a prime candidate for the fledgling Nazi Party, which he joined in 1920. Jailed after commanding an SA battalion during the Beer Hall Putsch, he served as Hitler's secretary in Landsberg Prison, when he transcribed and edited *Mein Kampf.* When Hitler seized dictatorial powers, he named Hess as his deputy.

With such a background, Hess's subsequent fall from grace seems more than bizarre. On 10 May 1941, he made a solo flight to Scotland

and then landed by parachute close to the estate of the Duke of Hamilton, whom he had met at the 1936 Olympic Games in Berlin. It is thought that Hess was on an unofficial peace mission. Hitler was incandescent with rage. Hess was suffering from 'pacifist delusions', he snarled. He ordered that Hess was to be shot on sight if he returned to Germany. Hess's captors came to believe that he was insane, but a psychiatrist who examined him testified at Nuremberg that he was of sound mind.

In court he was seen talking to himself, counting on his fingers and laughing for no apparent reason. He claimed that he did not recognize Göring, who asked to be seated away from him. Göring's request was denied. At first, Hess claimed that he suffered from amnesia and remembered nothing of his Nazi past, but during the trial he declared that his memory had returned, removing the possibility of a plea of diminished responsibility. Hess was convicted of crimes against peace – that is, planning a war of aggression – and conspiracy with other Nazi leaders. He was acquitted of war crimes and crimes against humanity.

Konstantin von Neurath

Honorary SS Lieutenant-General Konstantin von Neurath, *Reichsprotektor* of Bohemia and Moravia, was sentenced to 15 years' imprisonment, but he was released in 1954 because of illness. He died two years later.

Martin Bormann

Martin Bormann was called up in the First World War, but by then the conflict was nearly over, so he never saw action. Afterwards he joined the *Freikorps*. In 1924, he was sentenced to a year in prison as an accomplice to the murder of Walter Kadow. His friend Rudolf Höss was jailed for ten years. Released in 1925, Bormann joined the Nazi Party and became a leading fundraiser. He is thought to have bought police inspector Heinrich Müller's silence when Hitler's niece Geli Raubal was shot, perhaps by Hitler. Envious of the Blood Order decoration – at first only conferred on veterans of the 1923 Beer Hall Putsch – he expanded the qualifications to include himself.

From 1933 to 1941 he was private secretary to Hitler's deputy, Rudolf Hess. He then fulfilled the dual roles of head of the chancellery and private secretary to Hitler, which enabled him to control access to the *Führer*. He witnessed Hitler's marriage and his last will and testament, and he urged the execution of Göring. A worldwide search for his body took place after the war, but the mystery was solved when his remains were unearthed in Berlin in 1973. However, conspiracy theories abounded until 1998, when modern science finally laid all speculation to rest.

On 1 October 1946, 22 of the original Nuremberg defendants were found guilty and sentenced to death by hanging. They included SS Lieutenant-General Hans Frank, the governor-general of Poland; SS Lieutenant-General Ernst Kaltenbrunner, head of the SD; SS Lieutenant-General Joachim von Ribbentrop, Hitler's foreign minister; racial theorist Alfred Rosenberg; SS Lieutenant-General Fritz Saukel, organizer of forced labour; Julius Streicher, *Gauleiter* in Franconia; and SS Lieutenant-General Arthur Seyss-Inquart, commissioner for the occupied Netherlands.

They were all hanged on the morning of 16 October 1946, in the old gymnasium of the Nuremberg prison. The bodies were cremated and the ashes were scattered in an estuary of the Isar River. SS Lieutenant-General Martin Bormann, a former Nazi Party organizer and private secretary to Hitler, was sentenced to death *in absentia*.

United States tribunals

Although it was originally intended that the International Military Tribunal would sit again, the Cold War had started and there was no further co-operation between the participants. However, more military tribunals took place in the French, British, American and Soviet zones of occupation.

The United States held a series of trials of lesser war criminals, which were called the US Nuremberg Military Tribunals (NMT). As it happened, the Palace of Justice in Nuremberg was within the American zone of occupation, so the United States tribunals took place in the same building as the main trials.

On 9 December 1946, proceedings began against 23 German doctors, who were accused of participating in the Nazi Euthanasia Programme. The trial lasted 140 days. Eighty-five witnesses appeared and 1,500 documents were introduced in evidence. Sixteen doctors were found guilty. Seven of them were sentenced to death and were executed on 2 June 1948. The names of those who were hanged were Viktor Brack, Karl Brandt, Rudolf Brandt, Karl Gebhardt, Waldemar Hoven, Joachim Mrugowsky and Wolfram Sievers.

• After Viktor Brack had worked on the T-4 Euthanasia Programme, Himmler ordered him to find a way of sterilizing Jews so they could be used as slave labour without any fear of them procreating. He tested the procedures on Auschwitz inmates.

• Karl Brandt had been the head of the T-4 Programme, while Rudolf Brandt had handled Himmler's correspondence, including that relating to the Holocaust.

• Karl Gebhardt had been Himmler's personal physician. At Ravensbrück and Auschwitz, he had performed brutal surgical procedures on female inmates, opening their skulls or abdomens without an anaesthetic to see how long they could survive. He had also served as the president of the German Red Cross.

• Waldemar Hoven had worked on the T-4 Programme and he had also been a physician at Buchenwald, where he had carried out medical experiments related to typhus and the inmates' tolerance of a serum containing phenol. Many deaths had resulted from this programme.

• Joachim Mrugowsky had been the head of the SS Hygiene Institute in Berlin. He had distributed Zyklon B, a poison that was used in the gas chambers at the death camps and he had overseen Hoven's work at Buchenwald. In addition, he had experimented with poisoned bullets.

• Wolfram Sievers had been the director of the SS Institute for Military Scientific Research, where he had conducted extensive experiments using human subjects. He had also assisted in an anthropological study that had involved the murder of 112 Jews.

• SS Major Fritz Fischer had worked in the camp hospital at Ravensbrück, where he had conducted experiments on inmates, infecting them with typhus, smallpox, cholera and other diseases to test the effectiveness of vaccines. He was sentenced to life imprisonment, but he was released in 1954.

• *SS-Oberführer* Helmut Poppendick had been involved in medical experiments on concentration camp prisoners, including those at

Ravensbrück. He was sentenced to ten years' imprisonment, but he was released in 1951.

When the doctors had been tried, it was the turn of those who had been involved with the concentration camps.

• In 1947 the United States prosecuted SS Lieutenant-General Oswald Pohl and 17 other SS officers who had directed the WVHA, the organization that had administered the concentration camps. The main charge against them was that they had supervised the arrangements for the 'Final Solution'. Pohl and three of his fellow defendants were sentenced to death by hanging. Three others were acquitted and the remainder were sentenced to be imprisoned for periods that ranged between ten years and life.

• SS Brigadier Otto Steinbrinck was sentenced to six years' imprisonment when he stood trial alongside Himmler's close friend, wealthy industrialist Friedrich Flick. The charge was using slave labour and profiting from property taken from Jews. Flick spent seven years in jail while Steinbrinck died in Landsberg Prison in 1949.

• The production chief at Auschwitz, SS Lieutenant-Colonel Heinrich Bütefisch, was sentenced to six years' imprisonment when he stood trial alongside SS 'supporting member' Christian Schneider, a fellow director of IG Farben, the manufacturer of Zyklon B. Another director, SS Captain Erich von der Heyde, was acquitted.

Fourteen members of the RuSHA (SS Race and Settlement Main Office) were prosecuted for crimes against humanity, war crimes and membership of the SS. They included:

- Ulrich Greifelt, Reich Commissioner for the Strengthening of Germandom (RKFDV) – found guilty on all counts and sentenced to life imprisonment. Died in prison in 1949.

- Rudolf Creutz, deputy to Greifelt – sentenced to 15 years' imprisonment and released in 1955.

- Werner Lorenz, head of the VoMi – convicted of being an SS member, he was sentenced to 20 years' imprisonment and released in 1955.

- Heinz Brückner, VoMi office head – convicted of being an SS member, he was sentenced to 15 years' imprisonment and released in 1951.

- Otto Hofmann, head of the RuSHA – sentenced to 25 years' imprisonment and released in 1954.

- Richard Hildebrandt, successor to Hofmann – sentenced to 25 years' imprisonment and released in 1952.

- Fritz Schwalm, chief of staff of the RuSHA 'Immigration Office' in Lodz – sentenced to ten years' imprisonment and released in 1951.

- The heads of the *Lebensborn*, the health department and the legal department were convicted only of being members of the SS and were released.

Twenty-four officers of the *Einsatzgruppen* stood trial. Fourteen were sentenced to death by hanging. The following defendants were hanged on 7 June 1951:

—𝑆𝑆————————————————————————

- Erich Naumann, commander of *Einsatzgruppe B*.

- Otto Ohlendorf, commander of *Einsatzgruppe D*.

- Paul Blobel, commanding officer of *Sonderkommando 4a* of *Einsatzgruppe C*.

- Werner Braune, commanding officer of *Sonderkommando 11b* of *Einsatzgruppe D*.

The following defendants had their sentences commuted and were released:

- Walter Blume, commanding officer of *Sonderkommando 7a* of *Einsatzgruppe B*.

- Martin Sandberger, commanding officer of *Sonderkommando 1a* of *Einsatzgruppe A*.

- Willy Seibert, deputy chief of *Einsatzgruppen D*.

- Eugen Steimle, commanding officer of *Sonderkommando 7a* of *Einsatzgruppe B* and of *Sonderkommando 4a* of *Einsatzgruppe C*.

- Ernst Biberstein, commanding officer of *Einsatzkommando 6* of *Einsatzgruppe C*.

- Walter Haensch, commanding officer of *Sonderkommando 4b* of *Einsatzgruppe C*.

- Adolf Ott, commanding officer of *Sonderkommando 7b* of *Einsatzgruppe B*.

- Walter Klingelhöfer, officer of *Sonderkommando 7b* of *Einsatzgruppe B*.

- Heinz Schubert, officer in *Einsatzgruppe D*.

The following defendants escaped justice because of illness or death:

- Eduard Strauch, commanding officer of *Einsatzkommando 2* of *Einsatzgruppe A*, was handed over to the Belgian authorities and died in hospital in 1955.

- Otto Rasch, commanding officer of *Einsatzgruppe C*, was removed from the trial on medical grounds and died in November 1948.

- Emil Haussmann, officer of *Einsatzkommando 12* of *Einsatzgruppe D*, committed suicide before the arraignment.

The following defendants were sentenced to imprisonment:

- Mathias Graf, an officer in *Einsatzkommando 6* of *Einsatzgruppe D*, was released on consideration of time already served.

- Heinz Jost, commanding officer of *Einsatzgruppe A*, was sentenced to life imprisonment, but was released after ten years.

—*ss*————————————————

- Erwin Schulz, commanding officer of *Einsatzkommando 5* of *Einsatzgruppe C*, was sentenced to 20 years' imprisonment but was released after six years.

- Franz Six, commanding officer of *Vorkommando Moscow* of *Einsatzgruppe B*, was sentenced to 20 years' imprisonment but was released after four years.

- Gustave Nosske, commanding officer of *Einsatzkommando 12* of *Einsatzgruppe D*, was sentenced to life imprisonment but was released after ten years.

- Lothar Fendler, deputy chief of *Sonderkommando 4b* of *Einsatzgruppe C*, was sentenced to ten years' imprisonment but was released after eight years.

- Waldemar von Radetzky, deputy chief of *Sonderkommando 4a* of *Einsatzgruppe C*, was sentenced to 20 years' imprisonment but was released.

- Felix Rühl, officer of *Sonderkommando 10b* of Einsatzgruppe D, was sentenced to ten years' imprisonment but was released.

The judgement said that the facts of the case

> *are so beyond the experience of normal man and the range of man-made phenomena that only the most complete judicial inquiry, and the most exhaustive trial, could verify and confirm them.*

The defendants had committed

> *a crime of such unprecedented brutality and of such inconceivable savagery that the mind rebels against its own thought image and the imagination staggers in the contemplation of a human degradation beyond the power of language to adequately portray.*

The prosecution had put the number of people who had been murdered by these men at one million, but

> *it is only when this grotesque total is broken down into units capable of mental assimilation that one can understand the monstrousness of the things we are in this trial contemplating. One must visualize not one million people but only ten persons – men, women, and children, perhaps all of one family – falling before the executioner's guns. If one million is divided by ten, this scene must happen one hundred thousand times…*

In a separate trial of government ministers, SS Lieutenant-General Gottlob Berger, SS Brigadier Walter Schellenberg and SS Lieutenant-General Richard Walther were convicted for their roles in Nazi Germany.

They were sentenced to imprisonment and released in the early 1950s.

Other Allied trials were held for the SS concentration camp guards. In the western zone of occupied Germany 5,025 people were convicted. Eight hundred and six defendants were given death sentences and 486 of them were carried out. In the Soviet zone of occupation, it is estimated that there were 45,000 trials. Outside Germany, as many as 60,000 people have been convicted of Nazi crimes: 1,214 war criminals were executed in Poland alone.

Chapter Ten

ODESSA

There is some doubt that a formal organization called ODESSA – *Organization der Ehemaligen SS-Angehörigen* (Organization of former SS members) – ever existed. However, a number of former SS criminals, including Adolf Eichmann and Josef Mengele, certainly managed to escape from Germany at the end of the war and find their way to South America.

———⚡⚡———

azi-hunter Simon Wiesenthal learned of the existence of ODESSA while he was talking to former German counter-espionage operatives at the Nuremberg trials. The United States Army Counter Intelligence Corps (CIC) knew about ODESSA too, and they knew who ran it. According to a top-secret report dated 20 January 1947: 'The leader of this group is Otto Skorzeny, who runs it from the camp at Dachau, where he is interned. The men who take their orders from Skorzeny are being helped by the Polish guards to escape.'

When it came to his own escape, the daredevil Skorzeny did it in style. Three former SS officers, dressed in the uniforms of the United States Military Police, turned up and told the guard that they had come to collect the prisoner Skorzeny for the next day's hearing at Nuremberg.

Funding the operation

In the last days of the war Skorzeny withdrew to the 'Alpine redoubt' in Bavaria, an underground fortress where a group of Nazi fanatics intended to make their last stand. Art treasures and munitions factories had been moved to the caves to protect them from bombing. Adolf Eichmann also turned up. He had with him 22 crates filled with valuables stolen from his Jewish victims in the extermination camps, which included gold teeth and wedding rings. The Vienna State Prosecutor's Office estimated that 'Eichmann's gold' was worth $8 million in 1955. Key documents were also said to have been taken there. The prisoners who had been forging British bank notes in Sachsenhausen concentration camp were transferred to Mauthausen-Gusen concentration camp, near Linz in Austria. Adolf Burger, whose wife and parents had been killed in the death camps, recalled that they also forged Argentinian and other travel documents:

We printed Brazilian passports, Tunisian identity cards, British and American military passes and shipmasters' certificates. We even produced metal dies. Once we forged Dutch baptismal certificates, then there were official deeds from French cities or letterheads from the Palestine office in Geneva, with wording in Hebrew script. We forged British marriage certificates and a US army paybook.

Everything you would need, in fact, if you wanted to change your identity.

A witness once saw Nazis sinking crates in Lake Toplitz. Divers found one of the containers in 1959. When they prised the lid open with a crowbar, British £5 notes floated to the surface. Diving there is now banned. Most of the money found its way into the hands of a shady character called Friedrich Schwend, alias Wendig, who was arrested at the end of the war but soon released. After he had been issued with a Yugoslav passport bearing the name 'Wenceslav Turi', the CIC allowed him to leave Germany with his wife. He settled in Lima, Peru where he became 'head of ODESSA in South America', according to an informant.

Other funds were available to ODESSA, in Schwend's absence. When it became certain that Germany was faced with defeat, a number of wealthy Germans moved their money out of the country. By 1946, it was estimated that assets worth two billion Swiss francs were on deposit in Switzerland.

Escape routes

Skorzeny's ODESSA role was discovered when an American agent infiltrated a Nazi network known as the 'Brotherhood'. The former

Waffen-SS colonel was also thought to have run an operation called 'The Spider', which ran an escape route into Italy. Fugitives were transported in the German-driven trucks that delivered the American army newspaper *Stars and Stripes*.

The Catholic Church played a major role in the organization. In Rome, Austrian Bishop Alois Hudal assisted former SS men by finding accommodation, providing travel documents and making arrangements to get them out of the country. In 1937, Hudal published *The Foundations of National Socialism*, a book that praised Hitler. He sent a copy to the *Führer*, calling him 'the new Siegfried of Germany's greatness'. The bishop was helped by a former Nazi counterintelligence officer named Reinhard Kops, who sifted through the details of the new refugees arriving in Rome. Other Catholic clerics helped. It is not known if Pope Pius XII was involved, but Cardinal Giovanni Battista Montini (later Pope Paul VI) certainly lent a hand.

Many people lost their travel documents during the war, but it was easy to obtain a passport from the International Committee of the Red Cross on the recommendation of a priest. The archbishop of Genoa, Giuseppe Siri, set up a committee to help refugees get to Argentina. He put them in touch with the Argentine Immigration Commission in Europe, which was run by Franz Ruffinengo, a former officer in Mussolini's army. Juan Perón, who had become president of Argentina in 1946, wanted to turn the country into a military and industrial power along the lines of Nazi Germany and Fascist Italy, so he was keen to recruit 'technicians'. Meanwhile he established the anti-Semitic 'National Ethnic Institute'.

Perón's immigration policy in Buenos Aires was handled by Rodolfo Freude and Horst Carlos Fuldner. Freude was a blond-haired Argentinian whose German father had close ties with the Nazis during the war and Fuldner was a German–Argentinian former SS captain who had served in the SD. In March 1945, Fuldner had travelled to Madrid to set up an escape route for other SS men. When the Allies had demanded his extradition in 1947 he had fled to Argentina, a place where former SS men were granted immunity. Adolf Eichmann, Josef Mengele, Erich Priebke, Josef Schwammberger and Gerhard Bohne escaped this way.

Erich Priebke would have lived out his days as a free man if his arrogant nature had not led him to share his shameful past with a television audience. At the end of the war, Priebke was captured by the British, but he managed to escape. He was then hidden by a family in Sterzing, on the Austrian border. Eichmann and Mengele had also taken refuge there. In 1948, Bishop Hudal made arrangements for him to leave the country, so he fled to Argentina.

He had been living in Argentina for 50 years when he unwisely gave a television interview in which he admitted his part in the deportation of over 11,000 Italian Jews to Auschwitz. He said he had only been following the orders of SS Lieutenant-Colonel Herbert Kappler, the chief of the Gestapo in Rome. Kappler had been sentenced to life imprisonment by an Italian military tribunal, but his wife had smuggled him out of jail in a large suitcase in 1977, when he had been suffering from terminal cancer. He died in Germany in the following year.

Priebke's television revelations were only the tip of the iceberg, though. On another occasion he had shot 335 Italian civilians at the Ardeatine caves in Rome, while he was a captain in the *Waffen-SS*. He was exacting a reprisal for the shooting of 33 SS military policemen, who had been killed by Italian partisans on 23 March 1944.

The outrage over Priebke's TV interview led to him being extradited to Italy to face trial. SS Lieutenant-Colonel Karl Hass, a former SD man who had assisted Priebke in the massacre, was going to be the chief witness. Hass was hiding out in an Italian monastery when he was recruited by the CIC. He agreed to return to Italy so that he could testify against Priebke in return for immunity, but he changed his mind at the last minute. While attempting to escape from his hotel room by climbing down from the balcony, he slipped and fell. Still a captive, he was now injured as well, so he had to testify from his hospital bed. Hass was deemed to have broken the agreement that had given him immunity, so he was held under house arrest until his death in 2004. His testimony led to the conviction of Priebke, who was sentenced to life imprisonment under house arrest.

Josef Schwammberger was another SS war criminal who managed to escape to Argentina. During the Second World War, he was the sadistic commander of a number of SS forced labour camps around Krakow in Poland. Captured in the French occupation zone in 1945, he was sent by rail to the United States military authorities in Austria, where he was going to stand trial. However, he made his escape from a moving train. Although he travelled to Argentina on an Italian passport, he lived there under his own name, becoming an Argentinian citizen in 1965.

In 1973, the German authorities informed the Argentinian government that Schwammberger was on their top ten list of wanted Nazis, but it took until 1987 to locate him. He was extradited in 1989 and was eventually convicted of seven counts of murder and 32 counts of accessory to murder. Denied parole because of the unusual cruelty of his offences, he died in jail.

Gerhard Bohne also found the air in Argentina more congenial at one point. How much of a war criminal he had been is a matter for conjecture, but he had certainly been part of the T-4 Euthanasia Programme. The legally trained Bohne, then an SS first lieutenant, resigned his position in 1942 after accusing his colleagues of misusing motor vehicles as well as 'alcoholic and sexual excesses'. Captured by the Americans in Italy, he was released in 1946. He then returned to Germany, where he worked as a legal assistant.

In 1949, he fled to Argentina where he wrote for *Der Weg* (The Way), a German-language National Socialist journal that was published in the Perón era. After returning to Germany in 1956 he was admitted to the Bar in Düsseldorf, but in 1959 he was charged with complicity in the murder of at least 15,000 people. Bailed for health reasons, he escaped to Denmark and then travelled to Buenos Aires via Zurich. He was arrested in Argentina in 1964 and extradited to Germany two years later. However, the legal procedures dragged on until he had a heart attack in 1968. All charges against him were dropped in the following year.

Working for the West

The CIC was also using the Catholic Church's 'ratlines' (systems of escape routes) to smuggle American agents and informants out of Europe. The most notorious case was that of the 'butcher of Lyon', Klaus Barbie. A former SS captain, Barbie was on both the French and the American wanted lists when he cut a deal with the CIC.

'We simply knew very little about the Russians, about their army, their tactics, battle-plans and so forth,' said Jim Milano who used the ratlines, 'and there was a good deal of pressure on the secret service to get hold of this information.'

Himmler had fought tooth and nail to make the SS a communist-free zone. As a result, several Western organizations eagerly recruited former SS men in their war against Soviet espionage. When Barbie approached the CIC, they did not arrest him but instead used his skills by employing him as an interrogator. He was also ordered to infiltrate the Communist Party in Bavaria.

'In view of the great value he was to our organization, we had no great pangs of conscience,' said one of his American colleagues.

When the French demanded Barbie's extradition, the CIC simply arranged for him to flee to Latin America, where he worked closely with Friedrich Schwend and became an adviser to the Bolivian secret service. It is thought that Gestapo chief Heinrich Müller and Eichmann's 'best man' Alois Brunner disappeared in a similar fashion. Some former SS men even went to live in the United States or Canada. Both countries were happy to take communist-hating immigrants on board, even if they had been members of the SS.

Thanks to the Cold War, Barbie remained a free man for many years. He had not always been the 'butcher of Lyon', however. As a young man he had intended to study theology, but he gave up his further education plans when his father died. He was then conscripted into the Reich Labour Service (RAD), an organization that had been formed to reduce unemployment. In 1935, he joined the SD. After serving in the German-occupied Netherlands he was posted to Lyon, where he headed the local Gestapo.

From his headquarters in the Hotel Terminus, he oversaw the torture and death of over 4,000 people. He then condemned a further 7,500 innocent citizens to the death camps, including numerous children. Barbie personally tortured his victims in the most barbarous fashion. He burned them, beat them, half-drowned them, administered electric shocks to their nipples or genitals and pushed needles under their fingernails. On top of all that, he staged mock executions.

'It really amused him to see others suffer,' said one victim.

His most famous victim was Jean Moulin, head of the French resistance, who died from the treatment he received at Barbie's hands.

In 1945, Barbie was being pursued by MI5. Instead of running, he approached MI6, who gladly recruited the former mass murderer. However, some people found it impossible to overlook his heinous crimes. While he was in Hamburg he was beaten up by British soldiers and locked in a coal cellar for three days. His experience caused him to develop a grudge against the British, so he turned to the CIC, who welcomed him with open arms. He used his position to help other SS men escape. When the French learnt that he was in the American zone, they wanted him back, so in 1951 he was spirited off to Bolivia. Twenty years later he was tracked down by Nazi-hunters, but it was not until 1983 that he was extradited to France. At his trial, he refused to defend himself. He was sentenced to life imprisonment and he died in jail.

Alois Brunner was another big fish that got away. Brunner was responsible for sending at least 120,000 people to their deaths. He had been in charge of seizing and deporting Jews in Austria, Slovakia, France and Greece. In 1945, he kept out of the Allies' hands by the simple expedient of changing his name to Alois Schmaldienst. Although he was eventually detained by both the British and the Americans, he was soon released. He even went to work as a driver for the United States occupation forces.

When things got too hot for him in Germany, he escaped to Syria via Rome and Cairo. Former Nazis were welcomed there, especially after the foundation of Israel in 1948. First of all he worked as an arms dealer and then he was taken on by the Syrian secret service. However, Mossad, the Israeli intelligence agency, eventually discovered where he was. Israelis were not exactly welcome in Syria, so they let the postman

Former SS major Wernher von Braun, seen here with his arm in plaster, brought his knowledge of rockets to the US space programme

do the job of getting to Brunner. He lost his left eye when a letter bomb exploded in 1961. A parcel bomb blew off both of his hands in 1980.

Brunner has been sentenced to death twice *in absentia*. Rumours of his death have not been confirmed.

Well looked after

When SS men escaped at the end of the war, they were often well looked after. Money was smuggled out to them through the office Skorzeny had set up in Madrid and German manufacturers with factories in other parts of the world were asked to employ fleeing Nazis. Adolf Eichmann worked in the Volkswagen plant in Argentina, for example.

Some former SS members even went on to live a comfortable life at the expense of the British and American governments, provided they had some technical or scientific expertise to offer. The most famous of these was Wernher von Braun, the chief architect of the Saturn V launch vehicle and the rocket boosters that carried Apollo 11 to the moon. As an SS major, he had developed the V-2 ballistic missiles that had devastated London and Antwerp. These weapons had been built in an underground factory in Dora-Mittelbau, where thousands of slave labourers had been worked to death. It was not until 1979, two years after von Braun's death, that the United States Department of Justice set up the Office of Special Investigations. Its purpose was to apprehend all those who had committed crimes against humanity. Former Nazis were a prime target. It seems that former SS members could escape justice in numerous ways without the help of ODESSA. A number of other organizations also provided them with material assistance. One of them was the Comrades' Welfare Society founded by Hans-Ulrich Rudel, a *Luftwaffe* air ace who had escaped to Argentina with the aid of the Catholic Church. Rudel's organization helped with legal costs and it also sent parcels of food and clothing. Among those who received these care packages were the families of Rudolf Hess and Admiral Dönitz. Rudel acted as an agent for the agricultural machinery that was built by Josef Mengele's family firm in Bavaria and he also maintained close ties with Juan Perón. His closest associate, Willem Sassen, a Dutch SS member, worked closely with Augusto Pinochet, the president of Chile, and Alfredo Stroessner, the president of Paraguay. Life could be good in Argentina. Raucous groups of unrepentant SS veterans held 'Brownshirt parties' and toasted the 'good old days'.

In 1951, an organization called *Stille Hilfe* (Silent Aid) was set up to provide assistance to convicted Nazi war criminals. High-ranking former SS officers sat on its board, along with prominent members of the Church. Its first president was Princess Helene Elisabeth von Isenburg, also known as the 'Mother of the Landsbergers'. The Landsbergers were the Nazis who still languished in Landsberg Prison. A leading member of the operation was Gudrun Burwitz, *née* Himmler – the *Reichsführer's* beloved daughter, whom he had referred to as 'Püppi'.

At around the same time, the Mutual Aid Association for Soldiers of the Former *Waffen-SS* (HIAG) was set up. For years it was run by SS General Kurt Meyer.

One of his aims was to rehabilitate the reputation of the *Waffen-SS*. He maintained that its members were merely soldiers and had nothing to do with the crimes of the *Allgemeine-SS*. The organization's spokesman was Hans Wissebach, a member of the German parliament, or Bundestag, and a former member of the *Leibstandarte SS Adolf Hitler*. As well as the HIAG main office, there were hundreds of local and regional groups where former SS men could get together and reminisce. The HIAG was dissolved in 1992, but its journal *Der Freiwillige* (The

Volunteer) continued to be published. Its youth group – *Wiking-Jugend* (Viking Youth) – was banned in 1994.

All of the former members of the SS are now dead, or too frail to do any harm. However, the seeds that spawned the SS are still there. In 1979 the Aid Organization for National Political Prisoners (HNG) was set up along the lines of *Stille Hilfe*. Its aim was to help neo-Nazis 'who have, out of political conviction, committed acts of arson against accommodation of asylum seekers, inflicted bodily harm or been guilty of other criminal behaviour'.

The banned *Wiking-Jugend* has been replaced by the Friends of Ulrich von Hutten, a 16th-century poet and patriot who is romanticized in German literature as a freedom fighter. Its journal *Huttenbriefe* (Hutten Letters) calls for the establishment of a 'Fourth Reich', where there would be a need for a new SS.

Index

Bütefisch, Heinrich 270

C

Canaris, Wilhelm 54, 98, 193
Comrades' Welfare Society 287-8
Cooper, Thomas Haller 151, 153, 155, 156, 157, 158
Courlander, Roy 151, 153, 157-8
Cowie, Hugh 157, 158
Czechoslovakia
   invasion of 17, 56, 111-15, 208

D

Dachau concentration camp 60, 63, 67, 69, 83, 95, 125, 139, 172, 205, 207, 244
Daluege, Kurt 70
Degrelle, Léon 178
Delaney, Peter 159
Denmark
   SS branch of 181-3
Diebitsch, Karl 59-60
Diel, Lucas 160
Diels, Rudolf 71-2, 77, 83, 190, 192
Dietrich, Josef 'Sepp' 26
   and SS chancellery guard 63
   and Night of the Long Knives 79-80
   and SS-VT 142
   and invasion of France 145,

146, 147
   and invasion of Greece 163
   and Ardennes offensive 254
   on Eastern Front 258
Dirlewanger Brigade 249-52
Dirlewanger, Oskar 249-52
Dollfuss, Engelbert 102, 103, 193
Dönitz, Karl 105, 288
Drexler, Anton 15

E

Ehrhardt, Hermann 20
Eichmann, Adolf 55, 135, 174, 192, 193, 199, 213-16, 219, 223, 278, 281, 287
Eicke, Theodor 67-9, 78, 80, 83, 84, 95, 99, 141-2, 228-9
Einsatzgruppen 55, 129, 171
   and invasion of Poland 116, 117, 118, 119
   and invasion of Soviet Union 130-4, 166, 212, 213
   members prosecuted for war crimes 271
Enabling Act (1933) 29, 62, 204
Engelmann, Bernt 92-3

F

Fegelein, Hermann 193, 226, 227, 228
Feldmeijer, Johannes Hendrik

—᛭᛭—

—*SS*—

PICTURE CREDITS

Bundesarchiv: 7, 17, 21, 24, 31, 53, 59, 68, 85, 91, 107, 122, 134, 152, 218, 235, 251, 286

Topfoto: 9

Corbis: 45, 76, 185, 214, 255

Shutterstock: 163

ED Archives: 237